THE COMMONSENSE GUIDE TO ESTATE PLANNING

Robert H. Runde

J. Barry Zischang

BUSINESS ONE IRWIN
Burr Ridge, Illinois
New York, New York

This publication is designed to provide accurate and authoritative information in regard to the subject matter covered. It is sold with the understanding that neither the author nor the publisher is engaged in rendering legal, accounting, or other professional service. If legal advice or other expert assistance is required, the services of a competent professional person should be sought.

From a Declaration of Principles jointly adopted by a Committee of the American Bar Association and a Committee of Publishers.

Senior edtior: Amy Hollands
Project editor: Jane Lightell
Production manager: Bob Lange
Art coordinator: Heather Burbridge
Art studio: Jay Benson Studio
Compositor: Precision Typographers
Typeface: 11/13 Palatino
Printer: Book Press

Library of Congress Cataloging-in-Publication Data

Runde, Robert H.
    The commonsense guide to estate planning / by Robert H. Runde and
 J. Barry Zischang.
       p.   cm.
    ISBN 1-55623-678-6
    1. Estate planning—United States. I. Zischang, J. Barry.
 II. Title.
 KF750.Z9R86   1994
 346.7305′2—dc20
 [347.30652]   93–9618

Printed in the United States of America
1 2 3 4 5 6 7 8 9 0 BP 0 9 8 7 6 5 4 3

Preface

In the book you are about to read we have set our sights on some tough goals. We aim to expose you to a subject that you may want to know *nothing* about. You may not even want to think about it, because the subject seems so, well, deadly. Face it, your own demise is not a subject that anyone contemplates with relish. So getting you to focus on all the elements of proper planning and helping you to translate our ideas into action will be an accomplishment.

The two of us were determined to write this book so you would not only understand the issues, but also actually enjoy the process. We have tried to write in a personal style, drawing on our own experiences and those of our clients, families, and friends. We have tried to adopt a style that strikes a balance between sober reflection and sympathetic good humor. We have attempted, in other words, to minimize the pomposity that could infect a book of this sort.

The book uses the same approach that we take when we discuss estate planning with our clients, who represent a broad range of people at all stages of life. What distinguishes them, we believe, is what sets apart anyone who reads this book: the realization that ignoring such fundamental realities doesn't make them disappear.

A good friend of ours, a man of enormous wit, intelligence, and scholarship, once told us that he's a solipsist. That would have sent us scurrying for a dictionary except that he explained, rather flippantly, that it means he believes the world will end when he does—not actually, of course, but as far as he's concerned. We've revered and respected this man for years, and we hope he was being facetious, which is likely. The world doesn't end when you do; it becomes a sadder place for all those who love and care about you. How callous, it seemed to us, how downright cruel it is for someone to compound the grief of their own passing by making things difficult for those they leave behind.

You always have it in your power to be a positive or a negative force. Here's an example of what happens when you choose the wrong course. One of our most poignant clients is a youngish widow whose husband was a very successful self-made businessman. He died several years ago after a brief illness. When he became sick, he tried desperately, with visits to famous hospitals and experimental surgeries, to recover. But he pretty much knew, his widow reports, that it was no good.

He could have used those last months to put his affairs in such good shape that his widow would be well taken care of, his business would continue to thrive and prosper, and his grown children would ultimately be the beneficiaries of his foresight. Instead, he left things in such a mess that his family has spent a low six-figure sum paying legal bills in a rancorous attempt to straighten it all out. The wrangling has lasted for *years*, and one result is that his widow will spend the rest of her days worrying about her financial well-being. Naively, we once commented to her that if John, whom we never met, knew what a maelstrom his bad planning had created for his loved ones, he'd turn over in his grave. "Are you kidding," she shot back. "He's probably out there somewhere right now laughing his head off." To her credit, she's a big enough person to be able to say that with a smile.

What's the point? Just this: Why leave a legacy of hurt? Few people are so mean-spirited that they intentionally choose to destroy their family's lives as they exit. But many are so out of touch with the rhythms of life that they unintentionally leave a muddle in their wake. Our friend the solipsist, for example, either didn't stop to think about the implications of his lack of action, or he was so self-centered that he didn't care.

It amounts to love. Face it, most of the strategies and techniques we describe in this book won't help *you* at all. Many will actually cost you—time, money, and effort. The type of planning we are attempting to teach you is almost exclusively selfless. Using it will make the world more bearable for others. The rewards you will get will be mainly spiritual (not that we underestimate the value of doing things for the benefit of our souls, mind you).

But we digress. In these few prefatory pages, we wanted to reassure you that this work will not only give you some assistance in a difficult and little-understood part of your financial life, but also bring a smile or two and perhaps a shock of recognition along the way. We have spent our adult lives in service businesses and decades as financial and estate planners. Few preconceptions have withstood the harsh glare of real life.

So when we were approached by BUSINESS ONE IRWIN to write this book, we intended to draw on our experiences to give you a practical guide. We wanted to talk with you as we would if you came into our offices for advice. We did not want to write an abstract or theoretical tome—heretical, maybe, but not theoretical.

We had zero interest in putting so much labor into a work, only to have it gather dust on your bookshelf.

And we did not want to talk down to you. We respect your intelligence. Many of you are undoubtedly a lot smarter than we are, and all of you know a heck of a lot more about your own specialties. You simply have not had the privilege that we've had of spending decades dealing with the matters we describe in these pages.

A financial planner is uniquely situated to assist you—whether as a reader of this book or as a client—because if we are doing our jobs correctly, we take responsibility not just for the strategies you should employ, but also for the practicalities.

The two of us are not attorneys. So we do not draft the legal documents that will comprise your estate plan. Rather, our expertise lies in managing the estate planning process, from start to finish. When you work with a financial planner—at least, when a client works with *us*—the goal is first to map out the best plan, and then to see that it gets carried out. We work in the real world, so we take on the responsibility of seeing that abstract ideas become reality. Without such hands-on assistance, good ideas are apt to get stalled in a never-never land of good intentions.

In writing this book, we have tried to take the same approach. We have tried to show you at every juncture how to march methodically through each phase of the process.

Realizing that the whole topic is not a sexy one, we nonetheless soldiered on in the hope that we could at least make it vivid for you. This is, after all, supposed to be a practical, down-to-earth guide. We felt that if we presented estate planning realistically, spicing the lessons with generous portions of anecdotes and illustrations, a diligent reader could not only persevere but also actually enjoy the expedition. You will judge how well we've succeeded.

As you progress through the chapters, we would like you to hold us to two standards: Are we equipping you with the *essential information* (not every detail) that you need to know in order to construct an intelligently thought-out estate plan? And have we made the information easily accessible and interesting? If we have accomplished those objectives, we will be well satisfied.

Robert H. Runde
J. Barry Zischang

Acknowledgments

Being a rookie author, I'm not quite sure how you give proper thanks without either sounding presumptuous or making unforgivable errors of omission. Naturally, a gang of people has richly earned my gratitude.

At the top of the list is my dear wife, Lorraine. A more steadfast and stalwart mate would be hard to imagine. During the year that I spent every spare moment working on this book, she has needed every reserve of patience and good cheer. How she managed to constantly find them is a mystery and a tribute.

Similarly, my business partner, Michael Parry, has been the soul of understanding, support, and grace under pressure during this period. If I were under fire (which in my life I've seemed to be more or less continuously) and could pick only two people to help defend me, Mike would be one. The other would be Arnold Schwarzenegger.

My all-time favorite editor and friend of 25 years, Mark Howat, deserves special praise and thanks, both for his inspiration and for his high good humor.

The two most big-hearted people I know, Jinny and Sam Sammis, gave me both moral and physical support, being kind enough to let me hole up at their house in Vermont to bask in the undistracted silence while I climbed to the summit and down the other side of this writing project.

Two attorneys gave unstintingly of their time and talents and gently nudged me back on course whenever I drifted away from some law or concept. Richard Stein of Fisher & Stein and Nancy Blair of Blair & Potts can work with my clients anytime, or for that matter, join me for lunch.

Stamford Probate Judge Gerald Fox also gets a tip of the hat. If they were all like you, Gerry, the probate system wouldn't have such a bad rep.

Finally, but certainly not least, a large dollop of gratitude to my coauthor. Barry Zischang and I have been friends and colleagues for years, and we enjoy a cheerful relationship, even when he leaves me in the dust during road races.

Evidently, though, collaborating on a book can strain even the best of friendships. I know this because in the contract we signed with the publisher, there's a clause allowing them to pitch one of us out and hire a replacement to finish the book if we fight so much that the work is in jeopardy. Happily, I can report that such drastic action will not be necessary. We scarcely had a disagreement through the entire ordeal.

R.H.R.

* * * * *

This book is the result of much more than the collaboration of two authors. In addition to the tireless efforts of my good friend Bob Runde, there are a number of outstanding performances that deserve recognition.

My wife, Barbara Carter, is an established financial planner in her own right. She and her assistant, Bonnie Nardozzi, were a constant source of technical and administrative support.

I am also indebted to Jerry Randall and his crack team of legal and tax professionals at Connecticut Mutual Life in Hartford, Connecticut. Materials they had prepared proved invaluable in illustrating complex estate planning techniques in understandable terms. Patrick Smith and the legal eagles at ITT Hartford Life also pitched in with information on late-breaking developments.

The dedicated staff at Choice in Dying warrant particular praise. This book was written just as the new Patient Self-Determination Act was coming into effect. Their up-to-the-minute information on this new law and the latest developments regarding living wills and health care proxies made our job much easier in researching these topics.

And, I would like to thank our agent, Evan Marshall, and our editor at BUSINESS ONE IRWIN, Amy Hollands-Gaber. They each demonstrated forbearance, patience, and courage in dealing with not one, but two first-time authors.

J.B.Z.

Contents

GETTING STARTED

Chapter One

What Is Estate Planning and When Should It Begin?

Legacy *A bequest; a particular thing or certain sum of money given by the last will or testament. Anything handed down by an ancestor or predecessor.*

L *egacy.* It's quite a word, isn't it? It may have a different meaning for all of us. Yet the desire to leave our mark on this world is a common instinct that most of us share. The ancient Egyptians were very conscious of the need. You have to marvel at the pyramids and imagine what psychological forces caused them to be built. You may not make such an issue of your desire to be remembered. But you surely want your heirs to know you existed and left your mark— hopefully for the good—on this world as you passed through it.

Estate planning is the ultimate manifestation of our desire to influence the world, or at least our little corner of it, after we are gone. It doesn't matter whether you have great worldly wealth or relatively modest treasures. The people and entities that you care about—family, friends, institutions, or charities—can benefit greatly from your planning.

Whether you are a Pharaoh or just the sovereign's humble servant, whether you need a pyramid or just a simple memorial service, you want to be remembered. To a great extent, estate planning is about your vision of the monetary legacy you want to leave behind.

Estate planning is the legal procedure whereby you make your wishes known and direct others to have them carried out. Your estate plan thus fulfills your desire to express love and concern for your family. If you are sufficiently affluent, you may also wish to fund a charity or cause. In either case, you probably are motivated in large part by a desire to be remembered as a caring person. Philanthropists are good examples. Some led what they ultimately regarded as less-than-virtuous lives and then used their estate to be remembered for good works. The Nobel Prize was founded with wealth that came from the invention of dynamite, for instance. Most of us lead far less explosive lives, and our estate plans contain more modest goals.

Yet, we are all human, so our desire to leave a legacy is often outweighed by our reluctance to confront our own mortality. We reason that we're not going to die today, so we can put our planning off until tomorrow. Or next month. Or next year. Too many people run out of tomorrows before they run out of excuses, and the planning never gets done. You're busy with your career and your family, and rather than dealing with a traumatic issue, you tend to avoid it. Fully 75 percent of Americans die without a will, which is often a tragedy compounding a tragedy for those they leave behind.

PROCRASTINATION

People procrastinate because planning for death is a reminder that the day will come when the planning will be put into action. And we won't even get to see how our own planning turns out! This book is intended to help you overcome your inertia. We want to make it easy for you to get started. Our aim in this book is to guide you through the complex personal, legal, and tax considerations that hamper the process.

This is *not* a do-it-yourself manual. We strongly feel that everyone needs the objective and informed input of competent advisers, including attorneys, financial planners, insurance agents, and accountants. As professional planners ourselves, we believe that everyone should make appropriate preparations at each stage of life. Bluntly, Don't wait until after the third coronary to get started. Because you have read this far, we assume you feel pretty much the same way.

But the final decisions are always yours, and we hope to help you understand the concepts and techniques that make up your estate plan. That way, it can be a true expression of your wishes. By using this book, you have shown your willingness to overcome your lethargy. We hope that the ideas we give you will encourage you to develop and implement a plan of your own.

OUR LEGAL SYSTEM

This is a topic that we will deal with at various points in the book, but you should know a little something of the context right from the start. Estate planning is governed by a code of law as complex as any you are likely to encounter. The rules vary from state to state, though they fall basically into two categories: 42 states have a heritage that traces back to the English system, called common law; the other 8, known informally as community property states, trace their heritage to the Spanish (and in the case of Louisiana, French) system, called the civil code. One of the common law states, Wisconsin, has a hybrid system.

Not only are there those two broad categories, but also variations in the law from state to state. In some cases, the differences are dramatic, in other respects minor. If you spend your entire life rooted in one spot, this is unimportant. On the other hand, statistically the majority of the population moves every five to seven years. If you go to another state, you need to be certain that your estate plan conforms to local law. Moreover, if you own property in several states—a home in Boston, say, and a cabin in New Hampshire—you need to be aware that the result can be additional estate or inheritance taxes and a duplication of costs in settling your estate unless you take appropriate action ahead of time.

Here you are, just starting the book, and already we've given you two excuses to avoid estate planning. You don't want to confront your mortality, and you don't understand all the laws and rules that you must follow. We admit that it's a daunting process. But think of it this way: All those laws are designed mainly to protect the interests of the people you leave behind when you die. To help you, throughout the book we will present key elements of the laws in simple terms, with plenty of direction as to how to use them to your and your family's best advantage.

Whether or not you care to make your children rich, you undoubtedly do not want any unnecessary sums going to Uncle Sam's or your local state's coffers. Think about it. You worked hard, you paid your taxes, you saved for a rainy day. And when it's time to pass your legacy on to the next generation, the ravenous tax collectors may want 50 percent or more of all your worldly wealth.

How's that for an incentive to plan for your loved ones? Anyone who has accumulated enough assets to worry about taxes—or anyone who plans to—will find that the strategies and estate planning devices that we describe will pay for the cost of the book many, many times over. Staying well within the boundaries of our legal system, we will show you how to greatly reduce or eliminate altogether not only state and federal taxes, but also the costs of settling an estate.

STARTING TO PLAN—YOUR FIRST WILL

You're young, you're single, you're just out of school. No one depends on you financially. What? Me worry about a will? The answer, which might surprise you, is yes. (What did you expect in a book about estate planning?)

If you should die, someone—your parents, a brother or sister, some other relative or friend—is going to have to settle your affairs. If you have a will, your loved ones can settle things fairly effortlessly. But without a will, your family must petition the probate court to be appointed as the representative of your estate. It's not an extremely time-consuming or expensive process, but why put anyone through even minor aggravation on your behalf if you can easily prevent it? Even if your total estate consists of just a beat-up 1983 Chevy, $500 in the bank, and some student loan obligations, your closest relative or friend must labor unnecessarily through the probate process.

What does it cost to get a simple will written? Of course, costs vary tremendously from place to place and lawyer to lawyer. But in our experience, a basic will generally runs in the vicinity of $100, give or take. In midtown Manhattan, it may cost a couple hundred, at most; in Manhattan, Kansas, perhaps $50 to $75. The exact number is not important. The point is that a will is not a big expense, and, like estate planning in general, writing a will is an act you do out of love for the people around you.

On Page 74, we have reproduced a sample of a typical simple will. Don't make the mistake of simply copying the form from this book and signing your name to it, though. The estate laws are complicated and tricky, and if you make some small error, a court may toss your will out, meaning you died without a will.

Speaking of those student loans, you might want to think about whether you'd like to have those or any other obligations you have—credit card balances, for example—taken care of. You should consider taking out an inexpensive life insurance policy to cover your debts and what are often called final expenses. Those would include funeral costs as well as any possible medical bills not covered by your health insurance. The cost of buying an insurance policy would be minimal, and potentially it would be a help to your family.

We understand that you bought this book not because you are 21 years old and wonder whether or not to worry about your last will and testament. We realize that most people who take the trouble to buy and read a book about estate planning are much further along in their lives, with the attendant complexities. However, it also may be that, like us, you have children or nieces and nephews who are reaching the stage of life where they need someone to exhort them to begin making at least some rudimentary plans. In our view you should urge them to action.

Another document that every adult should have is a living will, sometimes referred to as a health care power of attorney. Often called the death with dignity document, a living will spells out the type of medical care you would want to have in the event you became incapacitated. Most notably, living wills specify that you do not want to be kept alive indefinitely by machines if all hope of your recovery is gone. The courts have ruled in a number of cases that you must make your preference known ahead of time if you feel that way; otherwise, doctors and hospitals are within their rights to do everything possible to keep you alive, regardless of your prognosis.

WHERE SHOULD DOCUMENTS BE KEPT?

This is a surprisingly controversial question. We are frequently asked by our clients whether a will should be kept at home, in a safe deposit box at the bank, in their attorney's office, or just where. Typically, an attorney will offer to keep your will for you. That way, it is safe and almost certainly won't be lost or misplaced. It has been our impression that some attorneys also believe that having custody of a will gives them an edge in terms of being selected to represent your estate after you die. Depending on the size and complexity of your estate, that's a job that could be more lucrative for the attorney than writing the will in the first place.

Years ago, when the world was simpler and more settled, there was probably more reason for leaving your will with your lawyer. Now, streamlined laws make it easier to get into a safe deposit box after a death. And law firms are much less permanent institutions than perhaps they once were. But the main point is that we have become such a fluid people. We move around; we marry, divorce, remarry; we change our allegiances. The concept of a family attorney that you work with throughout your life has broken down somewhat.

As a result, it's probably just as well to keep the original copy of your will yourself. Our preference is to house the original copy of the document in either a bank safe deposit box or a fireproof strong box at home. In addition, a copy should be stored in a readily accessible place—your desk, for instance, or wherever you keep other important papers. Finally, a copy also should be retained by your attorney, and it almost certainly will be in the normal course of events.

Inform your family that you have a will, and let someone know where both the original and the copies are kept. It's also a courtesy to tell the person you have named as your executor that he or she has been so designated. (You will specify a second choice in your will, in case your preferred person can't or doesn't want to take on the responsibility when the time comes; you can inform this second choice or not, as you feel appropriate.)

MARRIAGE

Once written, your will can be filed away—but it should not be forgotten. Your plan will need revision whenever you have a significant change in your life. For most people, the first big change is marriage.

When wedding bells chime, it's scarcely romantic to begin thinking of death immediately. But marriage (as well as divorce, incidentally) is a life event that *necessitates* writing a new will, even if you already have one. Our society makes the fundamental assumption that marriage is a sacred institution. Our laws grant many privileges to married couples that others do not receive. Married people are considered a unit in the eyes of the law, so they can pass property back and forth without any tax consequences, for instance.

So, should you rush straight from the church to your attorney's office? Well, go on your honeymoon first.

In the early years of marriage, a couple may have precious few resources, and it may seem that estate planning is the furthest thing from a necessity. This is true, but as we will stress repeatedly in this book, estate planning is about more than money. At bedrock, it is about people being sensitive to those around them. If you care about your spouse, you make sure that whatever size estate you have accumulated, it will be distributed according to your wishes with the help of a properly drawn will.

Of course, in those early years of adulthood, many of your assets will not be passed under your will. As we will discuss in detail later on, the will is just one vehicle for disposing of your property. You can title assets as "joint with rights of survivorship." That way if one of you were to die, the surviving spouse would automatically be the sole owner of the asset. Some things cannot be titled jointly, of course. If you have individual retirement accounts, those IRAs must be, as the name implies *individually* owned. You designate a beneficiary on them, as you do with a life insurance policy.

By using joint ownership and beneficiary designations where possible, you can minimize the assets that are governed by your will. Even so, it is an essential document that all married couples, no matter how recently wed and no matter what level of assets they have, should draw up. As we said earlier, if you neglect to write a will, you will simply make things more difficult for your mate in the event that you die.

DIVORCE

Almost half of all first marriages and a significantly larger proportion of second marriages fail. As with marriage, divorce is a life event that calls for a new will.

When you stop and think about it, how could a will continue to be valid after divorce? You certainly would not want your assets to go to your ex-spouse. At that point, you will want to reassess your objectives and construct a new plan.

You might, for example, want to make sure that your ex doesn't get his or her hands on any of your resources (beyond what the divorce decree specifies). So, you need a new will to ensure that your wishes are observed. Life becomes infinitely more complicated if, after a divorce, you remarry and one or both of you have children by prior marriages or you eventually have children together.

CHILDREN

Once you have children, estate planning is no longer an optional nicety. It becomes an absolute necessity. Heaven forbid both parents are killed in a common disaster. Who will take care of the kids? You certainly want to answer that question yourself, rather than leaving it to chance.

It's irresponsible for any parents not to deliberate over the contingent plans they would like to make for their children and then to spell out their wishes in writing. If you didn't do that, how would the judge who must make the decision know that you wanted your husband's sister Jennifer and her husband to raise the kids, rather than your brother Derek and his wife, but that you wanted Derek to manage your assets, which will be left to the kids?

You might also want to make explicit provisions for your children. In your wills, you may well incorporate trust provisions— usually called a minor's trust—to spell out how Derek is to manage their money for them and when he is to give how much to each child. This is especially true if your children are young. It can be equally essential if they are near or have recently entered adulthood, especially if your estate is a comparatively large one. You might well be concerned about having large sums conferred on your kids as soon as they become adults. Rather than leaving such decisions to chance or to the good judgment of your family and a probate court judge, you can and should express your own sentiments on the subject.

Here's something else to worry about: What if you died and

your spouse subsequently remarried? And then your spouse died leaving no new will. Where would your assets wind up? Some would undoubtedly go to the new spouse. There are legal safeguards, but if you do not go to the trouble of specifying your wishes, it is unlikely that your children will receive all the consideration—and assets—that you would have wanted.

As we indicated, the problem is trickier still if one or both spouses is divorced. It's far preferable to discuss how you would want things to be handled, in terms of both guardianship for your children and disposition of assets that you would want them to have, and then write wills that make your preferences explicit.

CHANGES IN FINANCIAL CIRCUMSTANCE

We can dream, can't we? What if you were to win the lottery in your state? What if your Uncle Zeppo died and left you a much larger bundle than you ever expected? Or what if that tip someone gave you on Googlionyx Corp. stock came in big time, and you made a major killing in the market? Of what if you hit the $3 million slot machine jackpot at Caesar's in Las Vegas or Atlantic City? Or, more realistically, what if you live a long and prosperous life, building up a very substantial estate through hard work and thrift?

Estate planning is a multilevel undertaking. As you read this book, you will learn the ins and outs. You will understand what estate tax consequences are and how to minimize them. You will receive an education in every phase of planning, in fact. But for now, think of it this way: If you had a lot of money to leave behind, would you treat it the same as if you had comparatively little? Undoubtedly you would not. And just as you would feel a little inadequate to deal with unexpected sudden wealth, so would your heirs, in all likelihood. Thus, you should assist them.

You do that from the grave by putting trust provisions in your will or by creating trusts apart from your will. That becomes a safety net, if properly thought out and constructed, that guards your heirs against squandering or being cheated out of their inheritance.

Sadly, the 1990s are teaching us that we don't always become more prosperous. Falling on hard times is also an occasion to revisit your estate planning. You may have been comfortable that your wealth was sufficient to provide for your family even if you died and the paychecks ceased. But if your wealth was in a real estate deal that went bad, or if your assets are tied up in a small business that is struggling and might flicker and die if you did, or if your fortunes have reversed for some other reason, maybe you better take another look. Any reversal of fortune should also occasion a review of your life insurance coverage.

MOVING TO A NEW STATE

Each state has its own approach to estate settlement. The 8 community property states take one view of assets owned by a married couple; the other 42 take a somewhat different approach. Some states have comparatively onerous inheritance tax levies; others have little or none. You would be making a potentially serious mistake if you did not consult an attorney upon moving to a new state. The lawyer might tell you that your will is still valid, or you might need to redo it. Living with such uncertainty, though, is foolhardy, especially since, in our experience, some minor adjustments (the lawyers call these *codicils*) might rectify a potential problem.

TAX LAW CHANGES

As with other laws, tax laws are in constant flux. Congress is always looking for ways to raise taxes without appearing to harm any segment of the population. They tinker here and there until everyone is confused and anxious. Estate planners, especially, worry about changes in law. It is axiomatic among planners that ''dead men don't vote,'' meaning that Congress—as well, presumably, as the legislature in your own state—may feel that raising estate taxes is a comparatively painless way to raise new revenues. As this book is being written, the $600,000 exclusion from federal estate and gift taxes that every American is entitled to is under attack. This exclusion has been in effect since the mid 1980s, but a move is afoot to pare it back to $200,000 in order to raise money to fund either a national health insurance program or long-term nursing home insurance.

Should there be a major change in estate tax laws, you certainly ought to consult your attorney or financial adviser. In that case, it is likely that you might need to revise or rewrite your will.

Have we missed anything? Quite possibly. Times change, lives change, laws change. And your planning needs to change with them.

Most people think of writing a will as a static undertaking. You finally get up the gumption to have your will drafted and then never want to think about it again. But estate planning, as we will show you in this book, is really a dynamic process. You wouldn't build a house and then never change it, remodel it, or trade it in for a new one. The same is true with your will. We recommend that it be reviewed every few years. Naturally, if something dramatic occurs that necessitates changes, don't wait. Most often, though, changes are more subtle and gradual. So, here's a test you can try at home: When your will is so yellow with age that the paper looks like parchment, it's a safe bet that you're overdue for a review.

Chapter Two

Setting Your Objectives

B efore embarking on a journey, it helps to know where you are going. Planning your estate is no different. To make effective preparations, you need to have a clear sense of what you want to accomplish. In our opinion, this is the single most important part of estate planning. Your professional advisers should not be so presumptuous as to tell you what to do. Rather, they should help you articulate what you want to do and then work out a program to implement your decisions.

The first order of business is to answer some questions. As financial planners, we spend a lot of time with our clients delineating the issues, weighing possible approaches, and helping to draw out their views. This is the first job of the planner: to put the issues in perspective and help the client decide what she or he really thinks. Often, people are unfamiliar with the problems, let alone the solutions. A quick example: You may want to leave everything to your spouse, and ultimately, after the spouse is gone, to your children. But what if your spouse remarries? What if your assets are large enough that federal estate taxes could be an issue? What if your present mate isn't your first? What if you have children who were born many years apart and have very different needs?

To help you crystallize your thoughts, let's look at some findings from a provocative recent study. Neuberger & Berman, a New York–based investment management and mutual fund company, commissioned the Gediman Research Group of Stamford, Connecticut, to ask people about their feelings toward estate planning. Called "Inheritance: The Problems and the Promise," the report contains findings that may mirror your own concerns. It may also suggest ideas and directions applicable to your own situation. The Gediman Group has graciously granted us permission to quote from the study.

THE FIRST IN LINE

Not surprisingly, husbands and wives consider each other far more important than anyone else. If you are married, you undoubtedly feel that way, too. Children, while they are next in line, are a distant second.

If you are happily married, or at least not estranged from your spouse, chances are you want the main thrust of your planning to be ensuring that your mate is well taken care of if anything should happen to you. And the law shares those sentiments. Spouses are given special treatment in several respects. Most states have laws specifying that your husband or wife has a right to at least one third of your "probate estate."

Your probate estate is made up of assets that you own in your name alone, which are distributed according to the terms of your will. If you were to leave your spouse less than one third of these assets in your will (one half in some states and under some circumstances), she or he could challenge that disposition in court.

In most states, assets that don't pass under your will, such as jointly titled property and life insurance, are not affected by these rules. There is a developing trend, our lawyer friends tell us, to include nonprobate assets in the calculation of the least amount you can leave your spouse. So you should be sure to ask your attorney to explain the situation in your state.

Chances are you want your spouse to get much more than one third of your worldly wealth. Most people want to leave everything to their husband or wife, assuming that they are not estranged. Often that strategy is fine. But if your estate is worth more than $600,000, the level at which the federal estate tax begins, then leaving everything to your spouse ultimately could generate extra money for the tax collector. (In our section on planning for larger estates, we'll show you how to avoid such a predicament.)

What if My Spouse Remarries?

One thing to think about as you plan is what you would like to have happen if you were to die suddenly or prematurely. How do you feel about the possibility that your husband or wife might find a new mate?

Nearly half the people interviewed for the Gediman study felt that leaving everything to their husband or wife was appropriate because they trusted their spouse to distribute the family's assets wisely. About a third said a spouse should not be "punished" for remarrying. Yet nearly 40 percent said they would want to use appropriate strategies to keep money in the family. Said one person: "I don't want some jerk marrying my wife for my hard-earned money. I'd use a trust to protect the assets for our children and grandchildren."

It's very possible to arrange your estate plan so your spouse has full use of the family's assets during her or his lifetime but does not have the power to will away at death those that belonged to you. Later in this book, we will show you ways that you can designate who the ultimate beneficiaries of your resources will be, which becomes more of a concern as your balance sheet builds up. You need to think about how you really feel, though, before you take such action. The most likely candidates for that type of protection are people who had substantial assets before they married.

CHILDREN

Kids might be a distant second, behind your spouse, but in all likelihood they are far ahead of whoever or whatever is third. If you have children, and haven't banished them from your home, chances are you will want your estate to consider them next, after your spouse has been taken care of. Yet, you also want to avoid conflicts over your inheritance, if possible.

Most people prefer to divide their assets equally among their kids for a variety of reasons: You love them equally; you don't want to show favoritism; or you don't want any bad blood among your children after you're gone. The Gediman report noted that "you can treat your children unequally while you're alive, but if you do it in a will, after you die it becomes 'official,' a kind of immortal black mark." One person surveyed had an interesting observation: "I don't want to be cussed from my grave."

In setting objectives in your own situation, though, it may be that unequal distribution is appropriate. For instance, what if one of your children has a handicap? What if some children are grown, but some still have college educations ahead of them at the time you die? What if some are rich and others struggling? These are issues you need to think about clearly when you are preparing your estate plan and to discuss fully with your advisers.

Our clients Bob and Betty, for instance, were updating their wills recently. They wanted to leave all their property to each other, but they were concerned about taking care of their children in the event that they both die before the kids are grown. The couple have three children: June, 23, who works at a bank; Mavis, 21, who's just finishing college; and Jimmy, 15, who is a sophomore in high school. Bob and Betty realize that Jimmy's situation is different from those of his sisters, because he would need a guardian if anything were to happen to his parents. The guardian would need funds to feed, clothe, and shelter Jimmy, not to mention for the same sort of college education that his sisters have already received.

If the couple's wills merely divided their estate equally among the three children, Jimmy would be shortchanged because a large chunk of his inheritance would be consumed in providing for his care and education, while his sisters' shares could be saved for their futures.

The couple decided to take what they felt was a more equitable approach, stipulating in their wills that Jimmy's needs be provided for first. Thereafter, remaining assets could be divided equally among all three children.

Interestingly, the Gediman survey found that people perceive that women have achieved economic parity with men. At least, parents did not feel a need to protect their daughters against economic inequality. Nearly 85 percent of those surveyed thought it unnecessary to leave more to daughters than to sons to compensate for the traditional reality that women generally will earn less over their lifetimes than men will. Undoubtedly, most people feel any inherent economic inequity can be compensated for if a woman marries a successful man. It's an interesting union of contemporary feminist and dated sexist notions.

Your will must also take into consideration the possibility that both you and your spouse might die before your children are grown. So for parents, one of the most important functions of planning involves naming the person or people you would want to care for your progeny.

In our experience, this is often a far tougher decision than the question of how much to leave to whom. Recently, a fairly sophisticated couple came to our office to discuss estate planning. When it came to designating guardians, they admitted to mixed feelings about who to name. The husband's brother was inappropriate, they felt, because he is a "53-year-old kid" and the wife's sister probably wouldn't be the right choice because she has "such screwy ideas," this rather buttoned-down couple felt. So, they were struggling between two sets of dear friends. Suddenly, it dawned on them that if *they* were having so much difficulty, how would a judge feel if they died in a common disaster and she or he was forced to make the decision without benefit of their views on the subject?

Single Parenthood

What if you are a single parent? Remember all the furor about the TV character Murphy Brown in the last presidential election? You really have to think this through, especially if, like Murphy, you have to contend with someone who is the child's natural parent but does not want to take responsibility. Another question is whether a person you did not want to marry would be the best guardian should something happen to you.

The question is just as complicated if you were once married to your child's other parent. With so many marriages ending in divorce, specifying in your will who should have custody in your absence has become an increasingly common predicament and an emotionally charged issue. If you have custody of your children, you have to consider whether it would be in their best interest for your ex-spouse to regain custody at your death. Of course, whether you could prevent that even if you wanted to is debatable.

Even if your former spouse got custody after your death, that's not necessarily a good reason that she or he should control the property and money you leave to your kids. There are several excellent alternatives, most notably the use of trusts, which we will deal with in later chapters.

Stepchildren and Adopted Children

The "Brady Bunch" syndrome complicates things still further, of course. In real life, unlike television, conflicting feelings and tensions can be almost Byzantine. In the Gediman survey, there was broad disagreement among the respondents about whether they felt compelled to leave the same amount of money to step-children as to natural children. While 29 percent felt that step-children deserved the same consideration as natural children, that view was more prevalent among people who had nurtured step-children from a young age. While 34 percent were neutral on the issue, 37 percent thought unequal treatment was more appropriate. Adopted children, as you might expect, fared much better. A large majority of parents thought they should not be discriminated against simply because they don't literally carry the family bloodline.

As you try to sort it all out in your own family situation, you realize how tricky the issues can be. Here's the worst case (or perhaps the best?): What if you have several children from a prior marriage, some adopted and some natural, then remarry and have more children with your second spouse? And what if she or he also has offspring from before your marriage?

First, our condolences. How do you deal fairly with everyone while you're alive, let alone after you're gone? No doubt, you do so by trying very hard and keeping your good humor. You and your new mate probably have more on your minds than your estate plan. The sheer logistics of day-to-day life must be stressful enough. But you would be absolutely derelict in your responsibilities to this passel of youngsters if you didn't spend time discussing all the implications for your new family configuration if one of you were to die.

In thinking your strategy through, you need to make certain that all the kids are treated fairly so if one or both of you were to die they would be properly cared for. You must also make certain you have adequate resources to discharge all these responsibilities. You may find there simply isn't enough money to go around. One or both of you may need to consider additional life insurance to cover all the overlapping obligations.

Sons- and Daughters-in-Law

Perhaps not surprisingly, the Gediman survey found that a majority felt that if one of their children married someone they disliked, it would not be grounds to punish the child by reducing her or his inheritance. Among people who were inclined to reduce the inheritance, most said they would use a trust with restrictive provisions.

"If my children marry creeps, that's their business—and their problem. Their poor judgment has nothing to do with me and with what I leave them," said one person surveyed. But another noted that "a son- or daughter-in-law I didn't like would have an effect on my inheritance decisions; I've worked hard for my money and I wouldn't want an outsider having control over our family money."

OTHER RELATIVES AND FRIENDS

If you are not married or if you have no children, your thoughts will probably turn to other relatives. Even if you are married and have children, there may be people who have always been a special part of your life: your parents, perhaps, or a favorite niece or nephew, or your grandchildren. Maybe your heart has always gone out to your younger cousin Tommy, who was born retarded.

Whoever you choose to leave your money to, you need to think it through. Are the people you wish to name capable of handling the money wisely? The very young, very old, or the handicapped obviously need assistance. You may serve them best by setting up a trust for their benefit and naming trustees who are more sophisticated in managing money. As you mull over the construction of your overall estate plan, these are questions you especially need to talk about with professional advisers.

OTHER BEQUESTS

If you have a favorite charity, you may want to designate it as one of the heirs of your estate. Of course, you want to make sure that the people you care about are considered first. But beyond that, many people have benevolent inclinations. For those who are financially well off, the incentives for leaving large sums to charities can be powerful. The tax benefits, as we will discuss in later chapters, can be strong motivators. You can get both estate tax *and* income tax breaks for making charitable donations—especially to charities approved by the IRS. It may be possible to enhance your retirement income while at the same time benefiting your favorite charity.

AND FINALLY . . .

In these opening chapters, we have tried to lay out in very broad form the issues you must grapple with as you consider your own mortality. For many readers, this is old stuff. You know, in general, who you want to benefit and how you want to accomplish that. Other readers will be tackling some of the difficult issues of estate planning for the first time—or for the first time in a long while.

Whichever group you fall into, as they say, don't try this at home. Don't try going it alone. You need the help of expert advisers, especially a financial planner, who will assist in setting strategy and who can expedite the process, and a good attorney, who can construct the estate plan you decide on. In the next chapter, we'll show you how to field the team of pros that can make it all happen for you.

Chapter Three

Assembling Your Planning Team

D epending on your situation, the number of players on your estate planning team can be as few as one or as many as three or four. Young newlyweds who need only simple wills can easily get by with just an attorney. Families with complex situations—business owners, for instance, and people with substantial assets—should be prepared to work with a more formidable team that may also include a financial planner, an insurance specialist, and possibly an accountant.

Estate planning is not a do-it-yourself job. We've seen will kits you can buy for nominal amounts in bookstores or by mail, and we're not impressed. Essentially, that amounts to trying to be your own lawyer, and you've heard the adage about that: Whether or not you're trained in the law, you'll have a fool for an attorney and a fool for a client.

Fielding your crack estate planning team will take some effort. Here's how to go about it.

FINANCIAL PLANNER

The planner is the professional you should start with. As a generalist, he or she is equipped to review your entire financial situation. More than that, the planner is a process manager. If the process doesn't work—and you don't end up with a successful estate plan—it's the planner who should assume the blame. If everything works smoothly, the planner can take a good share of the credit.

Most people need the process management function of the planner's role as much or more than they need other aspects of the job.

Put another way, a good planner will keep kicking you in the behind, and kicking the lawyer, too, to keep things moving. First, a planner establishes the human relationship to give the process a beginning, middle, and end (and even later, to provide periodic updates of the estate plan, if needed). Everyone tends to procrastinate, and the planner is charged with managing the undertaking so it gets done.

In our office, when we begin working with a new client we first prepare a comprehensive analysis that covers each aspect of the person's financial life. Out of that evaluation emerge recommendations in a number of areas. These form the broad outline of the estate plan, from which the attorney can get detailed information about your situation, add good ideas, and ultimately draft the necessary legal documents.

Finding a good planner may or may not be easy. It has become trendy for financial professionals to call themselves planners. But in many cases that's a misnomer. Stock brokers, for example, on occasion claim to be planners, though their expertise may lie solely in investments. Likewise, insurance agents can pretend to be planners, though curiously all their solutions involve purchasing insurance products—from them. There are advantages and disadvantages to working with a generalist rather than a specialist.

If a financial planner is worthy of that title, he or she will take an objective look at your entire situation and may uncover other financial issues besides estate planning that you should address. On the other hand, if you are certain everything else in your financial life is under control and you require assistance only in preparing your estate plan, a good attorney could be all you need.

Begin your search for a sharp financial planner by quizzing your accountant, your attorney, or both. They work regularly with other professionals in the community and can get a feel for a planner's breadth of knowledge and competence. They are unlikely to risk their relationship with you by recommending someone whose abilities are suspect. You can also call upon the two large national planners' organizations: the Institute of Certified Financial Planners (1660 Lincoln Street, Suite 3050, Denver, CO 80264) and the International Association for Financial Planning (Two Concourse Parkway, Suite 800, Atlanta, GA 30328). Each will give you the names of several of their members in your area.

When you have located some likely candidates, call for an appointment for a preliminary interview. Most planners are willing to spend an hour or so with you at no charge in the interest of getting acquainted. This initial meeting can be instructive. At the extreme negative end of the spectrum, we've heard tales of planners who immediately try to sell you something, typically life insurance. That instantly unmasks the person and should disqualify him or her as a professional you'd want to work with. Mostly, the planner should be asking informational questions and listening to your answers.

In interviewing prospective planners, *you* should be asking questions, too. Start with credentials. Ask whether the planner has a CFP (for certified financial planner) designation. That is the most widely respected credential in the profession because it signifies that the person has spent two years studying six subject areas, one of which is estate planning, and has passed exams in each of them. Moreover, it indicates that the person takes seriously the craft of financial planning, associates with like-minded people, and devotes some time to continuing education. The Denver-based IBCFP (International Board of Certified Financial Planners), which awards the CFP designation, requires ongoing professional education (just as certified public accountants [CPAs], architects, attorneys, and other professionals must keep their expertise sharp by maintaining their education).

Whether or not the planner is a CFP, ask what other qualifications or professional designations he or she has. And ask whether the planner is fee- or commission-based. If commission-based with a CLU (chartered life underwriter) designation, you are entitled to ask whether you'll be required to buy life insurance in order to receive the planner's assistance. Similarly, the ChFC (chartered financial consultant) designation indicates that the planner is insurance-based. The same organization, the American College in Bryn Mawr, Pennsylvania, that confers the CLU also qualifies insurance professionals for the ChFC, which requires mastery of a comprehensive curriculum similar to the CFP program.

It's also fair game to inquire about the planner's background. An acceptable answer might be "Until four years ago (or whatever), I was an investment banker (or stockbroker, financial journalist, or financial professional in some other capacity)." An answer that inspires less confidence would be "Until this year (or last week),

I was selling recreational vehicles (or encyclopedias, freezer plans, or plumbing supplies).'' Occasionally, you may speak with a planner who has a Master of Business Administration (MBA) degree or who is a nonpracticing CPA or attorney. We've found that these can be excellent backgrounds because they not only indicate a level of education that is largely transferable, but also a commitment to the financial services arena.

Once you've gotten beyond the pedigree, ask about the planner's approach. Typically, a planner is a generalist, the quarterback of your financial team. After a preliminary get-acquainted meeting, the planner should construct a report that tells you where you stand. If you have contracted with the planner only to do estate recommendations, you should expect to receive an analysis of your tax picture. Our reports contain side-by-side ''before'' and ''after'' illustrations of the potential estate tax burden. The ''after'' takes into account the strategic steps we recommend the client take in preparing a will and trusts. If you have asked the planner for more comprehensive assistance, expect to receive a lengthy document that evaluates all the areas of your financial life—your portfolio, income tax picture, cash flow, retirement calculations, insurance analysis, and education costs.

Planners should be up-front about what they propose to do for you. They should talk candidly about fees and commissions. Most planners derive their income from a blend of the two. In our practice, we quote a fee to a new client and mention that we might make specific investment or insurance product recommendations that could earn us a commission, but that the client is never under an obligation either to take our recommendations or execute them through us. Other planners work differently. Some charge minimal or no fees, but they ask you to make a commitment to make any appropriate product purchases through them.

Your assessment of a planner's candor is one of the most important grounds for deciding whether or not to work together, so think clearly about the issue of fees and commissions. On the face of it, there is nothing wrong with either approach as long as the basis of compensation is well understood by both sides up front. The problems can arise through misunderstanding. If you thought that you were hiring a fee-only planner (a very rare breed, by the way, and one that in our experience works mainly with very wealthy clients) you will quite understandably resent later product recommendations that clearly will generate commissions for the planner. On the other hand, discuss frankly with a commission-based adviser how he or she handles the potential conflict of interest—usually the higher the premiums you pay for insurance, the bigger the agent's commission.

Another equally important issue is compatibility. As in all your professional dealings, you certainly want to have a pleasant experience working with a financial planner. You wouldn't feel comfortable with a sourpuss dentist or an ingratiating accountant. It's even more essential that you enjoy your dealings with your financial planner because, as with your family physician, you may work with your planner for many years to come. So, pay close attention to your visceral reactions during the initial session. If you don't like the planner, it may not mean you won't hire him to help you with your estate planning; it probably does mean, though, that you won't want to work with him year-in and year-out on all your financial affairs.

Finally, if there's any doubt in your mind—and perhaps even if there isn't—it's a good idea to ask for references. Get the names of three or four clients the planner has worked with whose circumstances are similar to yours. When you call them, don't ask about their own situation, which is none of your business, but about the process they went through with the planner and their reactions. Ask how the planner worked with them, what they liked and what they didn't, and what the results were. If they were pleased, you'll know it quickly. You might also ask for the names of a couple of allied professionals that the planner works with, primarily lawyers and accountants. Your conversations with them won't be as illuminating, but the difference in perspective that they have can be helpful in making your assessment.

As we've said, expect to work first with the planner. He or she will begin the estate planning process and, more important, keep it moving along. You should expect to meet at least two or three times, and possibly more, before you start working with the attorney.

During the planning process, the planner will gather all pertinent information about your situation and aspirations, taking into account any complicated or unusual situations. A disabled child or needy parents necessitate special planning. Owning your own business or professional practice causes particular concerns. In addition to fact gathering, the planner will arrive at some preliminary recommendations. At that point, however, it's time to involve the lawyer, who can turn the information into a specific plan of action.

ATTORNEY

In most cases, it is best to work with an attorney who specializes in estate planning or who at least works in a firm that employs such a specialist. Over the years, we have been both awed and appalled by the amount of expertise (or the lack thereof) that lawyers have on this rather little-known subject. At worst, which we unfortunately have encountered on occasion, we have found attorneys whose only training in the subject was one course in law school many years before recommending simple wills without the least idea of potential tax implications.

Joe and Ann come to mind. He is an executive, nearing retirement, with a large national company based in New York City. She works part-time as a secretary. They were referred to us by friends of theirs who were clients of ours.

The couple wanted us to assist them with their investments. However, as we began questioning them about their situation, it developed that they had had new wills prepared not three months earlier. Unfortunately, the lawyer who'd done the job hadn't investigated their estate tax picture. As a result, he prepared simple wills, in which each of them left everything to the other, even though their assets were quite substantial. He took no cognizance of how that inappropriate approach could eventually cost their children unnecessary federal estate taxes. The couple had to tear up their fancy but worthless new wills and start over with a good estate planning specialist attorney that we recommended. They'd wasted $900, and they were not amused.

The point is this: You cannot assume that just anyone with a lawyer's shingle is the proper professional to assist you with something as involved as your estate planning. If you had some other legal need—divorce, for instance—you'd probably seek out a specialist. You wouldn't automatically assume that your family attorney or someone whose office just happens to be in your neighborhood could do the legal work for you. Unless you're certain that your situation is so simple that the most basic will is all you need, don't settle for a random attorney. One telltale sign that you'll probably need a more comprehensive estate plan is if all your assets together, including the equity in your home, your investments, your pension or 401(k) plan, and your life insurance coverage add up to more than $600,000. That's the level at which you have to start thinking of strategies to save on estate taxes.

Most people begin their search for the right attorney by speaking with their family lawyer. The drawback is that most legal practitioners will volunteer to draw up the estate plan themselves, whether or not they are qualified. Often they are. Sometimes they're not. If estate planning is not their specialty, they probably are neither schooled in the proper questions to ask you, especially in terms of your resources, nor necessarily familiar with the nuances involved in drafting various estate planning documents.

Only God knows when you are going to die, so it is axiomatic that you want the planning process concluded sooner rather than later. Estate specialists that we work with regularly promise to have drafts of the legal documents in a client's hands within three weeks of getting the go-ahead from the client. On the other hand, attorneys that our clients have asked us to work with occasionally have taken *months* to prepare the documents. We've never been sure whether that's because they have so many more pressing responsibilities that your will takes a low priority, or whether they procrastinate because they don't feel comfortable handling this task. If you were to die before this process was concluded, the tax consequences to your heirs could be disastrous.

If you are going to use your family attorney, don't be afraid to ask several straightforward questions. One might be: Do you, or does someone in your firm, do a lot of estate work? Another is: Are you familiar with the estate tax laws and can you assess the relevance to our situation? And a final question should be: How long will it take you to send out drafts of our documents? The preferable course, we believe, is to work first with the planner and let him or her help guide the choice of an appropriate attorney. If you would prefer to interview several candidates, ask your planner for the names of two or three lawyers.

A word about fees: Just as there is a wide range in competence among lawyers, there is also a broad spectrum of costs. Don't automatically assume that a specialist is beyond your means or that a general practitioner will necessarily come more cheaply. As our clients Joe and Ann discovered, you can pay a nonspecialist handsomely, especially if you happen to live in an expensive part of the country—in a large city on one of the two coasts, for instance.

In interviewing a prospective attorney, feel free to ask questions about cost. "What will you charge to do our wills?" is of course the most basic. In our part of the world, the answer can be anything from $400 to $1,500 for husband and wife, but in yours the costs may be dramatically different. No matter where you live, if an attorney wants more than $1,500 to prepare simple wills, you should shop around. Much more complex estate plans, though, can easily run you several thousand dollars, and in that case you really need to shop around.

Be careful. Not everything is necessarily included in the basic fee. You may have to pay extra for several documents. Powers of attorney, giving husbands and wives the legal authority to act for one another if either is incapacitated, are generally a good idea. In our area, an attorney is apt to charge you $50 or $100 each for powers of attorney. Living wills, the "death with dignity" documents, often cost a similar additional amount.

One document, the revocable living trust, can run up your bill a bit. This is more complicated than a will, although it is a will substitute, both because of its own nature and because it requires a companion, called the pour-over will. While brief, the pour-over will is still another document that must be created. In our experience, the revocable living trust package may cost you $1,500 to $2,500 per couple.

INSURANCE AGENT

It may not always seem necessary to involve an insurance specialist in your estate planning. However, it is often advisable to consider the role that life insurance can play. If your estate is modest in size, a qualified insurance agent can help you determine how much coverage you need for your survivors to live comfortably. If your estate is large or if you own your own business, you may find that your insurance agent's input can lead to significant estate tax savings.

How do you select an insurance agent? The answer is really the same as for any professional you choose to employ. Check for appropriate credentials. As we've said, a CLU or ChFC designation is an indication—not a *guarantee*—that the agent has diligently pursued professional education. Ask about experience. Check references. If you are really stumped, your attorney, accountant, or financial planner may be able to recommend someone they've worked with satisfactorily in the past.

Many agents choose to work with one primary carrier, with which they place most of their business. In Chapter 5 we will cover some of the criteria for selecting an insurance company. If the agent's business card does not list the name of a particular insurance company, feel free to ask whether he or she is indeed affiliated with one main company. Whether or not you are dealing with a single-company agent, you should make sure that you are comfortable with whatever company is being recommended to you. Pay especially close attention to a proposed carrier's financial strength and track record for meeting dividend and interest projections.

As with all of your advisers, you need to feel that you can trust your insurance agent. You want a person who will recommend the proper amount of insurance, the right type of coverage, and competitively priced insurance from a sound company. Each time you begin working with an insurance professional, you crank up a powerful salesman—at least you do if he or she is any good! One way to gauge an agent's or planner's recommendations is to ask that proposals from a number of insurance companies be solicited.

In our office, it isn't unusual to solicit hypothetical illustrations from three or four different companies and to invite representatives from several of them to meet with our clients, usually in our office, a neutral site where the client feels comfortable. That gives us a chance to review the need with the client beforehand and go through a post-mortem on each presentation afterwards. The dialogue is helpful in selecting the appropriate coverage.

In dealing with professionals, whether financial planners, attorneys, or insurance agents, just remember that these people work for you. You are the boss, and they are your servants.

II

TAKING STOCK

Chapter Four

Determining What You Are Worth

W hat's the value of your life? That metaphysical question is an imponderable. Depending on the context, though, you can give at least a practical answer. The context here, of course, is estate planning, and you cannot do your planning intelligently unless you know where you stand financially.

In this chapter, we try to help you estimate your current net worth. That's important because if you've achieved some level of affluence, your planning must take cognizance of the potential estate tax implications. In Chapter 5 we will help you calculate your long-term worth to your loved ones, which you need to know to determine what preparations you should make in case you die prematurely.

Figure 4–1 shows you in outline form how we compute a client's net worth. It's an actual balance sheet for one of our clients, one we thought was fairly typical of a person for whom estate planning ought to be a high priority. We've also included a blank version of the balance sheet for your convenience. Here's how you can prepare your own evaluation.

TAKING STOCK

The place to start is with your assets. If you have never totted up everything you own, that chore is probably overdue. In some cases, the value may be difficult to ascertain. But you should do the best you can.

You will want to organize your resources into categories. If you leave money in an IRA, 401(k), or other defined-contribution pension plan, you have choices as to how these funds are invested. You would include these assets in your listing, depending on which category they fell into. We generally like to array them from most conservative to most risky.

Let's begin with cash assets. These are fixed-value, meaning that they cannot lose value; a dollar is always a dollar. On the other hand, they can never grow in value, either; interest can mount up, but the underlying asset is always worth exactly what you invested, not a penny more or less. Therefore, cash-type investments expose you to the twin ravages of inflation and taxation. Assets like bank certificates of deposit (CDs), as well as checking, savings, and money-market accounts, are obviously cash assets. We also include Series EE savings bonds, fixed annuities, guaranteed investment contracts (GICs) in retirement plans, and the cash value that builds up in life insurance contracts.

Next are bonds. They are fixed-return assets since you are lending your money (to a government, municipality, corporation, or other entity), but they are not fixed-value. Bonds fluctuate in market value. Generally, as interest rates rise, bond prices fall and vice versa. This is important to consider in estate planning because in periods of fluctuating interest rates, bond values and hence estate values may also fluctuate.

Among the most popular types of bonds are municipal bonds (munis), especially insured munis. They fluctuate less in value than other types of bonds because they are not subject to the same forces that affect bonds in general. Intrinsically local investments, munis usually are purchased by residents of the particular state or municipality that issued them. Their interest rate is lower than that carried by other types of bonds, reflecting their tax-exempt status in the United States.

However, municipal bonds are not immune to default. There have been tragic cases of innocent investors losing their life savings in munis gone bad. Two ways to protect yourself when buying bonds are to buy bonds with top ratings from agencies such as Moody's and Standard & Poor's or to buy insured munis, on which the income stream is guaranteed by an insurance company specializing in munis.

U.S. government bonds insulate investors from any default risk. No one worries about the U.S. government going out of business. However, U.S. government bonds can change much more dramatically in price than municipal bonds as interest rates rise and fall. As a result, you need to update your balance sheet periodically to reflect the current prices of any government bonds or bond mutual funds you own.

Corporate bonds are still more variable in nature. They carry a higher risk of default since your only security is the particular company's promise to repay your loan to it, and consequently they must pay a higher interest rate. Thus the value of bonds (and the mutual funds that invest in them) are even more susceptible to the impact of interest rate swings. You should be aware of the ratings that your bonds have received from Moody's and Standard & Poor's. Generally, the higher the interest rate, the lower the rating and hence the less safe.

Some types of mutual funds are neither fish nor fowl; typically they are called balanced funds. *Balanced* implies some division in the fund's portfolio between bonds and stocks. (Other mutual fund designations, such as "growth and income," imply a similar approach.) A balanced fund might invest 30 percent to 50 percent of its assets in bonds and possibly a like amount in stocks while keeping a decent-sized cash reserve. The proportions can be changed dramatically depending on economic and market conditions. Because these funds are neither assets in which you entirely *loan* your money nor investments in which you entirely *own* an interest, we place them in a separate category.

Variable annuities may place you in a similar predicament, but one that's easier to resolve. A variable annuity is an investment you purchase from an insurance company. It's like putting your money into a mutual fund family, with investment choices that are likely to include stock funds, bond funds, even precious metals funds, and a money market account. Unlike a conventional mutual fund group, a variable annuity usually offers a fixed account as well, with your money gaining a set rate of interest, usually for one year at a time. All this is in a tax-deferred context because of the tax advantage that life insurance has. Unliked balanced mutual funds, however, it is easy to properly place your variable annuity shares on your balance sheet because such annuities have internal separate accounts that carry stated values. The dollars that you have invested in bond accounts should be listed in that section of your balance sheet, stock accounts in the appropriate section, and so on. Any sums you have invested in fixed or money market accounts belong in the cash portion of the balance sheet.

Ownership Assets

The two most common types of equity investments, by far, are stocks and real estate. Nearly every family has at least a small stake in one or both, even if it's only through ownership of a home or an investment in a corporate thrift plan.

Listing your positions in individual stocks or in stock mutual funds is easy. Unless you own stock in very small, unlisted companies, you need only turn to the financial pages of your newspaper to get the latest price of your securities. Updating the value of your stock portfolio becomes a relatively easy matter.

Real estate, on the other hand, is more subjective. Keep in mind that the point of this exercise is to give you a notion of your worldly worth so you can estimate any potential estate tax liability. Consequently, while you may not be able to figure an exact value for property you own, you at least need to find the right ballpark. You need to answer honestly the question: If I were to sell today, what's the most I could expect to receive for my property? Depending on the complexity of your portfolio, you might be able to compare notes with a real estate agent or two and get an approximate idea of value.

If you have invested money in a real estate limited partnership (as opposed to a real estate investment trust—REIT—which is traded and therefore has an easily ascertainable current value), determining the real value of your shares is very difficult. One attorney we know jokes that he first decides what value he wants to report to the IRS when he settles an estate, then works backward to arrive at that number. That's not such a joke when you consider the complexity of valuing partnership interests. If you purchased a stake in one of the large public real estate partnerships, you may be able to get a current market value from the company, or from one of the few brokerage firms that make a market in partnership shares.

We often see client portfolios that contain more unusual types of investments, typically limited partnerships invested in energy, for instance, or leasing or cable TV. Sometimes these partnership interests are held in a brokerage account, and the firm will attempt to value the holdings, especially if the account is an IRA.

Most often, you'll own the investment outside a brokerage account. The valuation approach we outlined regarding real estate partnerships is the same one you'd use for other deals. But don't drive yourself crazy. Again, we want to reiterate that you should take a *commonsense* approach. Such partnership interests ought to comprise a tiny fraction of your balance sheet, so spend an appropriate amount of time determining their worth.

Personal Use Assets

Beyond the realm of financial investments is a parallel universe of your personal use assets beginning with the most obvious, your house. As with investment property, you may be able to estimate the current market value of your house. But because of the decline in values in many areas since the mid-1980s, your estimate may not be very accurate. In the Northeast this has been a controversial issue for several years now because house prices have dropped, in some cases significantly.

It's not a bad idea to speak with a real estate agent about the likely current market value of your house. If yours is a unique home, don't use a run-of-the-mill agent. Find one who specializes in selling such homes and can imagine the type of buyer who'd be interested in your place, just as you'd ask an appropriate dealer to assess the worth of your original Jamie Wyeth print, not the local art emporium that specializes in clown portraits.

You may also have some collectibles—china, porcelain, artwork, antiques, stamps, or coins. If you have neglected to have your possessions professionally appraised, you should do so for more reasons than estate planning. A collection of even small value may exceed the coverage you have in your homeowners insurance. In such case, a loss due to fire or theft would not be completely covered. The same applies to precious metals. The sterling silver service you inherited from your grandmother should be appraised, as should your jewelry. The appraisal may not be exact and values change over time, but at least you have some evidence of value to present to the insurance company and, not incidentally, some insight as to the value of your estate.

Of course, such possessions may or may not ever actually be part of your estate. We have many elderly clients who over the years have given away their treasures to their children and grandchildren. As long as the gifts total less than $10,000 per recipient per year ($20,000 a year for a couple), you can give away an unlimited amount over your lifetime without encountering a gift or estate tax obligation.

You should also take more mundane personal property into account, but don't get carried away trying to figure out what your well-worn golf clubs are worth. In fact, once you've added up separately the value of everything you possess that has ascertainable value, you can probably plug in a number for the total of everything else. We usually use a range of $25,000 to $50,000.

An exception is cars. Unless you are driving a 1972 Pontiac with 190,000 miles on it and little usable life left, your cars should be listed separately.

Ownership

As you are tallying up your assets, be sure to note the ownership of each. If you are single, that's simple. But married couples, especially younger ones, generally own assets, particularly a home, jointly. You'll notice in the worksheet that we suggest making four columns: the husband's assets, the wife's, joint property, and the total. This is a key concept in estate planning, because the titling of assets often determines what sort of planning strategies are available. You can easily defeat the most canny estate plan by neglecting to properly title your assets. At the risk of oversimplifying, as a generalization the older you are and the larger your assets, the less appropriate joint ownership is.

We'll spend more time on the forms of property ownership and the tax implications of each later in the book. For now, realize that when you go through the exercise of determining what you are worth—a happy exercise, we hope—be careful to segregate your assets according to who owns them.

Nonbalance Sheet Assets

One asset that's difficult to evaluate is a pension. If it contains a survivor's benefit, your pension must be considered in figuring your estate. Say you are receiving $3,000 a month, and when you die your spouse will get $1,500 a month. After you die, your executor must hire an attorney or an accountant to calculate the value of your spouse's entitlement. The IRS demands that it be included as an asset of your estate.

Another nonbalance sheet asset that's more widely held is life insurance. Contrary to what most people think, under normal circumstances the life insurance benefits that your death produces (whether for your spouse, children, or whomever) are considered part of your gross estate. There are ways to get the insurance proceeds out of your estate. Most common is by using a planning tool called the irrevocable life insurance trust, which we strongly recommend and will discuss at length later in the book. However, we realize that insurance trusts are not appropriate in every situation, especially if you have a small estate, a nominal amount of coverage, or both. Therefore, we suggest that below your net worth you add in the death benefit value of life insurance on your life and your spouse's.

Liabilities

Once you have tallied up your resources, you need to subtract any liabilities. That figure gives you your net worth. For most, a mortgage is likely to be the biggest liability. You may also have a car loan, home improvement loan, lingering student loans, or standing balances on your credit cards. All of these reduce your net worth.

Having subtracted liabilities from assets, you can arrive at a net worth figure. Armed with that number, you have a preliminary estimate of your value for estate purposes.

Having gone through the exercise of determining what you are worth, you still can't know with complete precision what, if any, estate tax liability you may have. You could, for instance, give property away while you are alive or leave some of your assets to charity at your death. And there will be final bills and expenses that your estate will pay after your death. All these items would reduce your gross estate. Still, having a relatively accurate notion of the value of your current estate is an excellent place to begin thinking about what estate planning strategies are appropriate.

Figure 4–1 is a sample balance sheet from a financial plan that we prepared for one of our clients and Figure 4–2 is a blank balance sheet that you can use in evaluating your own finances.

FIGURE 4–1
Balance Sheet (August 6, 1992)

	Total	Husband	Joint	Wife
Assets				
Fixed investments				
Money market and savings	$ 224,614	$ 88,142	$ 136,472	$0
Certificates of deposit	509,671	163,829	179,536	166,306
Notes due	192,000	0	192,000	0
Life insurance cash value	81,350	81,350	0	0
Total fixed investments	$1,007,635	$333,321	$ 508,008	$166,306
Variable investments				
Real estate, market value	390,000	250,000	140,000	0
Total variable investments	$ 390,000	$250,000	$ 140,000	$0
Personal property				
Home	390,000	0	390,000	0
Bedford Condo*	73,000	0	73,000	0
Automobiles	43,000	0	43,000	0
Jewelry	45,000	0	0	45,000
Total personal property	$ 551,000	$0	$ 506,000	$ 45,000
TOTAL ASSETS	$1,948,635	$583,321	$1,154,008	$211,306
Liabilities	0	0	0	0
TOTAL LIABILITIES	$0	$0	$0	$0
Net worth	$1,948,635	$583,321	$1,154,008	$211,306
Invested capital	$1,397,635	$583,321	$ 648,008	$166,306

* One-third ownership.

FIGURE 4–2
Balance Sheet*

	Wife	*Husband*	*Joint*	*Total*
Assets				
Cash				
Savings accounts				
Checking accounts				
Money market funds				
Certificates of deposit				
Fixed annuities				
GICs				
Bonds				
Municipal				
U.S. Government				
Corporate				
Balanced Funds				
Equities				
Stocks and stock funds				
Real estate				
Limited partnerships (energy, cable TV, leasing, etc.)				
Business interests (net value)				
Personal Use Assets				
Home				
Cars				
Collectibles				
General personal property				
Totals				
Liabilities				
Mortgage				
Second mortgage				
Home equity line				
Investment loan(s)				
Car loan(s)				
Credit card balance(s)				
Student loan(s)				
Other debts				
Totals				

*Note that each spouse's estate is comprised of the total of his or her own assets plus one half of the couple's joint resources, minus their individual obligations and one half of joint obligations.

Chapter Five

Assessing Your Family's Needs and Purchasing Life Insurance

I f you are like most people, one of life's really uncomfortable experiences—right up there with dealing with an IRS audit or having root canal surgery—is facing a life insurance agent. Remember the classic scene in Woody Allen's wonderful movie *Take the Money and Run?* Woody plays a small-time criminal. Because he misbehaves while he's in prison, he is sent down into the hole to face the ultimate punishment: a week with a life insurance salesman. Two things about life insurance salespeople are apt to make your stomach churn. First, they're trying to sell you a product you don't understand at a price that may seem entirely unaffordable. Second, implicit in the deal is an unpleasant reality: You're buying this mysterious, expensive product not for yourself—you'll be dead when the investment matures—but for others.

As we've said about the process of estate planning itself, taking care of your family is something you do out of love. Oh sure, there are types of life insurance that allow you to recapture some of your premium dollars and their earnings later on. But the most basic use of life insurance is to provide protection, making up for whatever the rest of your estate may lack. Thus, it stands to reason that it's necessary for those people who have a small amount of assets compared with their obligations. Ironically, it is also useful for those who are fortunate enough to have very large estates, which need protection from estate taxes imposed at death.

This was brought home forcefully to us several years ago. A retired gentleman came into the office one day and said he needed help. His son, a thirtysomething, up-and-coming attorney, had died suddenly a few months before of a heart attack. The young man left behind three children, ranging in age from 18 months to 6 years old, a wife who hadn't worked in six years—and almost no assets. There was a modest life insurance policy that the man's law firm had supplied, a pittance in savings, and a mountain of obligations. Either he didn't believe in life insurance or he never got around to buying the proper amount. His father, our client, didn't know which. What he did know was that now his task was to assist his daughter-in-law and grandchildren as best he could. Instead of savoring his retirement, he was preparing to go back to work.

What the young lawyer left instead of assets were obligations. To start with, his wife had to pay the mortgage and a car loan each month. Though they didn't live extravagantly, she and her husband had a fairly large suburban home for their family of five and the attendant mortgage. After her husband's death, she wondered whether she would have to sell their home.

The car loan was easily settled. Since she no longer needed two cars, she sold one and used the proceeds to pay off the loan balance on the other one. But the largest obligations her husband left behind were almost invisible: raising and educating three kids, and then living comfortably herself for the rest of her years.

Several times over the years, we have heard clients casually shrug off their obligations. "Oh, she's young and attractive," they'll say of their wives. "If anything happens to me, she'll easily remarry." Maybe so, maybe not. In either case this seems to us like an especially selfish response to an exceptionally serious issue: If I love my family and may not be around to help care for them, will I have arranged my affairs such that my obligation will be discharged anyway? Or will I leave my spouse in a situation where she or he *has* to remarry in order to survive?

While we are on the topic of obligations, it's high time that we disposed of a few stereotypes. The typical family consisting of a working husband and a dutiful wife at home minding the kids is becoming less and less typical. This is not to disparage women who choose to make homemaking their profession. We think that's great. But many other women, out of desire or necessity, are pursuing full-time careers outside of the home. Many women are also finding themselves the primary breadwinner, either because of divorce or widowhood or because their careers have outpaced their husbands'.

Whether or not the woman is working outside the home, there will be obligations to meet in the event that *she* dies. If the wife is working, chances are the family is greatly dependent on her income for their standard of living. If she were to pass away, the husband's income alone might not be able to sustain the same lifestyle. This is even more critical if the woman is a single parent. Maybe Dad would step in and take care of the kids. But maybe Dad won't, or can't.

We really can't ignore the economic value of women who choose the traditional role of homemaker. What do you think it would cost to hire a housekeeper and full-time nanny for your kids? Big bucks!

Yet, we find all too often that the contributions women make are grossly undervalued. This shows up when we review our clients' insurance portfolios. We often find that there is at least some insurance on the husband, but often little or none on the wife. There are many reasons for this. One is that husbands tend to work for larger companies, which provide large amounts of life insurance as a corporate benefit. Moreover, they tend to earn more, which provides them with higher amounts of coverage through their jobs.

Another reason is that the couples themselves haven't thought about the need. And finally, most insurance agents are men, many of them graduates of the "old school." They were simply not brought up to recognize the economic power that women have today. So, very often the agents themselves are not pointing out the need.

Fortunately, this is changing. More women are entering the financial planning and insurance fields. Many of them have first-hand knowledge of what it means to be a working mother or a widowed or divorced parent. And more of us stodgy old men are having our consciousness raised to this new reality: Women play an essential economic role in every family, whether or not they work outside the home. Families need to be protected against the loss of the wife and mother every bit as much as they need to be protected against the loss of the father.

Next question: How much insurance do you need? This is one area where rules of thumb just don't work very well. Everyone's situation is unique. We have heard people say you should have an amount of coverage based on your earnings. Some people insist you should carry three times or four times your salary in life insurance. Such notions are dangerously simplistic. If your spouse is working and plans to continue doing so, if you have substantial financial resources, if your pension plan is well funded (or not), if your kids are grown—all these are important considerations. Three or four times your annual income may be way too much insurance, or woefully too little.

One of the things you should ask your financial planner or life insurance agent to do is to perform the calculations necessary to identify the proper amount of insurance. Most financial planners are equipped to do that analysis, as are better trained insurance agents. The evaluation is known by various names: Capital needs analysis, financial needs analysis, and survivor needs analysis are three of the most common.

All these programs work essentially the same way. The idea here is that if you have an obligation in the future, you can discharge it by setting aside an appropriate number of dollars in the present. Of necessity, those dollars will be fewer than you'd need if you waited until the time when the future obligation arrived.

That's because your dollars can be invested and can grow between now and the time you'll need them. That's the way Social Security (or any pension) is supposed to work. Put in a little money over a long period of time, and when you are ready to use the money, it will have grown enough to satisfy your need.

Let's take another example: college education. Suppose you have a six-year-old daughter. You want to prepare for the cost of sending her to a state university, which now runs about $12,000 a year in most places. If inflation in the cost of higher education runs about 6 percent a year, which is actually less than it has been averaging, then in 12 years when your child is ready to go off to college, you'll be facing an annual bill of $24,146 the first year, $25,595 the second ($1.06 \times \$24,146$), and so on. The question is how much money you would have to put aside today, given some assumed growth rate on your investment, in order to fund that child's college education.

For example, if you could achieve an 8-percent a year rate of return on your money, how much would you need? That's an achievable rate of return, by the way, since an investment that matched the return of the stock market over a long period would typically have returned more than 10 percent per year. In this example, in order to have $24,146 in 12 years, you'd need to invest $9,588 now and average an 8 percent return on your money, or to put $100 away each month. To have $25,595 in 13 years, you'd need to have $9,411 today, or to put away $93 each month for the next 13 years. This process is repeated for years 3 and 4.

Financial planners call that notion *present value*. The idea is that a small amount invested today can fill a large need tomorrow. The more time you have before the need arises and the better return your investment provides you, the less you must invest now.

The way you approach this subject in general, then, is to try to judiciously estimate all your future needs. Then subtract the resources you have available to meet them. The illustration in Figure 5–1 gives you an outline. Don't worry too much about the math. You can always find someone to run the numbers for you—a financial planner, insurance agent, or accountant. If you understand the concept and can plug in your own numbers, you'll be well on the way to an accurate assessment of your unmet need.

Sorry to say, you're going to have to begin with an exercise that most people find rather uninviting. You're going to have to figure out your current spending needs. The easiest way to do that is by examining your check registers. We ask our clients to take the past 12 months. It doesn't matter where in the year you begin, but try to get a full 12-month picture. Otherwise, you could be overlooking expenditures that fall only in a particular month (your homeowners insurance premium, say) or those that are higher in one season than another (winter heating bills, for instance).

There are several major categories of expenditure you don't need to be overly concerned about. Income taxes, for one, decline as your income shrinks, so for long-term planning purposes (such as retirement), you can include a smaller number than your current tax bill. (The way we actually calculate that number, by the way, is to figure out how much a family's basic living expenses are likely to total in retirement, then "gross them up," or in other words figure out what total a client would have to have coming in, including taxes, based on current tax law. See Figure 5–1.)

Similarly, in this evaluation you would not include FICA (Social

FIGURE 5-1
Capital Needs Analysis for the Roberts Family

	1992–1999	2000–2001	2002–2003	2004–2011	Lifetime thereafter
Income objective	$ 3,000	$ 3,000	$3,000	$ 2,500	$ 2,500
Social security	1,878	1,621	806	0	768
Robin's earnings	0	0	2,000	2,000	0
Monthly deficit	$ 1,122	$ 1,138	$ 194	$ 500	$ 1,732
Capitalized deficit*	$99,483	$27,897	$3,770	$34,425	$237,298

Total Deficit:	$403,973
Plus	
Mortgage	150,000
Funeral costs	10,000
Estate expenses	25,800
Credit card debt	5,000
Emergency fund	10,000
College fund	77,500
Total family needs	$682,273
Total family needs:	$682,273
Minus	
Current investments	$100,000
Life insurance	250,000
Additional life insurance needed:	$332,273

*Capitalized deficit represents the amount that would have to be invested today at 8 percent to maintain the buying power needed to retain the desired standard of living, assuming 6 percent inflation.

Security) taxes, which you pay only on *earned* income. And don't take into account the savings you're putting aside regularly for your children's college educations. Saving for retirement you don't need to consider, because you will no longer be doing so after you *have* retired.

When you have finished your evaluation, you have a good idea of how much you need each year for basic living expenses. Now, discount the number somewhat. If you were out of the picture, would your family have to spend quite as much? Probably not. The larger your family, the closer to 100 percent of current expenditures they would require.

Your planner may take this one step further. Some of your cash flow requirements will be impacted by inflation. Some will not. For example, a fixed mortgage payment will not increase no matter what happens. Some requirements will last forever. Some will not. Your car loan will eventually be paid off. College educations will end some time (though it may not seem so at the time).

On the other hand, your planner may take a more simplified approach and say that you need a certain amount of income during your preretirement years and a lower amount or none at all after you retire. We suppose we may get an argument on this score from punctilious financial planners. But in our view, attempting to be overly precise only gives people a false sense of security. There are so many variables in the equation. You can't predict with any certainty what the inflation rate will be. Even if you could, future changes in your family situation may be even more uncertain.

So, it's sufficient to get a basic idea of your needs. On the next few pages, we will present a case study that shows you how a simple capital needs analysis works.

Jack and Robin Roberts are the parents of two children, ages 10 and 6. Jack has a good job in a stable industry. Robin is not currently working outside the home, but she plans to return to her career as a real estate agent when her youngest child is in high school. Before having the children, Robin averaged $24,000 a year in commissions.

The Robertses have determined that Robin would need $3,000 per month to run the household if Jack were to die, assuming the mortgage were paid off. Once the kids are out of the household, Robin's need would drop to $2,500 and remain at that level for life. In addition, they wish to make sure there would be sufficient funds available to cover the cost of college, assuming an annual cost per child of $12,000 a year *in today's dollars.*

The Robertses figure that inflation will average 6 percent in the years ahead. They are confident they can earn at least 8 percent on their invested assets, for a real rate of return of 2 percent annually.

The analysis breaks the income needs out into periods conforming with Social Security payments. All three beneficiaries will be eligible until the older child turns 18. Then the 18-year-old drops off. When the younger child turns 16, Robin loses her own Social Security benefit. That's when our illustration assumes she will return to work. When the younger child turns 18, there are no further Social Security payments until Robin reaches age 60 and becomes eligible—depending on her income at the time—for Social Security widow's benefits. At 62, she would be eligible to file for her own Social Security benefit. She can collect the higher of the benefit she is entitled to by virtue of her own income or what she would get based on Jack's income, not both.

What do all these figures tell us? Jack and Robin are typical clients. They live in a nice home with a big mortgage—almost $150,000. If Jack dies, Robin would not go back to work until her oldest child (now age 10) was 16. At that point, she would be able to earn $2,000 a month. The analysis takes into account the eventual income that Robin could produce, as well as income produced by their existing investments and income that the death benefits resulting from Jack's life insurance policies would generate after his death.

After adjusting for inflation and the rate of return on invested assets, we find that a total of $403,973 would be needed to fund the Robertses' income needs. To that we must add the cost of paying off their mortgage (which was their desire), funeral costs, estate settlement costs, and debts, as well as providing an emergency fund. We also calculated the future cost of education; that number came out to be $77,500.

This brought the total need to $682,273. The Robertses already had $100,000 in savings, investments, and retirement plans. In addition, Jack had $250,000 in life insurance through his job. He thought that was plenty. The analysis showed he had little justification for feeling complacent. Without additional coverage of about $300,000, the family would not be able to achieve their objectives if something were to happen to Jack.

With such a large need, we would probably recommend term insurance on Jack. This coverage could be converted to a whole life or universal life policy later on, when the Robertses will have more discretionary income.

What if they lost Robin? They really hadn't thought about it. But the cost of bringing in full-time help for the kids and for housekeeping would be close to $20,000 per year, at least until the children were older. Our analysis indicated a need for at least $100,000 of life insurance coverage on Robin to help meet these needs.

As you study this needs analysis, a couple of things probably occur to you. For one, the younger you are, generally the greater your needs and the fewer your resources—unless you're very young and haven't had time to crank up the needs (because you're not yet married or haven't bought a home or haven't yet had kids). The older you are, the more likely you've discharged your obligations and have had time to build up your nest egg. Typically, the largest life insurance needs are found in people in their 30s and 40s. As the kids finish college, your mortgage declines, and your assets grow, the needs taper off until at retirement you probably have a lesser need for insurance (assuming you've done proper retirement planning—but that's a different book).

None of this discussion applies to people who possess substantial wealth or who own their own businesses. As we'll discuss in later chapters, their needs for insurance are calculated on an entirely different basis. Those needs can actually *increase* as they get older.

Another thing that may occur to you in looking over the capital needs analysis is how complicated the math seems. How do I figure out all these present values? How do I really know how much my family would need in order to live comfortably in my absence? How much *could* (or would) my spouse earn if I were gone?

Bearing in mind that this is the *Commonsense Guide to Estate Planning*, we urge you not to get too hung up by the inevitable uncertainties or complexities. Think of it this way: If you know what you're earning now and you subtract income taxes, Social Security tax, and savings, what's left is your family's living expenses.

If you earn $75,000 a year, pay $15,000 in federal income taxes, pay $4,000 in FICA, and save $6,000 a year (in a 401(K) plan or what have you), then the remaining $50,000 is what your family is spending each year to live. Without you, that might be a little less. But you wouldn't want it to be so much less that your family would be forced to alter their lifestyle significantly. Similarly, if your spouse is not employed now, try to envision what job—if any—she or he might be likely to take if you were to die. One excellent way to get a notion is to discuss this together.

After you have done at least a rudimentary form of this capital needs exercise, you'll have enough information to speak with someone who can run precise numbers for you. Any good financial planner or life insurance agent should be able to perform the analysis. Just make sure they don't skew the results by sneaking in unrealistic assumptions in order to boost the amount of your unmet need in order to sell you more insurance than you really need.

The inflation assumption is one key to determining capital needs. It should be either 5 percent or 6 percent per year. Since World War II, the cost of living has increased just under 5 percent per year; however, during the past quarter-century it's been about 6 percent per year, on average. The rate of return you can achieve on your investments should average 8 percent to 9 percent per year. In other words, you should forecast a 2 percent to 3 percent real (after inflation) annual rate of return.

When you are comfortable with the appraisal of how much (if any) additional life insurance you need, you should start thinking about what type of coverage to purchase. There's a profusion of different kinds of life insurance and endless variations on every theme. To oversimplify, a young person with large needs may be best off buying term insurance—a pure, unvarnished death benefit. No cash value. No permanent level premium. Large amounts of death benefit usually can be purchased comparatively inexpensively. The drawback is that not only do you never have any cash value to show for your premiums, but also you may run the risk of paying much more if you experience a serious health problem.

This occurs if your term policy has a reentry provision. At the end of a given period, often 5 or 10 years, you will be given the opportunity to take a new physical exam. If you pass, you can renew the policy at rates that are quite attractive. If you fail, your rates go up and could increase substantially.

Of course, if you no longer need the coverage, it doesn't matter, which is why term insurance is just what the name implies: coverage that you need for a specific, temporary need. If you need to continue the insurance, though, it could be a serious problem. Your only alternative might be to convert to a permanent plan of insurance. In most term policies, you can do this even if you flunk the medical exam.

You can buy term policies that have fixed premiums for as long as 10 or 15 years. This forestalls but does not eliminate the reentry problem. There are also policies that do not require reentry in later years, but they tend to be more expensive as the insurance company does not get to raise the rates for those whose health deteriorates.

You can use term life insurance for an obligation that is identifiable and finite, for example, insurance for the children's college costs. That will give you the most insurance for your money in the short run. At some point, though, most people should consider some form of permanent life insurance for their long-term needs (i.e., those that will last longer than 10 years). Again, this is a topic for another book. But in general such policies are available as either whole life, universal life, or variable life. We will briefly describe each of them.

WHOLE LIFE INSURANCE

This is the traditional type of insurance that your parents and probably your grandparents purchased years ago. It is permanent coverage with a level premium and an enforced savings feature that results in a cash value buildup within the policy. Traditionally, the cash value earned a very low interest rate. In the high inflation years of the 1970s, whole life began to look like a very poor investment. Thus, the insurance industry began to sharpen its collective pencil and revise whole life insurance contracts, to the point that they have become more attractive financially.

The advantages of whole life are a fixed premium, guaranteed cash value, and a guaranteed death benefit. True, these guarantees are not especially exciting. During the go-go years of the 1960s, 1970s, and 1980s, nobody looked much at guarantees. We've learned our lesson. The actual performance of these policies is determined by nonguaranteed dividends. The top companies have dividend performances that have been consistently strong over the years. The dividends are used to lower the cost of coverage or to increase coverage over time.

When you look at a proposal for a whole life policy, don't get too excited by the illustration. It is the dividends that make it look terrific. If dividends drop, which they have for most companies in the past few years, your policy will not perform as projected. On the other hand, if dividends go up, your policy may generate even more cash value than you originally anticipated.

UNIVERSAL LIFE

Unlike whole life, universal life does not have a fixed premium per se. The planned premium may or may not work out in the future. Like its cousin, universal life generates both cash value and death benefits. However, depending on the interest rate environment, they could be greater or lesser than those that build up in a whole life contract. To a much greater extent than whole life, universal life is a type of cash value life insurance that is a creature of interest rates. If rates in general tend to be higher in the future than they were when you bought a universal life contract, you'll do better than expected; if lower, you won't fare as well as you thought you would.

Universal life does provide flexibility. You can generally buy more coverage for each dollar of premium than you could with whole life. You can reduce or skip premiums from year to year. You can even pay a higher premium to build up more cash value if you are attracted to the tax-deferred nature of life insurance.

Universal life can be a very powerful financial vehicle. However, it can also be dangerous. Because of the lack of guarantees, the health of your policy must be continuously monitored.

Many people jumped at the chance to purchase universal life policies when they were first offered and interest rates were in the 12 percent to 15 percent range. Because universal life policies establish a separate investment account within the policy, those rates were enticing. After the cost of your insurance has been deducted, the investment account grows for you as your dollars gain a rate of interest. The cost of insurance is not guaranteed, but it is fairly stable and predictable. The course of interest rates is neither. Thus, people who bought policies when rates were 12 percent to 15 percent may be in for an unpleasant surprise. The premiums they thought they were committing to may be inadequate to support their insurance—let alone to build up value at the pace they had figured on.

Since there is no fixed premium, if a policyholder continues paying on the basis of the initial interest rate, and if rates drop substantially, sooner or later the universal life policy will run out of cash value. When that happens, the cost of keeping the policy alive will be far higher than expected. If the premiums fall short over any significant period of time, a policyholder can be asked to pony up ever larger amounts of money to retain the insurance. Or, the amount of insurance coverage may have to be reduced in order to coincide with the premiums being paid.

All this doesn't necessarily make universal life bad, especially at a time when interest rates have come down a lot. In the past few years, the rates projected by most universal life policies have been in the 7 percent to 8 percent range. At that level, the chances of future problems are probably somewhat diminished. Most seers anticipate that interest rates in the years ahead will be trending upward, if anything, not further downward. If true, that would make universal life policies quite attractive.

VARIABLE LIFE

This sort of insurance is more akin to mutual funds than to either of the two preceding types of permanent coverage. Variable life contracts allow the policyholder to direct the investment of cash values. The money can go into stock funds, bond funds, or money market accounts. Thus, performance is contingent on the policyholder being an effective investment manager. Generally, you get a choice of half a dozen or so investment options in a typical variable life contract. They range from conservative to quite aggressive. In our experience, variable life is not for the faint-hearted. You must be a risk taker who doesn't mind linking your insurance coverage directly to the performance of the financial markets. If you are more conservative or prefer an insurance policy that doesn't demand constant care on your part, variable life is not for you.

WHICH INSURANCE COMPANY?

Who should you buy from? This is a complex question. First, you should deal only with qualified agents, those whose advice you can understand, respect, and trust. Second, consider three criteria when you are evaluating a potential insurance company:

- The financial strength and security of the company.
- The company's performance history.
- The company's current projections.

Unfortunately, all too often, the focus is on projections. How foolish. Sales illustrations are merely forecasts of what will happen if nothing changes. They can be manipulated by agents. In the real world, interest rates will fluctuate, tax laws will change, and insurance companies' mortality experience will vary. It is far better to rely on the strength of the company and its track record than on current illustrations.

Ask your insurance agent or financial planner to provide you with the ratings of the company being recommended. These ratings are published by four major services: A.M. Best Co., Inc., Standard & Poor's Corp., Moody's Investors Service, and Duff & Phelps.

Opinions differ as to what is an appropriate minimum rating in order to justify consideration of an insurance company. In our opinion, you should be very careful in dealing with companies that are not rated at least A+ by A.M. Best and in the AA range by the other services.

Your agent should also provide you with historical performance information on companies being recommended. With a whole life policy, you want to see the dividend history of the company. Has it done a good job of paying dividends? How have its policies performed compared to similar policies issued by other companies? This information is available from A.M. Best & Co. All agents have access to it through the insurance carriers they deal with.

Comparing universal life policies can be a little trickier. First of all, universal life is a relatively recent phenomenon, with the vast majority of policies having been written since 1984. Obviously, you don't have a very long track record to evaluate. To compare proposals, you need to know more than just the current interest rate being credited. The cost of insurance and contract expense deductions are equally, if not more, important. It is difficult to get that information from a standard proposal. The easiest way to understand how these charges affect the performance of policies you are considering is to request illustrations from several different companies using similar assumptions.

To start with, the face amount of the two policies should be the same. Universal life is sold with two death benefit options, level and increasing. Make sure that the two illustrations assume the same option. Then ask that the same premium be paid into each contract for the same number of years. You should then look at how the contract performs at the guaranteed rate, an assumed interest rate 2 percent below the current rate, and the current rate.

Guaranteed rate. Do not be too dismayed if neither contract looks good on a guaranteed basis. Universal life is not designed for guarantees; it is designed for current performance. If that turns you off, you should consider whole life. But be prepared to pay a higher premium in order to receive that guarantee.

Assumed rate (2 percent below current). Which contract holds up better if interest rates go down? In general, a contract with better current pricing will do better at lower interest rates.

Current rate. If all goes well, which contract delivers more cash value? You may be surprised to see that it is a contract with a lower interest rate. This is a direct result of the impact of the cost of insurance and expense charges on the policies' overall performance.

Ultimately, the financial strength of the insurance carrier should be the key to your selection. Because of the lack of guarantees, the health of your insurer will be the ultimate determining factor in the contract's safety and performance.

To sum up this discussion, we suggest you first determine how much life insurance you need. If you are young or have severe budget constraints, purchase term insurance. It is far more important to have the right *amount* of coverage than it is to have the "best" type. If your needs are long term, a form of permanent insurance will work best, assuming you can afford it. Don't be pressured or seduced by promises of fantastic returns on permanent insurance. These policies can be attractive, but make sure you put your family's security needs first. Most of the time, you can convert your term insurance later, when you have more money.

P A R T

III

DISTRIBUTION OF YOUR PROPERTY

Chapter Six

What Happens to Your Property When You Die?

T he bereaved family has gathered in the oak-paneled offices of the dearly departed's attorney. Silence settles over the assembled group as the venerable barrister removes a document from the top drawer of his desk. The tension mounts as he opens the Last Will and Testament. Each relative anxiously awaits the reading of the will, eager to learn his or her fate.

That's the way it happens in Hollywood. In real life, the last will and testament is often a less-than-dramatic document, since it distributes only a portion of your assets. Depending on how you own your property, this may actually be a very small part of your total estate. To understand how your property will be distributed and where it will go upon your death, you need to look at the various ways that property is owned.

In addition to your will, there are six other ways that property can be held and distributed to your heirs.

OUTRIGHT OWNERSHIP

Property that you own in your name alone can include personal property of all types, such as your car, personal effects, jewelry, checking and savings account, investments, real estate, and so on. With respect to real estate, this form of ownership is known as *fee simple*.

Most property owned outright becomes part of your probate estate when you die. Each state has established its own rules and regulations for the process of estate settlement known as probate. But all have common goals. The probate process is designed to protect all parties with an interest in the estate. This includes not only the deceased's heirs, but also the deceased's creditors. It may also include the federal and local taxing authorities because income taxes may remain to be paid for money earned in the year of death— as well as for taxes still owed for previous years, in some cases.

As we will see in later chapters, there also may be estate and inheritance taxes due as well. The probate court's role in all this is to supervise the settlement process. We will spend much more time on probate later in this chapter and in Chapter 9.

JOINT TENANCY WITH RIGHTS OF SURVIVORSHIP

In this arrangement two people hold title to an asset jointly. At death, the survivor becomes sole owner. The asset need not go through the probate process. Joint tenancies of this sort are most common between married couples. (The reasoning: "I want my spouse to get the house anyway." So why go through the trouble of having it go through probate?)

Joint tenancies are not without drawbacks. First of all, you need to be certain that you want your joint tenant to inherit *all* of your share. If your joint tenant is not your spouse, then the matter warrants some thought. Joint tenancies will take precedence over your will. So if there are people who are not your joint tenant that you wish to provide for, your will must do that with other assets that are not jointly held. Even if your joint tenant is your spouse, there may be cause for rethinking the strategy. If your total estate is over $600,000, you will be interested in our chapters on estate taxation. One of the problems with joint tenancies is that planning becomes more difficult. All the jointly held property goes into the estate of the surviving spouse. So the surviving spouse's estate gets most heavily taxed. The solutions to this situation often require a dissolution of at least some of the joint tenancies.

TENANCY IN COMMON

In some cases, it is desirable to own property jointly with someone else for reasons other than estate planning. Let's say you and your brother, Tony, decide to invest in a condominium together. By owning it jointly, you can be equal partners in making decisions regarding the management of the property. When the time comes to sell the apartment, you will share in any profit in proportion to your ownership (which doesn't have to be 50/50). If Tony dies, however, he might not want his share to go to you. He has his own family to provide for. Tenancy in common means that he can leave his share to whomever he wants, and it will be distributed to his heirs by his will. The same would apply to you if you passed away.

COMMUNITY PROPERTY

Eight states—those with a civil code (as opposed to a common law) heritage—operate under the principal of property ownership known as community property. These states are Arizona, California, Idaho, Louisiana, Nevada, New Mexico, Texas, and Washington. A ninth, Wisconsin, has its own version called marital property.

Property owned by married couples in these states is considered to be equally owned by husband and wife. Regardless of who earned the most money or who actually bought the property, each spouse has an equal interest in it. There are a few exceptions. Property acquired before the marriage is separate property, as is property received by gift or inheritance. In some states it is also possible to waive rights to community property by signing a pre-nuptial (before-marriage) agreement. For the most part, though, virtually all income and property acquired during the marriage is community property. Each spouse's share is considered part of his or her estate and will be distributed through the probate process unless it is also part of a joint tenancy with rights of survivorship.

You may be curious to know why these nine states treat spouses so much better than do the 41 common law states, which permit spouses to accumulate as much property solely in their own names as they choose.

For the most part, the community property states are in regions of the country that were settled by the Spanish or French. Apparently, the Spanish and French legal systems were greatly influenced by Germanic and Gallic tribes, which were dominant in Europe during the time of the collapse of the Roman Empire. Because many tribal women were participants in battle, fighting side by side with their husbands, they were accorded honor and respect not found in the English tradition, which is the heritage for most of the United States.

Some of this seems to have been inherited by the people who eventually settled in France and the Iberian peninsula. The Spanish and French carried this civil code system with them, and it became part of the cultures of what are now our community property states.

PROPERTY DISTRIBUTED BY BENEFICIARY DESIGNATION

Some of the property you own outright may not pass under your will as part of your probate estate. Life insurance, annuities, individual retirement accounts, pensions, 401(k)s, and other retirement plans all pass to your heirs by beneficiary designation. This simply means that your designated heirs will receive the proceeds from these assets directly, without having them go through the probate process. This does not exempt the proceeds from any estate or inheritance tax that might be payable. It may, however, cut down on the time it takes to get the money to the person you named.

You need to take care to make sure that your beneficiaries are up to date. Your most recent designation is binding on the insurance company or institution managing your retirement plan. A change in your will has no bearing on your beneficiary designations. It is all too easy to forget to change beneficiaries when your circumstances change.

We won't soon forget the case of a man who named his wife as the beneficiary of his employer-paid life insurance. We'll call him Bob. At the time he did this, he also named his parents as contingent beneficiaries in the event his wife didn't survive him. This made sense at the time, since he and his wife had no children. Later, however, tragedy struck. Bob's wife died giving birth to their child. Soon afterwards, Bob was killed in an automobile accident. Their son escaped with minor injuries. But then another problem came to light.

Even though Bob had a will that named his son as his heir, he had never changed the beneficiary designation of the $100,000 life insurance policy he had through his job. The insurance company had no choice but to pay the proceeds to Bob's parents, who were still contingent beneficiaries. Fortunately, Bob's parents did the right thing: They used the money to help care for their grandchild. However, this created a number of income and estate tax issues for them, which would not have been necessary if Bob had gotten around to updating his beneficiary designation.

Another consideration is the age of your heirs. It is generally a mistake to name minor children as your beneficiaries. If they are below the age of majority in your state when they come into money, the probate court must step in.

Even if your will named someone to take care of their money, that designation would not apply to the money from your life insurance, annuity, or retirement plan. You will need to consider a separate trust arrangement such as the one we describe in Chapter 8. The legal age of majority in your state is listed in Appendix I on page 298.

TRUSTS

One of the most flexible methods of owning and distributing property is the trust. We cover trusts in depth in Chapters 8, 9, and 13. You can place property in a trust during your lifetime or at death. Assets that go into a trust while you are alive will not have to go through probate; assets passed to a trust by your will generally must be probated.

It's important to bear in mind that a trust operates independently of your will. In fact you may have completely different beneficiaries for your probate estate and your trust estate. In our later chapters we'll give you some tips on how to use trusts effectively in your estate planning.

What does it mean to you? Simply this: In planning your estate, it is vital that you consider how your property is owned and how it will be distributed. It is not enough to draw up a will and forget about it.

YOUR EXECUTOR

To understand how the various forms of property ownership inter-
act in an estate, it helps to look at the process of estate settlement
through the eyes of the person who has to do it. The person who
is in charge of settling your estate is usually called your executor,
though a number of states by law have replaced the term *executor*
with a modern unisex alternative, *personal representative*. Although
it is becoming a little archaic, we'll stick with executor, since that's
such a widely recognized term.

By whatever name, the person who winds up your affairs after
you die has a number of essential, if mundane, tasks to attend
to immediately upon your demise. Once everything is done, the
executor's role is complete. Generally, getting the job accomplished can take anywhere from about a year, if your estate is
uncomplicated, to many years if there are complex tax issues or if
your will is contested.

Now suppose that your Aunt Millie has just died. You are named
in her will as her executor. You must do several things immediately.
First, you have to notify the probate court that Aunt Millie has died.
The funeral home will help you with some of the other early chores,
such as assisting you in obtaining a death certificate (make sure to
get several *original* copies) and helping you begin the probate process. Unless Aunt Millie's will is challenged, which is comparatively
uncommon, the probate court will help you expedite settlement of
her affairs by formally appointing you as executor.

Matters become trickier, obviously, if Aunt Millie died without
a will, or if there is some question as to where it is or whether it
is authentic or the most recent version. The point of this book is
to help you do things in an orderly way, so we will assume that
she left a will, that you had no trouble locating it, and that there's
no question about its authenticity.

Notifying the probate court of a person's death and searching
for his or her will are such high priorities that, depending on the
laws in your particular state, you will be obligated to attend to
these initial formalities within days of the death. Once you are
appointed (if you are appointed by the court in the absence of a
will, you are apt to be called an *administrator* rather than *executor*),
you have official status to begin acting. Early on, you will need to
attend to a number of chores.

You have to publish a notice to interested persons and creditors of the estate that you are the executor and any legitimate bills against the estate should be presented or sent to you. You may have to post a bond, which is insurance against the loss of any estate funds due to your negligence or dishonesty.

Another early task is to open up an estate bank account. You are responsible for administering the estate. So you should make certain to keep the estate's affairs segregated from your own. A checking account is sufficient, particularly if it is interest bearing. Into that account you should deposit any income the estate receives, and out of that account you write checks for all estate bills.

Remember the estate, like a corporation or a trust, is an entity. It has assets and liabilities, responsibilities and obligations. You are its steward. Generally, you should not commingle your own and the estate's affairs. Obviously, this prohibition is somewhat less important if you are not only executor but also sole beneficiary, such as a surviving spouse or an only child. Still, until you get things under control, it's advisable to maintain strict separation.

Next, you begin assembling an inventory of the deceased person's assets. Finding them all and valuing them properly can be one of your most time-consuming responsibilities. In some states the probate courts require an accounting only of the probate assets, those that were individually owned outright. Other states require a complete accounting of both probate and nonprobate assets, such as life insurance and jointly held property. From a practical standpoint it doesn't make much difference.

Whether or not your state's probate court requires it, you must total up all the deceased person's assets, including life insurance, trust property, jointly held property, and any other nonprobate property the person owned. This is necessary in order to determine whether or not federal and state death tax returns need to be filed.

If the total estate exceeds $600,000 after deducting the costs of settling the estate, a federal estate tax return (Form 706) may have to be filed, and taxes may be due. In some states, inheritance tax returns must be filed even if the estate is less than $600,000. Since one of your main jobs is to pay all creditors, you will not be able to settle the estate until any taxes due are paid.

Whether the probate court in your state requires an accounting of all assets or merely looks at probate assets being distributed by the will, as executor you still have a big job to do. Some of your tasks are quite easy. You have only to call or visit banks to get date-of-death balance figures for all accounts. Understandably, you may not have had the presence of mind to save the newspaper on the first business day after your loved one or friend died. If you didn't, you'll need to go to the library to look up date-of-death values on publicly listed investments, such as stocks, bonds, and mutual funds. (The date-of-death values are published in the next day's edition of the newspaper.)

Other assets may be considerably more difficult to value. You might need to hire a professional to appraise real estate, a business interest, jewelry, precious metals, art, antiques, or anything else of unusual value.

By and by, settlement of the estate starts falling into place. Doggedly, you pursue all assets. Creditors submit their claims in due course. Typically, they have six months to do so. You are responsible for evaluating the bills, authenticating them, and paying those that are valid. If a bill comes in late, technically you could reject it. But you probably won't if it is valid. You should talk this over with the beneficiaries, but doubtless no one will want to stand on technicalities to stiff a legitimate creditor.

A more difficult problem is how to pay the bills if the estate lacks sufficient liquid assets. As executor, you are responsible for solving this dilemma. Again, you should talk it over with the beneficiaries. You may need to sell an asset, though forced liquidation is not usually advantageous. It's a reality, though.

We happened to attend an estate auction in Vermont recently, and it set us to thinking about such things. The deceased couple's treasures of a lifetime—some impressive antiques, others just old junk—were dragged out into the yard and pawed over while a fine drizzle misted the air. It was an achingly sad sight, but as executor you may have to preside over such a proceeding. Hopefully you won't.

Worse, you may have to sell real estate. This can present you with a dilemma because buyers have a way of sensing when a forced sale is compelling the seller to accept a below-market price.

While the settlement process is going on, an executor needs to be circumspect about distributing assets to the heirs. Some money, investments, or other assets may be given out. And certainly the nonprobate assets will have already been passed along independent of your actions as executor, via beneficiary designation or joint ownership of property, or through trusts. However, you need to hold the rest of the assets back until you've sorted out and met most of the legal and tax requirements.

When the estate has finally been settled, you can distribute the balance. Even then, you might consider it prudent to hold back a small amount, just in case some unforeseen bill crops up.

So far, so good. But let's take a look at some of the things that can go wrong—terribly wrong. Let's say that your Aunt Millie, who never married, left a will naming you; her niece, Sarah; and her brother, Uncle Ernie, as equal heirs.

How nice, you might say! She even named you as the executor. But her insurance was payable to your cousin, Sarah. Her house was titled jointly with your Uncle Ernie. All she really had to probate was stuff like the things that we saw at that sale in Vermont. Maybe she meant to distribute everything equally. But she didn't!

Because of the way her property was titled, your interest may actually be quite small. Worse yet, all expenses of the estate have to be paid out of the probate estate. So, you do all the work, yet watch as the inheritance you thought you were going to receive is eaten away by expenses. To add insult to injury, as executor you have to sign the checks!

This example highlights one of the biggest mistakes we see in estate planning: the failure to coordinate various types of property into an integrated estate plan. If your Aunt Millie's intention was to leave each of you one third of her property, it was not enough for her to name all of you equally in her will. Instead she would have had to take into account the value of her property that was not going to pass under will, namely her life insurance and her home.

This brings us back to planning. Yes, the will is a vital document. But it is of little value if it's not coordinated with the property that is distributed by means other than through the probate process. In the following chapters, we will show you how to do a proper job of leaving your property in a coordinated way.

Chapter Seven

The Will

More controversy, not to mention misunderstanding, than you might think surrounds wills. Most people feel, if they think about it at all, that estate planning begins and ends in the writing of a will. On the other hand, a surprising number of commentators are highly critical of the will, considering it at best a partial answer to the need to plan and at worst a document that causes more harm than good. Taking the commonsense approach, as always, we feel that the truth lies somewhere in between. When you have finished this chapter, which we believe is the heart of this book, we'd like you to understand that you should certainly have a will, but that your estate planning begins rather than ends with its execution.

By most accounts, our modern privilege of writing a will began in 1540, when the English Parliament passed the Statute of Wills, allowing everyone the right to designate how their property should be disposed of after death. In the United States we consider it a fundamental liberty, although virtually every state passed laws limiting that right. For example, in most states it is impossible to cut your spouse entirely out of your probate estate.

If you try to leave your spouse out of your will, she or he can choose to employ a strategy called "electing against the will." That ensures that a spouse receives a minimum share of your estate, based on the laws in your state. (This applies only to assets distributed by your will, in other words, your probate estate.)

Despite this and other limitations on what you can accomplish with a will, it is still an essential document, in our estimation. Yet, you'd be surprised how many prospective clients come to us either with no will or with a wildly outdated one. They are often shocked to hear what would happen if they died, and sometimes they don't believe us when we tell them. A few of the undesirable results could be that your spouse would not receive all your assets; your children might not be taken care of in the way you would want; the cost of administering your final affairs could be much higher than you expected; people you've never met could put their hands in your wallet; people you have met but didn't necessarily invite to share in your riches (your parents, brothers and sisters, aunts and uncles, cousins, nieces and nephews) might receive a portion of your worldly wealth.

The problem is that, as they say, taking no action is also taking action. Let's put it another way. If you don't express an opinion, you force the state to step in and determine how your assets should be apportioned. When you think about it, if neither you nor the state specifies, then who should?

INTESTACY

The operative laws are called the laws of intestacy. Your will is technically called your *last will and testament*. Thus if you have no will, you are said to be *intestate*. These laws vary from state to state. But in general terms, they spell out the methodology for distributing your assets. At the risk of overgeneralizing, we could say that usually (in most states) a spouse is entitled by law to receive just 30 percent to 50 percent of her or his deceased spouse's estate if there is no will. For example, in Pennsylvania, the spouse of a person who dies without a will would get just $30,000 plus one half of the deceased mate's assets. In neighboring West Virginia, the spouse receives just one third. Iowa, Montana, Virginia, and Wisconsin have laws specifying that a spouse gets all of your estate. In Georgia, a surviving husband or wife receives an equal share with each child of the union, but no less than one quarter of your assets. (Appendix A contains the current intestacy guidelines for each of the 50 states.)

If this information brings you up short, here's another attention grabber. The expense of dying without a will is substantially higher than if you have one. The probate process is more cumbersome. An administrator is apt to be named by the probate court, and that person charges your estate for the tasks that need to be performed. Moreover that person must be bonded, and the expense is passed along to your estate. During the process, which can be excruciatingly slow, your spouse may not have access to your money and indeed will be lucky to get an allowance from the income that your estate may generate.

At this point, you may be having a nightmare. You may be imagining that you are sitting up in heaven, watching the proceedings from above, feeling either sick at heart that you left your affairs in such a sad state or getting angry at The System for treating your loved ones so shabbily. Since you can't count on divine intervention from beyond the grave, why not take care of business in the here and now?

If you're starting to sweat a little, let's turn up the heat. Suppose you have minor children, and you and your spouse are both killed in a common accident. Granted, that doesn't happen often, but it happens. Without a will, you have given the probate court the right to make decisions concerning your kids: who will take care of them, who will manage your assets for their benefit, even how much will be left after the administrative process picks your pocket.

Your best hope is that a well-intentioned judge makes wise decisions, that your kids are cared for sympathetically by whomever you would have designated, and that your assets are treated respectfully by the system. Without being rude or gratuitous, we would point out that in real life, the situation may fall short of this ideal. Sitting up in Heaven—or wherever—you'll obviously be powerless to influence the outcome. So, out of love for your family, why not take care of it forthwith!

Although writing a will falls a good deal short of having an intelligently thought-out estate plan, we believe it should almost always be step 1. You can take care of a lot of business in your will. Here's step-by-step guidance.

THE PRELIMINARIES

Most wills first specify something you'd think would be obvious: that all rightful obligations of your estate should be discharged. (See Figure 7-1 for a sample will including these standard provisions.) If you left this mortal coil owing, say $600 to MasterCard and $247 to Sears, those bills have to be paid—not to mention funeral expenses, any final medical bills, and the normal bills we all receive each month.

Next, your will should mention the payment of any appropriate state or federal inheritance or estate taxes. Depending on the state where you live and the size of your estate, there may or may not be any tax obligation. Elsewhere in this book, we tell you how to keep the tax man at bay. Suffice it to say here that if taxes are owing, your will authorizes that they be paid.

In your will you can exempt your executor and trustee(s) from having to post a bond. By making such an exemption, you are saying that you have implicit faith in the ability of the people you have designated to act on your behalf, and you aren't worried that they may misappropriate your assets. If you die without a will, the court will require that a bond be posted by the people appointed to serve your estate. Aside from leaving to a court decisions that rightly should have been yours, by not leaving a will you are costing your heirs money. Posting bond is not inexpensive, especially if you have a large estate. Typically, the cost correlates with the value of your estate, though the decision concerning the amount of the bond rests with the probate judge. Here are some approximate costs for obtaining a bond (although insurance premiums vary): $10,000 bond, $100; $250,000 bond, $900; and $500,000 bond, $1,600. Thus, the premium could cost you more than the expense of drawing up the will in the first place.

The opening clauses in your will could be considered throat clearing. So far, you haven't really expressed any sentiments that could be called dramatic, but rather you have simply stated the obvious. At this point, though, you begin to express some unequivocal and important opinions, including who you'd like to handle your affairs for you in your absence both in terms of settling your estate and, even more important, taking care of your children if both you and your spouse die while they are minors.

EXECUTOR/ADMINISTRATOR

Traditionally, *executor* is the name given to the person whose job it is to wind up your affairs. In old-fashioned parlance, *executor* is

FIGURE 7–1
Last Will and Testament

I, Homer Simpson, a resident of and domiciled in the Township of Washington, County of Bergen and State of New Jersey, do hereby make, publish and declare this to be my Last Will and Testament and hereby revoke any and all other Wills and Codicils heretofore made by me.

FIRST: I direct my Executrix hereinafter named to pay out of my estate all of my just debts and funeral expenses as soon after my death as may be practicable.

SECOND: I give, devise and bequeath all the rest, residue and remainder of my estate, of whatsoever character and wheresoever situate, both real and personal, whether acquired before or after this Last Will and Testament and all the property over which I have a power of appointment to my wife.

THIRD: In the event my wife, Marge, shall not survive me pursuant to the terms and conditions hereof, then I give, devise and bequeath all the rest, residue and remainder of my estate, of whatsoever character and wheresoever situate, both real and personal, and all the property over which I have a power of appointment, wheresoever situate and whatsoever nature, whether acquired before or after this Last Will and Testament to my children, Bart and Mitsie equally share and share like or to the survivor of them.

FOURTH: For the purpose of this Last Will and Testament no person shall be deemed to survive me if he or she shall die within 120 hours of my death.

LASTLY: I hereby nominate, constitute and appoint my wife, Marge, Executrix of this my Last Will and Testament with power to lease, manage, mortgage, sell and convey any and all of my said estate of whatsoever character and wheresoever situate, both real and personal, at such time or times, term or terms as she may deem to be in the best interest of my estate, and I direct that she be not required to give bond in any jurisdiction wherever she may be called on to act. In the event my wife shall not survive me or she is unable, unwilling, or for any reason declines to so qualify or having qualified resigns, I hereby nominate, constitute and appoint my cousin, Tina, Executrix, of this my Last Will and Testament with power to lease, manage, mortgage, sell and convey any and all of my said estate of whatsoever character and wheresoever situate, both real and personal, at such time or times, term or terms as she may deem to be in the best

FIGURE 7–1
Last Will and Testament (continued)

---

interest of my estate and I direct that she be not required to give bond in any jurisdiction wherever she may be called on to act.

IN WITNESS WHEREOF I have hereunto placed my hand and seal and hereby publish this my Last Will and Testament, this 28th day of May in the Year of Our Lord, One Thousand Nine Hundred and Ninety Three.

SIGNED, SEALED AND PUBLISHED AND DECLARED BY Homer Simpson as and for his Last Will and Testament in the presence of us, who at his request and in his presence and in the presence of each other, have hereunto subscribed our names as attesting witnesses.

_____ residing at _____

_____ residing at _____

---

the male term, *executrix* the female. If your attorney uses the latter, check to see if he's still writing with a quill pen.

It may help you decide who to nominate as your executor if you understand just what the role is. That's why we spent time in Chapter 6 explaining the duties. The person you elect does not need to possess any special expertise; executors need only handle things to the best of their ability, exactly as you would handle your own affairs. Conscientiousness and integrity are the most important traits, by far. Competence and specific skills can be hired; they will often come from the attorney chosen to help settle the estate.

Married people almost invariably name each other as their executors, which is generally as it should be. A typical will also designates a successor in case your spouse dies first, perishes with you in a common disaster, or is incapable of acting on your behalf when the time comes. If you are executor for someone other than your spouse, then you should speak at length with that person and, at the time of death, with the family.

It is ideal if you have worked things out with the person who asks you to be executor. Find out preferences about the service and burial or cremation. Are there any wishes that are not in the will?

Let's say that your favorite aunt, who is a widow and childless, would like you to attend to her affairs. While she is alive, you should speak with her at some length and with candor about her desires. She may want to be buried in a particular outfit. There may be a particular type of service that she would favor, a special clergyman or other person she would want to conduct the service, and dear friends or relatives she would like to have speak at the service. She may have very definite ideas as to who should receive her most cherished mementos.

The best way to ensure that her wishes are observed is to have her jot them down ahead of time. Ideally, she should write down her preferences in a sort of letter to her executor: My niece Elsa is to receive my antique opal pendant; my nephew Freddie, my cherished Queen Ann chair; and so on. If she is reluctant to, or unable to, you might consider interviewing her and tape-recording the interview. Obviously, this is most appropriate for elderly people. But even in middle age, it is wise to make your wishes known— or, if you are at the other end of the transaction, to determine a relative's or friend's wishes so you can observe them.

GUARDIANS

Frequently we find ourselves telling clients that one of a parent's most irresponsible acts is failing to specify a substitute for themselves, a guardian for the kids, should something happen to them. Imagine how heartbreaking it would be if you looked down from heaven and had to watch powerlessly as your children were ill served by The System.

For most parents, that's an unspeakable thought. Yet, we have found over the years that deciding on a guardian is perhaps the most difficult task people confront in writing their wills. Maybe the gravity of it makes it so difficult. We would say, however, that for anyone with minor children, naming a prospective guardian is the most compelling reason for going to the trouble of writing a will.

What could be closer to your heart than naming someone to raise your children if you were to die prematurely? In a million years, you wouldn't want to leave such a thing to happenstance! Yet, a surprising number of people do.

Granted, the chances are remote that a husband and wife might both perish while their children are young. Even if such a catastrophe occurred, there might be an obvious solution: your parents, your sister and brother-in-law, your spouse's parents, your best friends. But if you haven't given the issue some forethought and made your wishes known in your wills, you and your spouse are leaving the resolution of such a disaster to chance. Specifically, you are forcing a judge to determine the fate of your children.

In our experience, probate judges are decent, honorable, sensitive people, many of whom have served in this capacity for years. They are capable of weighing the evidence and making an informed decision regarding your children's welfare. But they are not you. Choosing someone to act on your behalf in such a tender matter obviously demands a fair amount of care. Some of our clients feel comfortable naming prospective guardians, while others agonize over the choice.

"Bill and Sue," they might say, "are great people, but their values aren't quite the same as ours." Or, your mother and father are perfect, but they are already in their sixties, and the kids are still little. Or, Timmy and Laura would be ideal, but they live in Detroit. Or, Vanessa and Johnny would be great, but they don't have much money.

Start with this truth: no one could ever replace the two of you. Not grandparents, stepparents, aunts and uncles—no one! A person gets one mother and one father and no matter what, whether they ever know them, whether they like them, whether they live with them, no one could ever take their place entirely. Keeping that in mind, it behooves you to figure out the next best alternative: Who would do the wisest and most compassionate job in your place?

We would caution you to use that test and invest much less importance in age or place or circumstance. Sure, your mom and dad are a generation older than you, two generations beyond your kids. But we know several situations where loving, caring grandparents have raised their children's children and done an excellent job. Sure, Timmy and Laura live in Detroit; so what's wrong with an urban upbringing? Granted Vanessa and Johnny are far down the socioeconomic ladder; so what? If it's that important, buy plenty of life insurance on yourselves.

The only hesitation you should have is in the case of someone whose values don't coincide with your own or someone who is demonstrably unable, for whatever reason, to take on such a large responsibility as rearing your children for you.

The best approach is to discuss your intentions with the people you choose. Try to be open and frank in your conversations, especially when it comes to financial issues. You may want to name the guardians as trustees of trusts that you establish for your children. That decision has to do with your assessment of the prospective guardians' financial acumen.

TRUST PROVISIONS AND TRUSTEES

Traditionally, many if not most trusts were written in the context of wills. That is changing, as trusts become a more common part of the estate planning landscape, rather than the exclusive province of Vanderbilts and Rockefellers. Still, the majority of trusts are created within wills. And the naming of trustees is largely a function of wills. Because we consider the proper use of trusts such an important element of estate planning, we have devoted the entire next chapter to the subject, as well as Chapters 14 and 17.

LEAVING YOUR ASSETS

As we've discussed, your will is only one of a number of vehicles for passing your property along to your heirs, and perhaps not even the most popular one. Survivorship rights to joint property, particularly real estate, are probably more prevalent, especially between husbands and wives. Increasingly, beneficiary designations are disposing of more and more assets, not just through life insurance but also through IRAs, pensions, 401(k) and profit sharing plans, annuities, and revocable living trusts.

So, what should you leave via your will? The quick answer is: the less the better. The drawbacks to leaving property via your will can be summarized in three words: *cost, delay,* and *publicity.* The process of probating your will can be costly because attorneys too often bill an estate on the basis of a percentage of the probate assets. The delay stems from the nature of the system. Since your will is a legal document administered by a legal entity, the probate court, it is subject to the attendant rigors.

Have you ever heard of a *fast* court proceeding? In contrast, a joint owner of property gets it immediately upon your death, and a beneficiary can have a check in as little as a few weeks. At its speediest, the probate process runs six to nine months. It is not uncommon for more than a year to elapse between your death and the distribution of your property. Then, if there is a contest over your will, forget it! Disposition can be sidetracked indefinitely.

Finally, the probate process entails publicity. For most people, that is not a real issue. Face it, the world just isn't that interested in most of us. But since a will is a public document, whatever it contains is a matter of public record. If someone wanted to, they could look your will up in the local courthouse, where it gets filed after you die. They could read its provisions and learn what assets you had.

Most people would not go out of their way to avoid probate so as to maintain their privacy, but that's a side benefit of keeping to a minimum the part of your life that is subject to public view. Some people, especially very wealthy or very private folks, would actively want to take steps to avoid such scrutiny.

For all these reasons, some commentators dismiss the will as a document of little importance. We disagree. Most of our clients place substantial reliance on their will as the foundation of their estate plan. In fact, the majority probably don't realize how much they could deemphasize their will if they wanted to. In truth, we should probably go further than we do in encouraging other approaches. But because people are comfortable with the concept of a will, we try instead to help them get the most mileage out of it.

HOW TO DISINHERIT

In addition to naming your executor, trustee, and guardian and passing along some of your assets, your will is good for several other purposes. One is negative. You can, if you wish, use your will to disinherit someone.

This can get a little tricky. As we mentioned, you should not try to disinherit your spouse, because husbands and wives can always fall back on a legal right that spouses have called electing against the will. Exactly what minimum a spouse is entitled to is spelled out in each state's laws of intestacy. If the law in a particular state says that a spouse gets half your wealth, then basically that's the least your mate can receive no matter how much of a grinch you wanted to be. The law holds no one else in such high esteem, though.

Remember the movie *Rainman*? In that film, Tom Cruise's character was chagrined to learn that his father had left him an old car and some rose bushes. Period. ''Well, at least I got the rose bushes,'' he fumed. ''I definitely got the rose bushes.'' If you want to jab a thorn into one of your kids, or someone else, your will is the place to do it. You can leave them a bush. Or your old pocket watch that hasn't worked since the Eisenhower administration. Or one perfect rose.

WHAT SHOULD NOT BE IN A WILL

Some things are better left out. It's not generally advisable to specify the type of funeral arrangements you want. Say you'd prefer cremation and a memorial service. Or perhaps you want a Masonic funeral rite or burial in a certain cemetery.

Rather than spell these wishes out in your will, make them known in a letter to your loved ones. For one thing, you cannot compel your family to treat your final arrangements in the way you'd prefer. The best you can do is express yourself on the subject and hope they will honor your requests. For another, your will probably won't be read until after the arrangements have been made and you've been buried or cremated, which makes the will an unsuitable vehicle for such requests.

Similarly, you should not spell out in great detail in your will who gets what. As we noted, if you want your daughter Susan to receive your mother's heirloom pearl necklace and your son Willie to get the antique clock that has been in the family since Grover

Cleveland was president, put those requests in a letter accompanying your will. If you put such bequests directly in your will and later change your mind—or circumstances change—you'll have to spend time, effort, and money rewriting the will.

Using a codicil or referring in the will to a letter you write to your heirs allows you to change your mind easily (though, of course, you need a lawyer to do the codicil for you). When grandson Wedgie runs off with a traveling nudist circus, you can effortlessly transfer your 12 place settings of bone china tea service to niece Nora. Wedgie, presumably, will never be the wiser.

Generally, you are well advised not to attempt to be too controlling from the grave. It's bad enough to play the ruler when you are alive, treating your family and friends like your subjects—if you are guilty of that sort of behavior. It's totally unacceptable, both philosophically and practically, to exert undue influence once you're gone. For one thing, it often doesn't work. You can cause more expense and trouble than your loved ones are likely to get into on their own. Then again, what you accomplish by acting petty or spiteful is to give your family confirmation of their darkest fears—that you had little respect for their abilities.

Mind you, we're not contradicting ourselves here. As you have gathered by now, our strong orientation is toward proper planning. Often, as we will discuss in the next chapter, that can involve preventing your heirs from spending your assets immediately. In our office, we have dealt with a number of clients who received large settlements as a result of accidents, and invariably, whether a child or an adult is involved, the recipient prefers to receive staged payments over many years so as not to be tempted to squander the money all at once.

No, that's not what we're driving at. What we're advising against is going to an extreme. Don't try to govern from the grave. Be sensible, but allow your family to lead their own lives and make their own mistakes. After all, you did.

Chapter Eight

Basic Trusts

T he term has a certain resonance. *Trust.* It has a rich aroma. You can almost taste it. *Trust.* It conjures up the feeling of a mahogany-paneled library in a private club, where the members are sipping brandy and debating the merits of this season's new opera production.

But trusts are not just for the rich and famous. Trusts can play a vital role in the estate planning of everyday people. If you are concerned about the ability of your heirs to manage the money you leave them or if you are worried about the administrative and tax expenses they will have to pay, you need to know about trusts. This definitely applies to anyone with young children, older "problem" children, or aged parents whom they wish to provide for. Of course, it also applies to the very affluent who wish to keep Uncle Sam's tax bite to a minimum. In this chapter, we'll give you a basic overview of trusts. Chapter 17 goes into more depth on the variations and uses for trusts.

Just what is a trust? Very simply, it is a legal entity created to hold and manage property for the benefit of beneficiaries. The person who creates and funds the trust is called the grantor (or alternatively, the donor or settlor). The beneficiaries are the ones for whom the trust is set up. The trustee is the person designated to run the trust. This person is responsible for carrying out the directions laid down by the grantor in the trust document. This includes deciding when to make distributions to the beneficiaries, making investment decisions, and keeping track of accounting and tax matters.

As mentioned, a trust is a separate legal entity. It can owe state and federal income taxes on its net taxable income after allowable expenses. Quite often, trusts have no tax liability because they get a tax deduction for any income they pay out to beneficiaries. Naturally, the beneficiaries pay taxes on any income they receive from a trust. It makes sense for the trust to pay out income because in the 31 percent income tax bracket, the trust is taxable at about $10,000. However, individuals who are in the 31 percent income tax bracket who receive income from the trust pay taxes only on income exceeding about $50,000. This may change under recent tax proposals.

How do ordinary people, who are not Rockefellers and Kennedys, use trusts? Let's look at the example of a typical middle-class family consisting of a husband, wife, and two young children. Call them the Jones family. They aren't rich, but they own a home, have a little savings, and have some money set aside in a 401(k) pension plan. The couple's wills were drawn so as to leave all their respective assets to each other. The wills state further that if both of them die, either together or separately, before their children reach adulthood, Uncle Max will act as guardian for the children and their inherited property.

Here are a couple of problems. Uncle Max is terrific with the kids. He loves them and would raise them as his own if they came under his care. Unfortunately, Max hasn't a clue when it comes to managing money. He's honest, but simply not capable of investing the inheritance properly for his niece and nephew. Perhaps worse than that, much of the Joneses' estate would fall under the jurisdiction of the court. The Joneses named their children as contingent beneficiaries of their insurance policies and the 401(k) retirement plan. No one told them they were creating a potential problem. If the Joneses children are under the age of majority at the time the proceeds are payable, the courts must step in. Even though Uncle Max was named in the will as guardian, responsibility for money left directly to the children, outside of the will, could be given by the judge to someone else. Worse still, when the children become adults, they will receive the money. Will they be mature enough to handle it? Or will they blow it? It is out of Max's hands, and the court's, too, for that matter.

So, although the Joneses are not wealthy, they can make very effective use of trusts in their planning. Before seeing their lawyer, they need to think a few things through. First of all, if Uncle Max is not the right person to manage money for the kids, who is? As the term *trustee* implies, they need to find someone they can trust to do the right thing for their children. Honesty is a must. So is competence in financial matters. The search may start with family members (other than poor Uncle Max).

Trustees are allowed to charge fees for their services. This is fair because, frankly, being a trustee does entail putting in some time and effort. However, a family member may be willing to waive the fee entirely or charge only a modest fee to cover his or her expenses in running the trust. A close family friend might be another alternative.

Bear in mind that the person selected will have some work to do. They will need to collect all the money that is payable to the trust after the deaths of Father and Mother Jones. This money may come out of probate through the will, from insurance and annuity policies, or from retirement plans. Next, bank accounts and investment accounts have to be opened. The trustee is required to act as a "prudent man" (or woman) in managing this money. This means that investment decisions cannot be overly aggressive. The trustee is charged with the responsibility of earning a reasonable rate of return for the Joneses' children, while at the same time protecting the original value of the inheritance. This does not mean that the trustee has to stick the money in a passbook savings account at an FDIC-insured bank and forget about it. If that's all there were to it, we might as well let Uncle Max be the trustee. Rather, the trustee should take a balanced approach that may include taking some prudent risks in investments that have the potential for a greater return. The trust document itself can specify which investments are permissible and which are not. The trustee can then select from these choices to put together an investment portfolio geared to the specific needs of the children.

One of the things that should be avoided is a conflict of interest. An obvious example would be a trustee borrowing money from the children's trust for a business venture that his bank refused to finance. If the deal goes bust and the trustee can't pay back the money, where does that leave the kids? Two things can protect the Joneses from such conflicts of interest. First and foremost, they should pick a trustworthy trustee; second, fiduciary obligations of trustees leave them vulnerable to a lawsuit if they engage in such transactions.

If you are at all concerned about the potential for trouble, you can require that the trustee post a bond to indemnify the trust against his or her malfeasance or negligence. This bond can be obtained through a property and casualty insurance agent. To be safe, we recommend waiving this bonding requirement only in situations in which your faith in the trustee is absolute.

In addition to managing the trust's assets, the trustee must also decide when to make distributions. The Joneses' attorney can insert instructions to allow the trustee to give money to Uncle Max to defray the expenses of raising the children. The trustee is responsible for making sure that Uncle Max's requests are reasonable. So, even if the Joneses' older boy persuades Max that he simply *must* have that new Corvette, it is up to the *trustee* to "just say no!"

Finally, the time will eventually come to disburse trust assets to the children. The trust can be written to list the age or ages at which this will occur. A common approach is to stagger the distributions. In the Joneses' case, the family decided to pay out 25 percent of the assets at age 21, another 25 percent at 25, and the balance at 30. (A more typical distributing approach would be to pay one third at 25, one third at 30 and the balance at 35.) The theory is that the children will have the chance to mature as they receive the money and will have the opportunity to learn from their mistakes. We have seen situations where clients have been so skeptical of their children's financial sense that they have provided that the assets remain in trust until age 45 or even 50!

While the trust is in force, the trustee must keep accounting records of trust income, net worth, and distributions. A tax return must be filed each year. If the trustee hires an accountant, these fees can be charged to the trust.

As you can see, being a trustee is quite a job. The age of the trustee you select is one factor to consider. It is a good idea to name a backup in the event that your original trustee becomes unable or unwilling to serve. In some cases, it is perfectly acceptable to have the children's guardian also serve as trustee. But, as in the case of Uncle Max, that may not always be the best choice.

What if you scratch your heads and come up with nobody among your family and friends? You can employ the services of a corporate trustee, typically the trust department of a bank. There are some advantages to this approach. Bank trust officers are professionals whose business it is to manage money for widows and orphans. They tend to be conservative money managers. Bank trustees also provide continuity. While the personnel may change, the trust department will live on to continue to serve as trustee. While we're talking about continuity, we should discuss the impact that bank failures can have on this relationship. Trust assets are held separately from the bank's own assets and are not subject to the bank's creditors if the bank goes under. The only exception would be funds invested directly in the bank's savings, money market, or CD accounts. These funds are protected by the FDIC, but only up to $100,000 per account. If you designate a bank trustee, make sure it is clear that under no circumstances is the trustee to invest more than $100,000 in the bank's own accounts or those of any other bank.

There is one more advantage to using a hired trustee. Institutional trustees tend to be less emotionally involved in the day-to-day lives of the beneficiaries. This can make them more objective in their management of the trust. As we have mentioned, the trustee may be placed in a position to turn down a request for funds from a beneficiary. This creates an obvious conflict that may be easier for an independent trustee to deal with.

There are compensating disadvantages of corporate trustees as well. They will certainly not waive their fees, because that's how they make their living. They also may not be as empathetic or sensitive to the unique needs of the beneficiaries as would someone closer to the family. There is also a practical matter. If you have a modest estate, bank trust departments may not be interested in your account. In general, smaller banks in smaller towns will be more accommodating even if your estate is in the hundreds of thousands, rather than millions—and many will do a fine job. At the other end of the spectrum, larger banks in big cities won't even talk to you unless they know they'll have $5 million or more to manage in the trust.

Once you settle these issues, you are ready to create the trust. You can use either of two types of trusts. The simplest is a testamentary trust, which is established by your will and takes effect upon your death. In the Joneses' case, the trust is contingent upon the death of both parents since it is only after that event that management assistance would be desired.

The other possibility is an *intervivos* trust, also known as living trust. *Intervivos* is one of those Latin terms that attorneys like to use, but we'll stick to the more user-friendly *living trust*.

In contrast to a testamentary trust, which takes effect only after your death, a living trust can come into being during your lifetime. You can transfer your assets to the trust and they are managed by the trustee, usually you. Assets that are not placed in the trust will "pour over" into it from your will. The proceeds of life insurance, annuities, or retirement plan accounts can be directly payable to the trust. An advantage of the living trust is that assets placed in the trust or payable directly to it by beneficiary designation are not subject to the delays and expense of the probate process. You are not actually giving these assets away. You have the right to take the assets back at any time. For this reason, they are still part of your estate. You will continue to owe taxes on any income earned by assets in this trust. The disadvantages of a living trust are less than you might suppose. They include the cost of setting it up and the administrative costs of maintaining it. These administrative costs will include accounting fees as well as any charges for transferring the title of your assets.

Which type of trust should you use? See Chapter 9 on the probate process. If avoiding probate is important to you, a living trust makes sense. If you are primarily concerned with providing financial management assistance for your young children, a testamentary trust will be a simpler, less expensive option.

Now, let's get back to the Joneses. They have selected their trustee and thought about the trust provisions. Their attorney has drafted a trust. The final step is the most important. The Joneses need to make sure that all their assets are coordinated with the trust. Their intent is that the surviving spouse should inherit the entire estate. The survivor's will is the document that directs these assets to the children's trust. However, it is critical that all beneficiary designations be revised. The Joneses can continue to name each other as beneficiaries of their life insurance policies, annuity contracts, and retirement plans. However, they must name the trustees rather than their children as the contingent beneficiaries. Otherwise, the proceeds will go directly to the kids, defeating the purpose of the trust. Failing to take this step is one of the most common mistakes people make in estate planning.

We have just reviewed basic trust planning for a typical family with young children. The same principles can be applied to a variety of other situations.

PROTECTING THE YOUNGER CHILDREN IN YOUR FAMILY

We often encounter situations involving families who have both younger and older children. The couple's older son and daughter are through college and out working on their own. The youngest child, however, came along later in their lives. (Whoops!) So the "little guy" may be just starting high school when the older kids are grown.

Now, if Mom and Dad both die, the youngest child is in an entirely different situation from his older siblings. Funds must be made available to cover his upbringing and higher education. If the parents' estates are divided equally among their three children, is this fair? A large chunk of the younger child's inheritance will be spent providing things that the older children have already received.

Dealing with such a situation is a matter of personal choice. One solution, using a trust, is to set aside enough money from your estates to cover these remaining "upbringing" costs for the younger children. Once those obligations are met, the remaining proceeds can then be divided equally among all your kids.

PROTECTING CHILDREN FROM MULTIPLE MARRIAGES

You know the story. Boy meets girl. Boy marries girl. They have babies. They get divorced. They then repeat the process and re-marry. They have more babies. And so on. Suffice it to say that children and stepchildren create special estate planning challenges. Trusts can help.

Again, you must first figure out what you want to do. You have property and so does your spouse. How would you want that property divided between your children from your previous marriage(s), your spouse's children from previous marriage(s), and the children you've had together in this current marriage? This is a very subjective decision and we can offer no better advice than to sit down with your mate and talk it out. You almost certainly will want to make sure that the children you've had together are provided for. If you are still responsible for the support of young children from your prior marriage(s), you need to take care of them, too. It may be that dividing your estates equally among all the children is not practical. The needs of the younger children may be much greater than those of their older siblings and half siblings. You may find that your estates are simply not large enough to go around equitably. At this juncture it may be time to call your life insurance agent!

In the meantime, once you have an idea of how the assets should be divided, your attorney can set up trusts for you. These trusts can be either testamentary or living, although it might be more advisable to use the living version because it will be easier to create separate trusts for separate classes of beneficiaries, including your children, your spouse's children, and your children together. As with all trust planning, it will be most important for you to coordinate your property ownership, beneficiary designations, and wills with these trusts. Otherwise your property may not go where you intended it to. Your financial planner and attorney can be of great assistance here, but you must take the initiative to make them aware of the issue.

PROTECTING CHILDREN WITH SPECIAL NEEDS

Some children will never grow up or be self-sufficient. Whether due to genetic disorders, disease, injury, or emotional problems, many thousands of people will always be in need of assistance. One approach is simply to cut these children out of the will. They can't be trusted with the money, and the hope is that other family members will step in and help. At least some of the people who are homeless on our streets are victims of that approach.

For a family with adequate means, there is a kinder, gentler course. A trust can be created to help provide for children who will need assistance as long as they live. This can be either a testamentary trust or a living trust. The key provision is that the share of the estate allocated to the impaired child remains in trust for his or her lifetime. Naturally, it is important to designate trustees and successor trustees who are likely to be around to provide these services for many years.

Another major issue you need to grapple with is what amount of money should be set aside for such a child. You may not want to effectively disinherit your other children in favor of the one who needs permanent help. But, since you may wish to provide substantial assets, you might consider buying a life insurance policy to provide extra funds for the special needs.

Or you can carve out a portion of your estate for your impaired child and divide the balance among the others. There are no universal guidelines. The facts and circumstances of each case, combined with your personal feelings about the issue, will dictate the appropriate approach. For example, a bequest to a disabled child could affect eligibility for medicaid. Thus leaving even a small amount of money to a trust could be self-defeating, since many families of modest means may have no alternative to allowing the child to become a medicaid and public assistance client when he or she reaches adulthood. Other families will do whatever it takes, including using a trust, to prevent that from happening.

PROTECTING AGED PARENTS

People are living longer and longer, which is wonderful. Unfortunately, many of them will outlive not only their financial resources, but also their ability to manage their money. Inflation and taxes will erode the buying power of their pensions and savings. Social Security helps. But eventually things can get tough. More and more, we see clients who must assist their aged parents financially. It is not unusual to see a couple in their 50s and 60s providing financial support to parents in their 80s, 90s, or beyond. Just ask Willard Scott! What would happen if you predeceased your parents? This is another situation in which a trust can help. An outright bequest to a parent is not advisable. If the parents are mentally alert, that's great. But the older the parents are, the more likely they may be slipping.

If the parents are ill, a trust would be even more appropriate. In any case, leaving money to older people may be inadvisable because of the potential estate tax consequences. The dollars could wind up being taxed twice in a relatively short period of time, once in your estate and again in theirs. And there would be no guarantee that these assets would go from your parents to your children.

One technique is to use a testamentary trust within your will. If you and your spouse are comfortable that each of you would continue to assist the other's parents should one of you die, a trust in your will could be the way to go. It would specify that after both you and your spouse are gone, assets would pass to a trust for the benefit of your parents. The assets should be sufficient to produce the additional income needed. The trustee would also provide the parents with help in managing their financial affairs. The selection of a trustee is very important. Obviously, a relative who has a personal interest in helping care for your parents would be ideal.

Such a trust can be arranged so that assets remaining after your parents' deaths are to be distributed to your children or other heirs. This protects the assets themselves should your parents enter a nursing home and fall under medicaid. The income would likely go to the nursing home, but the principal itself would be safe.

Your attorney may also advise using an irrevocable trust while you are alive for this purpose, which would work well, especially if you wanted to place assets in the trust today for their benefit.

PROTECTING YOUR SPOUSE AND CHILDREN

Older couples can provide the same protection for themselves. A Qualifying Terminable Interest Property Trust, inevitably known as a QTIP Trust, is a wonderful tool in this situation. An examination of the QTIP's name reveals a lot about what it does. *Qualifying* means that assets left to such a trust qualify for the unlimited marital deduction from federal estate taxes. This is a critical provision because *no* estate taxes are due when the marital deduction applies. *Terminable Interest* means that the trust will dictate who ultimately receives the property after both spouses pass away. The benefit of this feature is that your intended ultimate heirs, usually your children, are protected. If your surviving spouse remarries, his or her new spouse could otherwise be entitled to a portion of your estate. A QTIP forecloses this possibility. Furthermore, since the assets are controlled by the trustee, there is less danger of an elderly person being gulled out of the family's fortune by a scam artist or bogus charity.

QTIPs are also used in second marriages. In the classic example, a man remarries a younger woman. He wants to take care of her if he dies, but he wants to make sure that his kids ultimately inherit his money. The QTIP will help ensure that. We should also point out that there are lots of women in similar situations, marrying younger men. They can use QTIPs in exactly the same way, and they probably should!

SAVING TAXES

There are numerous ways to use trusts for the purpose of limiting estate taxes. In Chapter 9 we deal with the Credit Shelter Trust, which can exempt up to $1.2 million of your assets from federal estate taxes. Chapter 14 deals with the irrevocable life insurance trust, which can exclude all your life insurance benefits from estate taxation. Chapter 17 deals with even more sophisticated trust planning techniques, which are used by the very wealthy to legally prevent the long arm of Uncle Sam from reaching for their pockets.

SAVING PROBATE COSTS

Whether or not your estate is large enough to be taxable, some of the costs associated with settling your estate are inevitable. As we said earlier, there are several excellent ways to avoid the bulk of these expenses.

We really don't believe you should go crazy trying to avoid probate because the estate taxes your heirs will pay will be the same whether or not your assets are probated. However, if paying attorneys less and avoiding the publicity and delays associated with probate are attractive, you can certainly consider a revocable living trust as part of your strategy. We'll show you how in the next chapter.

Chapter Nine

Probate: Myth, Reality, and the Revocable Living Trust

M ore than a quarter-century ago, a man named Norman F. Dacey sparked an estate planning revolution. As with all revolutions, this one was long overdue and represented a reaction almost as excessive as the ills it set out to cure. A self-proclaimed estate planner of 35 years duration, Dacey wrote a book called *How to Avoid Probate!* In it, he wrote a prescription for sidestepping the ills of the probate system. Dacey's publisher has reissued the book every few years and claims to have printed 1.5 million copies. It has spawned a clutch of imitators over the years, some with catchy sounding names.

Dacey's premise was that probate was an evil to be avoided at all costs. Before we describe a more moderate course of action for you, we'd like to tell you why we take some exception to Mr. Dacey. Like rhetoricians down through the ages, Norman Dacey goes to excess in deploring the evils of the probate system he's trying to crack. But, for all his rhetorical flourishes, Dacey's book contains prodigious scholarship. He cites scores of cases, studies, inequities, and downright thievery by lawyers and judges. Perhaps that sort of argumentative overkill was necessary during the early years of Dacey's crusade. But today it seems dated and even crude. The overwhelming majority of estate attorneys we have dealt with are competent, honest people, who work hard to help their clients through a difficult time.

Dacey was definitely on to something, even if he oversold it. In our estimation, attorneys are not the enemy, but they must be made to see that when we are clients, they are our servants—not the other way around. Unquestionably, the probate process can be arduous, time-consuming, costly, and often infuriating. In many cases, if you can allow your heirs to sidestep the process you'll be doing them a very good deed, not to mention saving them significant dollars and time.

Let's be very clear what we are and are not talking about. None of the discussion in this chapter concerning probate has anything to do with taxes. The federal estate tax is calculated on your *total* assets, *not* just those that are subject to the probate process. Whether you've given your assets away before you die or pass them upon your death, they are covered by the tax law. A key point you must master is that *the probate process has only to do with the costs and time involved in settling an estate. It has no bearing on any potential tax liability.* We emphasize the issue because over the years we've found that it is perhaps the major misconception regarding estate planning.

With that distinction firmly in mind, let's take a clear-eyed look at the probate process. Dacey calls it "legal larceny," and "private taxation." We prefer to think of the system more magnanimously.

IF YOU ARE SOMEONE'S EXECUTOR

To show you how the system works in practice, imagine that you have been named executor of someone's estate—that of your spouse, perhaps, or another family member or friend—and that the person has just died. You are numb with grief, but you must attend to a number of things, some of them immediate necessities. The first concern, funeral or memorial service arrangements, you probably discussed ahead of time with the person who died, especially if she or he was elderly. If the death was sudden and involved a younger person, you will talk with the family about what is appropriate and what the deceased would have wanted.

Once you have gotten past the urgent necessities surrounding the death, as executor you need to begin the methodical process of winding up the person's affairs.

You begin the assignment by assembling an inventory of the deceased's assets. Finding them all and valuing them properly can be one of your most time-consuming responsibilities. Depending on the state in which the person lived, you may need to report to the court only what are called "probate" assets, the ones distributed by the will. However, you will still have to gather a list of nonprobate assets for potential inclusion on federal and state tax forms.

Opinions vary on when to involve the probate court. We have had clients who waited as much as a month or more, but we don't advise delay. Once the funeral services are over and you have gotten yourself together enough to begin addressing these difficult issues, you should begin taking action. Among the earliest steps you'll need to take:

- Opening the deceased persons's safe deposit box. That used to be a sort of cat-and-mouse game because banks sealed boxes as soon as they learned of the death of one of their depositors. Many states now allow anyone who has authorization to go into the box, regardless of whether one of the owners has died.

- Applying for an estate bank account. As executor, you are going to have to accept income on behalf of the deceased and pay bills, so you need a bank account. At some point, you will also need a federal tax identification (ID) number. For this, you apply to the IRS.

- Notifying the probate court that the death has occurred and beginning the process. At its best, the probate process is court supervision of your estate under the watchful eye of a kindly, well-intentioned judge. Such orderly disposition of your affairs runs smoothly for the most part, in our experience. Undoubtedly, outrages such as those reported by Norman Dacey still exist, but they are the extreme exception. In general, an executor is apt to find the probate court a rather canny ally, and often the long-term administrators are more knowledgable and useful than the judge.

HIRING AN ATTORNEY

One of an executor's most important decisions, and certainly a task that will have a major financial impact on the estate, is deciding on an attorney. This is an indispensable early decision, since the lawyer can help you at every stage of the process, from getting a tax ID number and filing the first notification with the probate court through the entire process.

Too often, unsophisticated executors make inappropriate selections. They hire a lawyer just because they are acquainted, unmindful of whether the professional in question has any probate experience. Inexperienced executors are also untutored in the art of defending the estate against unjustified legal bills. It is tempting to simply engage an attorney who has been a family friend or one who was a friend of the deceased. That can work out just fine if the attorney is scrupulous and conscientious enough to let you know of any problems that develop beyond the scope of her or his expertise.

In fact, under the right circumstances, hiring a friend can be an excellent approach. For example, if the estate is fairly simple, almost any attorney can probably help you. If you are the executor of your spouse's estate, for instance, and basically everything has been left to you, there's no reason not to call on a lawyer who's a family friend.

But if you are charged with managing the final affairs of a family member or friend whose situation was complex, perhaps because of substantial assets, a business, or property in several states, you should be much more careful about whom you employ. In such cases, begin by asking professionals you know to recommend attorneys who are estate specialists. You may know of a good financial planner or be working with one, or the deceased may have been. You may know an accountant who can suggest referrals. When you have the names of several candidates, call each one and interview them. Some questions you ought to ask include:

- How would you handle this case?
- How long would you expect the settlement process to take?
- What working relationship do you like to have with an executor?
- How do you charge your fee? Do you work on an hourly basis, or are you paid according to a percentage of the estate's assets?

The latter is controversial and in flux. An anecdote makes the point. Not too long ago, one attorney made a Norman Daceyesque remark to another lawyer within our hearing. Making no attempt to be secretive, the first attorney told the second rather matter-of-factly that he was going to charge "top dollar" to an estate he was settling "because the old lady had no immediate family, and her nieces and nephews all live on the other coast."

We hope this is the exception rather than the rule. But it illustrates a point: There is little restriction on what an attorney can bill. One state has taken the lead in curbing this practice. Rather than allowing attorneys the unfettered opportunity to charge whatever the traffic will bear, Florida has prohibited lawyers from charging solely on a percentage basis. The alternative is an hourly fee, charged for however many hours the attorney works, which seems reasonable enough.

A good way to defend yourself, if you become executor of someone's estate, is to make it clear from the inception how you prefer to pay for legal assistance. When you interview prospective lawyers, tell them that you want to pay them by the hour and that you don't want to pay *their* hourly rate when an underling, such as a paralegal, is actually performing the tasks. Many of the chores of settling an estate are routine, and the paralegal or secretary will be handling them. Thus, the estate should be billed accordingly. The bottom line is that right at the beginning you should ask any lawyer you are considering to give you a ballpark figure of what you can expect the total bill to be.

Before leaving the subject of executors, a word about your own fee, if any. Generally speaking, family members do not receive compensation for their time and effort. If you are the surviving spouse or substantial heir, however, you might charge a fee if that would mean reducing the estate's federal estate or state inheritance tax. Fees are legitimately deductible estate expenses.

If you are not a significant heir, and if you put in considerable time and effort, you may be justified in asking for compensation. You may be taking enormous responsibility if it is a large or complicated estate. The laws and even customs on this subject tend to be vague. So you need to be guided by your attorney and by the probate court as to what's appropriate. However, your fee should bear some defensible relationship to the value of your time. One persuasive basis would be to charge by the hour, keeping careful track of the time you actually spend.

DELAY

Cost is not the only downside to the probate process. Delay is another disadvantage. If you leave assets to your spouse via your will, the process tends to run fairly smoothly and speedily, especially if your estate is not too large—under the $600,000 that is excluded from federal estate taxes. However, there are many stories of hapless widows forced to subsist on meager incomes while their husband's assets were frozen in the probate process.

Generally, the problem occurs more frequently at the death of the second spouse. Often at that time several beneficiaries are involved. The estate may be larger than it was at the time of the first death. The beneficiaries may be scattered around the country, making communication more cumbersome. The executor may not be a beneficiary, or even a family member. If you *are* a beneficiary, the process can seem excruciatingly slow.

We've had plenty of clients who were ready to strangle someone (they didn't know whether it would be the probate judge or the attorney settling the estate) before all the technicalities were cleared up and the assets distributed.

Why all the holdup? There are many steps in the process. Some of them involve the probate court, others the process of paying death taxes and obtaining waivers. Beneficiaries must be polled on how assets should be treated.

PUBLICITY

Finally comes the issue of publicity. For most of us, the world couldn't care less about our situations. However, some people *are* subject to public scrutiny. In any case, probate is a public process. You can go down to your local probate court and look up any past will.

We've done so, both for particular purposes and just out of curiosity. This may sound like a macabre pastime, but actually there's a certain poignancy about the past. If you don't think so, take a field trip to the appropriate court in your town and ask to look at the will of someone who died 40, 50, or 60 years ago. Particularly if you are familiar with your community and if the family name is familiar to you, you'll be amused to see what assets the deceased person had.

All the money amounts will look so small. The house was valued at, say, $27,500. Bank accounts totaled $9,780. And so on. The language of the will may sound archaic by contemporary standards. The point here is not so much that this is a humorous exercise that you can try at home. The point is that someone else can do this to you!

AVOID PROBATE!

So how, you're asking yourself by now, can I avoid all this folderol? Basically, there are three ways. You can own property jointly with someone else. You can designate a beneficiary for some of your assets. Or you can use a trust. Each of the three techniques has advantages, and each has drawbacks.

Joint Ownership

As we noted in Chapter 6, when you own property with someone else, that becomes a legal matter, especially if you own it as so-called joint tenants with rights of survivorship. If you die, your co-owner then automatically becomes the owner of the asset by operation of law. Thus the asset avoids the cost, delay, and publicity of probate.

It might seem tempting simply to own everything jointly, especially if you are married. In fact, that can be a very appropriate strategy if you are young. Newlyweds, for instance, are generally inclined to hold all their assets jointly unless there are unusual circumstances.

If partners came into the marriage with significant resources, for example, because of an inheritance, those assets may continue to be owned individually. An individual retirement plan must be individually owned. Aside from those instances, however, it would be wise to maintain joint ownership. If something were to happen to one partner, the survivor at least would instantly and automatically own everything.

As life goes on, though, strategies that used to work perfectly begin to creak and crack. When you reach mid-life and beyond, the value of your assets—your estate—will no doubt have increased significantly. Then you have a new issue to cope with: the possibility of estate taxes. No longer will it be appropriate to own everything as joint tenants because that could foil proper tax planning. In our practice, we find ourselves constantly explaining to older couples that the habits of a lifetime no longer will serve them well. We will talk in detail later in the book about how to arrange your affairs so as to take maximum advantage of the federal estate tax exclusion. The point here is that holding all your assets jointly will most likely frustrate that objective. So, one of the things we do a lot of is to disentangle our married couples' joint property.

That strategy can be reversed later on, though. Once one spouse has died, it may be a good idea to put some or all your assets back in joint name, for instance with one or more of your children or other heirs. We had a client, let's call her April, whose father left everything to his brother Steve. Uncle Stevie then wanted to leave the modest combined assets to April and her two brothers. So he made each one a co-owner of one of his assets—bank accounts, U.S. savings bonds, and what not. It worked beautifully. When he died in a nursing home, Uncle Stevie left the easiest possible estate to settle.

Don't get confused. Simply opening joint accounts is not real tax planning. That's a different and much more complicated endeavor, as you'll see in Chapter 14. But as an estate settlement technique for the young and the very old, it has great attraction.

Beneficiary Designation

Obviously, you can't use this approach for any but a select few types of assets. You cannot designate a beneficiary to your house, say, or your stock brokerage account. Though you can do something *like* a beneficiary designation on a bank account—it's called a payable on death, or POD, account—that's really more akin to joint ownership than it is a beneficiary designation.

Beneficiary designations can be made on two basic types of assets: tax qualified retirement accounts and insurance products. Whenever you have a pension, of whatever sort, you are required to specify who you want the proceeds to go to upon your death. If you are married, the beneficiary must be your spouse, unless your spouse consents to some other designation. Naturally, life insurance contracts also allow you to name a beneficiary, as do other insurance products, such as annuities. You may, for example, own one of the several types of annuities sold by insurance companies. If there is a balance in your investment at your death, the money passes directly to your beneficiary, unless you have already annuitized the contract for your life only, that is, begun receiving set monthly payments for the rest of your life.

The best part about such a transfer is that, as in joint ownership, you receive the deceased person's assets almost instantaneously. An insurance company only needs to get verification from the executor of an estate (usually by receiving a copy of the death certificate) in order to release the proceeds from a life insurance policy. The beneficiary will usually receive a check within a week or two thereafter.

Obviously, since you are a direct beneficiary of the death benefit proceeds, the money is not subjected to the probate process. No probate judge passes on it, and no lawyer can count that money in levying a fee if legal charges are based on a percentage of your probate estate.

Beneficiary designations carry some of the same problems as jointly held property. The most natural thing to do is to name your spouse as beneficiary of all of your insurance, retirement plans, and of your life insurance. If you have a modest estate, that approach is usually appropriate. If your estate is larger, you could be sabotaging efforts to keep your family's taxes to a minimum.

Revocable Living Trusts

In the last chapter, we dealt at length with trusts. So here let's just quickly review the concept of a trust. A trust is a legal entity. It has a tax ID number, and a formal and formidable mandate, called the trust document, establishes it and its own personnel, the trustees. Very much like a corporation, a trust is a type of citizen. And like a corporation, you as its creator have wide latitude. The law allows creation of trusts for many different types of purposes. Trusts can be established to help avoid taxation. They can be set up to manage property for people (the very young and the very old in particular) who can't manage their affairs themselves. A trust can be intended to expedite the passage of property from one person (the grantor) to another person (the recipient or beneficiary). It's the latter variety that we're speaking of in the context of planning to avoid probate.

If you want to carry probate avoidance to the highest level, you can do so fairly easily. A number of our clients have. Good examples are Barbara and Jane, two widows in their mid-70s. The pair, lifelong friends who'd lost their husbands a number of years ago, had heard about a device that was being promoted with the too-cute name, "loving trust." This strategy relies on the technique of giving your assets to a trust so the assets are out of your name. Because you might not care to make an irrevocable gift of your entire worldly wealth, the trust allows you a change of heart later on if you so choose. But if you don't, it snaps shut at the instant of your death, and essentially you die owning little or no property. This approach is called the revocable living trust—*revocable* because you are able to change your mind later if your circumstances or attitudes change and *living* because you create the trust while you are alive.

Barbara and Jane came to see us as a result of an estate planning seminar we had conducted. They felt that revocable living trusts were appropriate for them. They reckoned that because they were widows whose children were scattered around the country, their estates could be vulnerable after their death to undue legal bills. The ladies didn't know too much about revocable living trusts, just that the technique seemed appropriate in their situations. They were right. With our help and the assistance of an attorney we recommended, each of them established a trust. While they are alive, they are the sole trustee of their own trust. After death, one of their surviving heirs becomes the trustee of the deceased woman's trust.

After the legal documents had been executed, we helped them retitle all their assets. That part of the process can be exceedingly time consuming. As they say, don't try this at home. However, being professionals, we have a better feel for the ins and outs of financial institutions (stock brokerage firms, transfer agents, mutual fund companies, and banks). And we have one additional weapon: administrative assistants, who are paid to be patient and persistent. Some financial institutions are easy to deal with—stock brokerage firms and mutual funds are two of the best examples. Banks can be balky about retitling, but they generally come through after a little prodding. Real estate is quite easy, since the attorney simply files a form, called a quit-claim deed, at your local courthouse.

When all is attended to—it takes a minimum two months from start to finish—virtually all your property has been retitled in the name of your trust. You get exactly the same investment statements you got before. It's just the titling that has changed. When you sign things, it's as trustee rather than individually. But in no other way has your ability to control your investments been altered.

The important change occurs when you die. Instantly, at the moment of your death, your *revocable* trust becomes *irrevocable.* Any asset in the trust is not part of your probate estate. Furthermore, you execute a will that is a companion to your trust. It's called a pour-over will because it calls for any asset that's not titled in the name of the trust—such as your car—to become part of the trust after your death. When you die, the successor trustee takes over from you. In Barbara's and Jane's cases, several of their children were named to that role. They could then distribute their mothers' assets (to themselves) without any need to report to the probate court. Of course, they would be responsible for all the same functions that an executor must perform, particularly paying bills and filing estate tax returns if necessary. But the costs, delay, and potential publicity of probate were mostly eliminated by the trust.

Another advantage of the revocable living trust is its flexibility. It can be drafted to provide for your spouse, as well as to coordinate with the tax-saving credit shelter trust covered in Chapter 13. It can also be named as beneficiary of your insurance policies and other assets that provide you the opportunity to designate a beneficiary. Unlike jointly held property, 100 percent of which goes to the survivor, these trusts avoid probate yet give you the flexibility to distribute your property among a variety of heirs.

Why doesn't everyone manage their affairs so as to sidestep the probate process? Ignorance is one main reason. Practicality is another. The vast majority of the population is so unsophisticated when it comes to estate planning that *most people don't even have a simple will.* Our local probate judge tells us that 75 percent of the folks who die in our area do so intestate (the fancy term for "without a will"). It's hardly surprising, then, that few people take the trouble to go to the other extreme and intelligently plan their affairs using a revocable living trust.

Not everyone should worry about probate, either. As we said earlier in this chapter, we believe that too much has been made of avoiding probate. A dozen or so years ago, there was near hysteria in the financial press on that subject. An evangelistic fervor seemed to take hold. Let's keep it in perspective. If a competent family member is executor of an estate and a competent and *honest* lawyer is handling the legal end, the difficulties of the probate process can be kept to a minimum.

Besides, it's almost impossible to totally avoid probate. It's not practical to put *everything* you own in trust. What about your car? Your personal effects? Your furniture? To some extent, the time and money you save your heirs will be offset by the time and money you have to spend setting the darned thing up and transferring your assets to it.

When should you consider using a revocable living trust? Anyone who has any substantial amount of assets should at least consider using this technique. Those for whom it may make the most sense are people who own property in several states (and don't want to pay probate costs in each of them) and elderly single people whose children or heirs do not live nearby. For them, a revocable living trust will virtually assure a smooth estate settlement.

One final word on the revocable trust. Some lawyers are lukewarm to the idea and may even try to talk you out of it. Attorneys that we respect come down on both sides of the issue. However, if you feel that avoiding probate is an important goal of your estate planning, by all means talk to a number of lawyers until you find one who is willing to assist you properly.

IV

PROVIDING FOR YOUR LOVED ONES—AND YOURSELF

Chapter Ten

Deputizing Others to Act for You While You Are Still Alive

Y ou are hale and hearty. You are at the top of your game, in charge of your world. So you have trouble imagining that it could ever be otherwise. As children and young adults, everyone feels immortal. Even through much of the rest of our lives, it's hard for most of us to imagine ever needing to rely on other people to make basic decisions concerning our welfare.

Among our own clientele, we have noticed a striking tendency. At some point, generally in their 50s, most people begin to sense their mortality. That's when they start to take seriously our advice that they make sure their affairs are in order. As our population ages and as advances in medical science allow for the preservation of life, we need to plan for the sorts of occurrences that can incapacitate us without killing us. Here's an example. Suppose your elderly bachelor Uncle Beasley, who lives alone, has a stroke. All sorts of issues will arise. Who has the authority to make decisions concerning his care? Who can put him in a nursing home, if that turns out to be appropriate? Who can pay his bills for him?

These issues fall into two principal categories: taking care of the person and taking care of the person's affairs, both personal and financial. In the next chapter, we'll discuss living wills, the death with dignity documents that allow you to make your wishes known in advance if you would prefer not to be kept alive by artificial means after hope is gone that you will recover from injury or disease. We also describe the durable power of attorney for health care, in which you deputize a spouse, a relative, or a friend to make decisions regarding your medical care if you are in no shape to make such decisions yourself. In this chapter, then, let's look at the other side—empowering people to handle your financial affairs when you can't.

DURABLE POWERS OF ATTORNEY

You may have encountered the power of attorney in other contexts. For example, if you are selling your house but can't be present at the closing, you will want to give your lawyer a *limited* power of attorney to sign the appropriate documents for you. If you have hired an investment manager, you may have given him or her a limited power of attorney to buy and sell stocks and bonds or mutual funds for you. In these cases, you grant very narrow authority for one specific purpose, and that power of attorney is valid only while you are in good mental condition. If you fall ill and are not competent to make decisions, the limited power of attorney is invalid.

It is possible to give someone much more authority. Thinking back to poor old Uncle Beasley—whom we left rather unceremoniously incapacitated following a stroke—let's suppose you're his favorite niece or nephew. You get a frantic phone call from his neighbor, Mrs. O'Reilly. The ambulance has been summoned. He's admitted to the hospital. Now what? Presuming that you have his medical care under control, we can easily envision you settling back in a chair and letting the enormity of the situation sink in. What do you do now? The doctors say he's going to be in the hospital for a while and then will probably need to be transferred to a convalescent facility. He is likely to be paralyzed for some time. Right now, he can't speak and can't move the whole right side of his body. He'll need therapy. Who's going to take care of Ginger, his beloved golden retriever? What about his mail? Bills? And so forth.

Change a detail here or there, and most of us can easily envision ourselves in the role of caretaker for a family member or friend. Moreover, we may have to do so at a distance because we're such a far-flung people. It's a huge responsibility, but doable, as are most things in life, given the right tools.

The most powerful tool in this case is called the durable power of attorney. It's such a powerful weapon, in fact, that you should be discrete as to whom you give it to—and even more discrete in using one that's been conferred on you.

The *durable* designation means that it endures an incapacitation on the part of the person who gave you the power. That's important because the time when you need to use the power is precisely when the person who gave it to you can't act for himself or herself. *Power of attorney* means you have permission to take just about any action the person would take himself. You can write checks for the disabled person, manage investments, or assume obligations (such as hiring services). Essentially, a power of attorney gives you the ability to do just about anything the person might do.

It is a good idea to have your bank review your power of attorney if you're concerned about using it because not everyone respects a power of attorney. Our clients and the lawyers we work with tell us that banks, in particular, can be snippy about honoring a power of attorney. Occasionally a bank will be so officious that you'll have to go to court to get an order compelling the bank to allow you to handle the disabled person's affairs.

That's what you would do without a power of attorney: go to court. The idea of a power of attorney is to facilitate a sharing of authority. Then, when the time comes that you need to look after someone, and presumably you have your hands full taking care of that person's affairs, you don't need to assume the additional burden, delay, and expense of trudging off to court to get permission to act.

Most often, powers of attorney are given by spouses to each other. We advise our clients, half-jokingly, that they should not give each other such potent authority if they are not secure in the relationship. We say it light-heartedly so as not to insult our clients, but it's no joke. If you are having marital difficulties, definitely do *not* give your spouse such a potent weapon. In fact, we could give you plenty of advice on that subject, both of us having been divorced and remarried—but that's a different book.

Less common but often just as important is getting a power of attorney from an elderly relative or friend. Uncle Beasley, if he is getting along in years, should consider giving you his power of attorney while he's in good health. Then neither of you needs to worry about some sudden adverse change in his condition. Of course, Uncle Beasley may justifiably be reluctant to grant so much authority over his affairs. If you are considering conferring such authority, you need to think very carefully about it; and if someone is asking you to take that responsibility, make sure you have a long and frank conversation about expectations. This is very serious business, and there must be implicit trust on both sides of the equation.

As you and Beasley are doing this planning, you may also want to speak with him about other tactics you can use to facilitate your role as his helper. At least one bank account could be put into joint name so you'd have some resources to call upon if he had an emergency. You should probably be a joint signatory of his safe deposit box. You should discuss with him the details of how he wants funeral arrangements and burial handled when the time comes, and so forth. If Uncle Beasley gets to the point at which he's having trouble attending to his day-to-day affairs, even though he's home, you (or someone else he's close to) will have to help him out.

PERSONAL REPRESENTATIVES

When a person cannot easily manage his or her affairs unaided, a personal representative may be appropriate. This is a lower level of assistance, much less far-reaching than a power of attorney. Many elderly people confer personal representative status on their children and nieces or nephews.

Some of our clients, for example, can get around with difficulty, but find that that the effort of, say, going to the bank is too daunting. So they name someone as their representative. One old codger we know informed his bank that he wanted his niece to act on his behalf. So she handles everything for him, including writing out his checks and taking them to the bank. All he has to do is sign his name. She has no power over his affairs; she simply assists him. She also balances his bank statements, pays all his bills, and goes to the post office or drug store or supermarket. When the time comes, she assembles all his tax documents and takes him to the accountant.

This sort of relationship is informal. No legal document sanctifies it. The relationship relies on the continuous mental activity of the elderly person. To a large extent it is based on trust. To feel completely comfortable relying on a personal representative, you have to have total confidence that your helper will never take advantage of you. Betrayal must be unthinkable.

When a relationship of this sort is working well, the older person doesn't feel that he or she is a burden and the younger assistant doesn't feel put upon. A lot has been written lately about the "sandwich generation." Middle-aged people sometimes feel overwhelmed by having to raise their children, care for their aged parents, and work full-time besides. There are ways to overcome these feelings of stress. Without being crude and crass, an older person can offer some dignified financial compensation.

One of our clients recently called to ask whether his wife and her mother could come to the office. They had a very small matter to discuss, he said. When the two women—Evelyn, who is in her mid-70s, and Linda, who is fortysomething—came in, it developed that Evelyn wanted to turn over some of her nest egg to her daughter Linda and son-in-law John. It seems that Linda had been helping her mom for several years, and mom wanted to help out by giving her daughter enough money to finance a long-postponed kitchen remodeling. (The tricky part was the amount of the gift, some $25,000. In order to avoid estate-tax consequences, we advised her to spread it over two years.)

That may be more help than the average person wants—or can afford—to provide in return for assistance. But help can come at whatever level both parties are comfortable with.

We know a lot of people who have regularly devoted one day a week to helping a senior citizen, and part of the day was always spent going to lunch at a nice restaurant, with the older person picking up the check, naturally. We also know of people who have volunteered to endow a particular expense. For example, grandparents quite often offer to pay part or all of their grandchildren's college bills. One way to do that, a comparatively easy way, is to start early and put a small sum away each week or month.

The personal assistant role can take on more formality as a senior citizen becomes more frail. Without making the assistant a co-owner of assets, an older person can inform the bank that the younger person will manage his or her affairs. The best way to do that is by making a personal visit to the bank, speaking with the branch manager, and writing a note expressing the wish that the bank permit the assistant to handle the necessary affairs. If the younger person is going to inherit the assets eventually, it may not be a bad idea to make some accounts joint. If there's a safe deposit box, putting both signatures on the card facilitates things.

In giving all this advice, we are assuming that there is a very high degree of confidence and trust between the personal assistant and the elderly person. We want to stress that you must be careful! Just as you may be able to, we can tell horror stories about older people being duped or swindled out of their life's savings by ingratiating con men and women. Sometimes families watch helplessly as such swindlers ply their nasty business. We advise that you be cautious about granting anyone you aren't completely certain of too much power over your affairs.

CONSERVATORSHIP

Of all the estate planning issues, this is probably the most emotionally charged. A probate court judge we know says this is "the booming end of this court's business." He attributes that to medical advances. It's also, he says, the unhappiest of his responsibilities. (The happiest: adoption. "Then, everyone is joyous," the judge observes.)

Conservatorships fall into two categories: supervision of a person's estate while they are still alive, and power to determine where the person lives and how their medical care is to proceed. This is obviously the most comprehensive authority one person can have over another. Holding a power of attorney gives you far-reaching authority. But having a power of conservatorship confers on you virtually limitless authority.

When you hear of abuses by unscrupulous family members, they're generally in this area. There are harrowing stories. If you saw the delightful Disney film *Beauty and the Beast*, you may remember that one of that cartoon's scariest episodes had nothing to do with the beast, who, after all, seemed to be mostly roar anyway.

Rather, it involved the heroine's father, whom an angry spurned suitor was trying to have committed to an insane asylum.

Does that still happen? Such doings have the reek of the medieval, a time before due process was invented. But then you read of recent outrages. Clearly there can be cases where grasping relatives and conniving lawyers and judges take advantage of aged, helpless people. Those cases are rare, though, because of safeguards built into the system. More typically, when there's disagreement over a person's care, court hearings are held.

Conservatorships are granted by a court, usually the probate court. It's certainly possible for an older person or an infirm person of any age to designate someone to care for them. You can grant a power of conservatorship just as you would confer a power of attorney. However, most families find the subject a difficult one to broach until one member is on the verge of needing institutionalization, and then it's often too late. Either the person is no longer capable of making a rational decision or is too frightened to do so. At that point, the family petitions a court.

"These hearings are often very contentious," says our friend the probate court judge. "The children quite often disagree about what should be done about their parents, and the parents usually resist going into a nursing home." In his court, the proceedings give the benefit of the doubt to the senior citizen.

Before anyone is appointed as conservator of the elderly person a number of steps must be taken. Medical reports have to be filed with the court, specifying several doctors' opinions as to the fitness of the person. In addition, someone may be appointed as a temporary guardian. Generally an attorney, the temporary guardian has the responsibility of being an advocate for the senior citizen. Only after the judge weighs all the evidence and conducts one or several custody hearings will a decision be made.

Whether or not it is acrimonious, all this can be time-consuming and expensive. In our view, if you can avoid the inevitable rancor of judicial proceedings, everyone benefits.

The only way to do so is by discussing the issue ahead of time. No one expects such conversations to be easy. Deteriorating health and mental fitness are not happy developments. The way to ease the pain, however, is not to ignore it, but to deal with it honestly and openly. Easy for us to say, you may be thinking, and just so.

Still, if you have a family meeting or a series of meetings to explore the possibilities, that process will probably be rewarded. At that point, you may be able to devise the proper strategy and make plans covering various contingencies. If nursing home care is inevitable, in most parts of the country the application process is so cumbersome that you must make your plans ahead.

We have clients named Charlie and Nora. Not long ago, Nora called us in a panic because Charlie, who is 85, had fallen in the bathtub and was in the hospital. Fortunately, he recovered—more or less—and came home after a two-week stay. But the accident, caused by a small stroke, scared them both, and their children as well. Their daughter Nancy lives in Seattle, but she hopped the first plane to the East Coast and stayed for a month. During that period, after Charlie came home from the hospital, we had a series of family meetings, even involving their son Bud by phone from Boston. The prospect of Charlie entering a nursing home was unappealing, but Nora is also in her 80s and feared she wouldn't be able to care for him at home if he had further seizures. Nancy couldn't stay indefinitely because of her own family responsibilities. And Bud's job precludes him from caring for his parents, except from a distance.

The strategy that developed from these sessions was twofold. Charlie authorized his wife and daughter to be his conservators. Should he be incapacitated, they have the complete authority to make decisions concerning his care. At the same time, Nora began investigating nursing homes in the area. She found that they vary considerably in both the care they offer and in cost. Moreover, most have lengthy waiting lists, and all require extensive applications with complex financial questionnaires.

For Nora, everything seems to be a struggle these days. The most routine details of daily life seem to cause her inordinate difficulties because of her age. So wading through nursing home applications and compiling financial data seem like monumental chores. However, since she has the advantage of time, they're not insurmountable obstacles.

The process of obtaining what's called a voluntary conservatorship for Charlie was not entirely uncomplicated. Nora had to apply to the probate court for the appointment. The judge spoke with both Nora and Charlie, as well as with their daughter Nancy. Because the relationship was voluntary, Charlie can terminate it at any time. He has only to give the court 30 days written notice. Since conservators of a person's property have such considerable power, a judge can require that a bond be posted. However, in Charlie's and Nora's case, that was unnecessary because the conservators—Nora, and Nancy as the backup, are next of kin.

When the appointed conservator is a more distant relative, a friend, or an attorney, a probate judge will usually require the conservator to purchase a bond. It's simply insurance to protect against mistakes or fraud, which could jeopardize the person's assets. The bond is usually in the amount of the total assets, and the premiums are paid by the person being protected, not by the conservator.

Now that they've done all this planning, Charlie and Nora—and their children—have the comfort of knowing they are prepared for the unexpected. Should another, more serious episode occur, they have the tools in place to ensure that Charlie's care should proceed without a hitch.

Compared with what are usually considered the more central issues of estate planning, wills and trusts, the provisions we've been discussing in this chapter may seem small. On a more basic level, though, they are perhaps *more* important. After all, your will disposes of your *property* after *you're gone.* But what could be more critical than your *personal care* while you are *still here?*

Chapter Eleven

Living Wills

U p to now, we have mostly been discussing estate planning as a way to help provide for those you care about after you are gone. However, modern medicine has opened up a whole new set of issues that you sometimes have to address while you're alive.

Advances in medical care have produced many miracles. Injuries and illnesses that were invariably fatal to earlier generations are now curable. This progress has not been without unpleasant side-effects. For example, it is now possible to sustain life well beyond the point at which there is any chance for recovery. Patients who are in irreversible comas or the final stages of terminal illness can be fed through tubes and their hearts and lungs can be kept functioning by mechanical respirators.

The most famous example probably is Nancy Cruzan, who lived in Missouri. In 1983, at the age of 25, she was critically injured in an auto accident. Among numerous injuries, she lost the flow of blood to her brain for 12 to 14 minutes. Nancy lapsed into what's called a persistent vegetative state. Her doctors had to insert tubes through her nose and into her stomach to provide food and water. She remained totally unresponsive. After months of attempted therapy, her doctors pronounced her condition hopeless. However, Nancy was not dying. In fact it was estimated that she could live for another 30 years, as long as she continued to be fed through the tubes.

Finally, Nancy's parents made the gut-wrenching decision to ask that the feeding tubes be removed and that she be allowed to die. The doctors refused. Although they were sympathetic to the Cruzans' dilemma, Missouri law prevented them from stopping the feeding. Even though Nancy was no longer a functioning, conscious human being, she was alive. Missouri law was concerned with preservation of life, not with quality of life. The Cruzans went to court. After years of litigation, the case was appealed all the way to the United States Supreme Court.

On the face of it, the Supreme Court's decision was bad news to the Cruzans. By a 5 to 4 vote, the justices upheld the Missouri Supreme Court's decision. However by an 8 to 1 majority, the court also ruled that had Nancy made her intentions known beforehand or appointed someone to make those decisions for her, then her wishes could have been honored.

Armed with this ruling, the Cruzans produced three witnesses who confirmed that Nancy had discussed her wishes with them before the accident. According to their sworn testimony, Nancy had said that she did not want to be force-fed or machine dependent "like a vegetable" if she were ever in a hopelessly critical condition.

On the basis of the Supreme Court's ruling and the testimony of Nancy's friends, the Missouri court authorized removal of the feeding tubes. On December 26, 1990, Nancy Cruzan was allowed to die.

The degree to which patients like Nancy are aware of their suffering is not known, although that's a controversial issue. It is clear that their families and loved ones face a host of agonizing questions.

- Is the patient suffering needlessly?
- Can the family afford to pay the cost of the life-prolonging measures, even beyond the point at which all hope for recovery is gone?
- What are the moral and religious implications?
- What would the patient have wanted?

Due to recent changes in the law, you have the legal right to express your wishes and beliefs before you become incapacitated. On December 1, 1991, the federal Patient Self-Determination Act (PSDA) went into effect. People entering health care facilities now must be informed of their right to refuse treatment and their right to make their wishes known in advance.

You do so either through a living will or by designating a health care proxy, often called a durable power of attorney for health care. A so-called proxy is a person to whom you give the power to make decisions concerning your medical care in the event that you become unable to do so—for example, because you've had a stroke or because you are on medication that impairs your ability to make decisions. Before executing a living will or naming a health care proxy, you should consider a number of possible situations that you and your loved ones may face.

What if you were in an accident like Nancy Cruzan's? All Nancy required to keep her alive was food and water, administered by feeding tubes. Even so, the medical bills piled up. On the other hand, a miracle might have occurred. Would you want your family to hold out for the million-to-one shot, or would you want them to terminate the artificial feeding? It's an issue you need to think about.

Let's look at another situation. You are terminally ill. You have some good days, but mostly bad ones. Sometimes the pain is pretty bad. Your condition worsens. You lapse out of consciousness periodically. Several times you are near death, but the doctors are able to bring you back. Finally, you reach the point at which you are no longer able to communicate. However, the doctors and their machines are able to prevent you from dying, even though they can't do anything to make you better.

We wouldn't presume to tell you or your family what you should do in such a situation. This is one of the most personal and perhaps most critical choices you will ever make. However, we do suggest that you discuss this matter with your family, friends, clergy, and doctors, as well as with your financial advisers. It may help you to think about what is truly important to you.

Ask yourself the following:

Do I want to avoid long-term pain and suffering once my situation becomes hopeless?

Do I want to fight on indefinitely until the bitter end?

Do I want to avoid being a financial burden on my family?

Are all financial considerations secondary to my religious and personal beliefs about the value of life?

We must emphasize at this point that we are *not* talking about committing suicide. Rather we are talking about withholding or withdrawing medical care when a person's health has reached the point at which medical science is extending the natural process of death rather than prolonging life. You have the right to decide for yourself.

What is the best way to express your wishes? The majority of our states and the District of Columbia have passed legislation that specifically provides for living wills or the designation of so-called health care proxies.

Courts in the remaining states have tended to accept such documents as the best evidence of a patient's intentions. You'll find a list of the states that have adopted such legislation at the end of this chapter. We have reproduced a sample living will, courtesy of Choice in Dying, a nonprofit New York–based organization. Copies of living will forms for your state are available from Choice in Dying. (The organization's address is: 200 Varick St., New York, N.Y. 10014.)

Very simply, a living will leaves instructions for the type of care you would want or not want in the event you become hopelessly injured or ill. You can make your feelings known about any number of medical procedures including:

Cardiopulmonary resuscitation (CPR), used to restart the heart and lungs after they've stopped.

Intravenous (I.V.) therapy, used to provide medication, water, and food through the veins.

Feeding tubes, placed in a person's stomach through the nose to provide food and water to patients who are comatose or otherwise incapable of eating.

Respirators, used to keep patients breathing artificially.

Pain medication, which can control the degree of pain.

Once you have gone through this soul-searching, you are ready for these steps:

- Check the laws in your state.
- Put your wishes in writing, using your state's accepted forms. Even in states that don't formally recognize such forms, it can be helpful to have your written request.
- Sign and date your advance directives. Have them witnessed and, if possible, notarized.
- Keep a card in your wallet stating that you have a living will.
- By all means, make sure that your physician has a copy.
- Discuss your directives with your family and friends.

The advantage of a living will is that it is very simple to fill out and put into effect. The disadvantage is that the situation you find yourself in might not be so simple. What if it isn't clear whether or not your situation is hopeless? What if your family is not happy with your present medical team? What if there's a 25 percent chance that an experimental procedure could restore you to at least a semblance of normal life? A 10 percent chance? 5 percent? (Chances are, though, experimental procedures are not covered by your health insurance, which would put a financial burden on your family and reduce your estate.)

If you can't make the choice, who should? In some states (again, see our list at chapter's end) you can designate a health care proxy in your living will. In other states you must establish the proxy in a separate durable power of attorney for health care (DPAHC) document. In either case, whomever you designate as your proxy will have the right to make a broad range of decisions for you in the event you cannot make them yourself.

Because this person is empowered literally to make life-and-death decisions, you must choose that stand-in very carefully. You obviously need to trust her or him and be sure that your surrogate understands your wishes. The person also needs to have good judgment and the fortitude to make difficult decisions.

Typically, married people designate their spouse. But you may appoint a friend or family member or anyone else you feel certain you can rely on. You should also appoint a backup. Discuss your wishes thoroughly with your designated proxy so that she or he will feel comfortable that the decisions made on your behalf are what you would have wanted under the circumstances.

If you decide to execute a power of attorney for health care, we strongly urge you to consult an attorney in your home state. An ideal time to do so would be when you implement some of the other estate planning techniques we describe in this book. Although federal law now requires that you be informed of your rights upon admission to a health care facility, it may be too late by then. Nancy Cruzan was already unconscious by the time she got to the hospital. The new law would have been of no use to her unless she had taken the time to execute a living will or power of attorney before her accident.

STATE LAWS GOVERNING LIVING WILLS AND APPOINTMENT OF A HEALTH CARE PROXY

The following list indicates that a state recognizes (whether by legislation or court cases) the following:

- A living will only.
- A health care proxy only.
- Both a living will and a health care proxy.

The details of each state's laws vary considerably and are changing rapidly. We suggest that you contact your attorney or Choice in Dying for the latest information on your state's current regulations.

Alabama	Both
Alaska	Living wills only
Arizona	Both
Arkansas	Both
California	Both
Colorado	Both
Connecticut	Both
Delaware	Both
District of Columbia	Both
Florida	Both
Georgia	Both
Hawaii	Both
Idaho	Both
Illinois	Both
Indiana	Both
Iowa	Both
Kansas	Both
Kentucky	Both
Louisiana	Both
Maine	Both
Maryland	Both
Massachusetts	Both
Michigan	Both
Minnesota	Both
Mississippi	Both
Missouri	Both

Montana	Both
Nebraska	Has no provisions for either living wills or designation of a health care proxy.
Nevada	Both
New Hampshire	Both
New Jersey	Both
New Mexico	Both
New York	Both
North Dakota	Both
Ohio	Both
Oklahoma	Living wills only
Oregon	Both
Pennsylvania	Health care proxies only
Rhode Island	Both
South Carolina	Both
South Dakota	Both
Tennessee	Both
Texas	Both
Utah	Both
Vermont	Both
Washington	Both
West Virginia	both
Wyoming	Both

CHOICE IN DYING

Formerly Concern for Dying and the Society for the Right to Die

Instructions for Using the Connecticut Living Will Document, the Appointment of a Health Care Agent Document, and the Choice In Dying Living Will

Connecticut's law on living wills and health care agents changed in 1991. The Connecticut documents we are enclosing comply with the 1991 law.

The Connecticut Living Will Document Concerning Life Support Systems

The Connecticut living will document concerning life support systems and the document concerning the appointment of a health care agent are printed on one form.

Please read the Connecticut living will carefully before you complete it, especially the "Questions and Answers" that start on page 2 of the document. Note that it will be carried out only when you are in either a terminal condition or a permanently unconscious state and are no longer able to make decisions yourself. We have left space for you to add personal instructions. You must clearly state your wishes about artificial respiration, cardiopulmonary resuscitation or artificial means of providing nutrition and hydration ("tube feeding"). Please read that section very carefully.

The Connecticut Document Concerning the Appointment of a Health Care Agent

The appointment of a health care agent document lets you appoint a health care agent to convey your wishes about life support systems to your physician when you are no longer able to make decisions yourself. Like the living will document, the health care agent document will be carried out only when you are in either a terminal condition or a permanently unconscious state. Please read the document carefully before completing it. You **must** tell your agent and alternate agent (if you appoint one) what your wishes are. (The best way to do this is to complete a Connecticut living will document in addition to completing the appointment of a health care agent document.) If you do not, your agent(s) will not be able to act for you. The agent(s) should be given photocopies of both your Connecticut living will document, the appointment of a health care agent document, and the Choice in Dying Living Will.

Choice In Dying's Living Will

Connecticut's living will document concerning life support and appointment of a health care agent only become effective when the person who signed them is in a terminal or permanently unconscious condition. Some people wish to have life-support withdrawn or withheld in other conditions – for example, in case of advanced Alzheimer's disease, or minimal consciousness as a result of a stroke. Because the Connecticut living will may not cover those conditions, and you may want to, you should complete the enclosed Choice In Dying living will **in addition to** the Connecticut living will. Please read it carefully before completing it.

Although the broader and more comprehensive Choice In Dying living will is not specifically approved by Connecticut law, the United States Supreme Court has suggested that such a document should be honored in every state.

The Connecticut Durable Power of Attorney for Health Care

A durable power of attorney for health care is a document in which you may appoint another person to make medical decisions for you if you are not able to make your own decisions but are **not** terminally ill or permanently unconscious (for example, if you are temporarily unconscious due to a head injury). Choice In Dying does not distribute this document because it does not address end-of-life decisionmaking.

(over, please)

If you wish to receive a copy of this document you may contact:

John Flannigan
Constituent Services Officer
Office of the Attorney General
55 Elm Street
Hartford, CT 06101
(203) 566-6027

What to Do With Your Documents

Give photocopies of the completed documents to your health care agent (if you name one), to your doctor(s) and to family members or close friends who might be concerned with your medical care. Keep the signed original forms in a safe place that will be easily accessible to others in case of an emergency – not in a safe deposit box – and let someone know where they are.

Be sure to keep your health care agent(s) and health care provider(s) up to date with your wishes about medical treatment, especially if your medical condition changes.

The Living Will Registry

Choice In Dying's Living Will Registry offers you the opportunity to safeguard your documents in our files for safe, permanent storage and easy retrieval. A one-time fee of $40 ($35 for Choice In Dying members) makes you a lifetime member of the Registry and entitles you to the following:

• Analysis of all your documents to make sure they are properly completed
• Automatic notification of any changes in your state's law
• New documents when your state's law changes or when you move to another state
• Regular reminders to review the information in your file
• The security of knowing your documents are safe and always available to your family and doctors if needed

Other Services from Choice In Dying

Choice in Dying's publications provide further information about various aspects of the right to refuse treatment. Please use the form on the enclosed publications list to order.

The annual membership fee of $15 entitles you to the latest information on right-to-die developments, including any changes in the law that might affect you; a subscription to our quarterly Newsletter; a wallet-size membership card, to alert people in case of an emergency that you have a "living will" document, a health care agent document, and/or a Choice In Dying living will; and a discount on all our publications, videos and special services.

By contributing you will join the ranks of supporters who have kept Choice In Dying in the vanguard of the patients' rights movement for over 50 years. Please remember that we are a not-for-profit group that depends on supporter contributions. Your donation will help us to continue our work to protect the rights of all Americans to a natural and dignified death.

Thank you.

ADVANCE DIRECTIVE
Living Will and Health Care Proxy

*D*eath is a part of life. It is a reality like birth, growth and aging. I am using this advance directive to convey my wishes about medical care to my doctors and other people looking after me at the end of my life. It is called an advance directive because it gives instructions in advance about what I want to happen to me in the future. It expresses my wishes about medical treatment that might keep me alive. I want this to be legally binding.

If I cannot make or communicate decisions about my medical care, those around me should rely on this document for instructions about measures that could keep me alive.

I do not want medical treatment (including feeding and water by tube) that will keep me alive if:
- I am unconscious and there is no reasonable prospect that I will ever be conscious again (even if I am not going to die soon in my medical condition), or
- I am near death from an illness or injury with no reasonable prospect of recovery.

I do want medicine and other care to make me more comfortable and to take care of pain and suffering. I want this even if the pain medicine makes me die sooner.

I want to give some extra instructions: *[Here list any special instructions, e.g., some people fear being kept alive after a debilitating stroke. If you have wishes about this, or any other conditions, please write them here.]*

The legal language in the box that follows is a health care proxy.
It gives another person the power to make medical decisions for me.

I name _____ , who lives at _____

_____ , phone number _____ ,

to make medical decisions for me if I cannot make them myself. This person is called a health care "surrogate," "agent," "proxy," or "attorney in fact." This power of attorney shall become effective when I become incapable of making or communicating decisions about my medical care. This means that this document stays legal when and if I lose the power to speak for myself, for instance, if I am in a coma or have Alzheimer's disease.

My health care proxy has power to tell others what my advance directive means. This person also has power to make decisions for me, based either on what I would have wanted, or, if this is not known, on what he or she thinks is best for me.

If my first choice health care proxy cannot or decides not to act for me, I name _____

_____ , address _____ ,

phone number _____ , as my second choice.

(over, please)

LWGEN

I have discussed my wishes with my health care proxy, and with my second choice if I have chosen to appoint a second person. My proxy(ies) has(have) agreed to act for me.

I have thought about this advance directive carefully. I know what it means and want to sign it. I have chosen two witnesses, neither of whom is a member of my family, nor will inherit from me when I die. My witnesses are not the same people as those I named as my health care proxies. I understand that this form should be notarized if I use the box to name (a) health care proxy(ies).

Signature _____

Date _____

Address _____

Witness' signature _____

Witness' printed name _____

Address _____

Witness' signature _____

Witness' printed name _____

Address _____

Notary [to be used if proxy is appointed] _____

Drafted and Distributed by Choice In Dying, Inc.—the National Council for the right to Die. Choice In Dying is a National not-for-profit organization which works for the rights of patients at the end of life. In addition to this generic advance directive, Choice In Dying distributes advance directives that conform to each state's specific legal requirements and maintains a national Living Will Registry for completed documents.

CHOICE IN DYING INC.—
the national council for the right to die
(formerly Concern for Dying/Society for the Right to Die)
200 Varick Street, New York, NY 10014 (212) 366-5540

5/92

CONNECTICUT

**DOCUMENT CONCERNING WITHHOLDING OR WITHDRAWAL OF
LIFE SUPPORT SYSTEMS *and* DOCUMENT CONCERNING THE APPOINTMENT
OF HEALTH CARE AGENT**

*Please see page 2 of this form for the Document Concerning
the Appointment of a Health Care Agent and important
information on how to complete the documents*

**DOCUMENT CONCERNING WITHHOLDING OR WITHDRAWAL
OF LIFE SUPPORT SYSTEMS**

If the time comes when I am incapacitated to the point when I can no longer actively take part in decisions for my own life, and am unable to direct my physician as to my own medical care, I wish this statement to stand as a testament of my wishes.

"I,_____ , request that, if my condition is

(name)

deemed terminal or if I am determined to be permanently unconscious, I be allowed to die and not be kept alive through life support systems. By terminal condition, I mean that I have an incurable or irreversible medical condition which, without the administration of life support systems, will, in the opinion of my attending physician, result in death within a relatively short time. By permanently unconscious I mean that I am in a permanent coma or persistent vegetative state which is an irreversible condition in which I am at no time aware of myself or the environment and show no behavioral response to the environment. The life support systems which I do not want include, but are not limited to:

> Artificial respiration
> Cardiopulmonary resuscitation
> Artificial means of providing nutrition and hydration

(Cross out and initial life support systems you <u>do</u> want administered)

I do not intend any direct taking of my life, but only that my dying not be unreasonably prolonged."

Other specific requests:

This request is made, after careful reflection, while I am of sound mind.

_____

(Signature)
_____

(Date)

This document was signed in our presence, by the above-named_____

_____ , who appeared to be eighteen years of age or older,

(name)

of sound mind and able to understand the nature and consequences of health care decisions at the time the document was signed.

Witness_____

Address _____

Witness_____

Address _____

$\boxed{2}$

DOCUMENT CONCERNING THE APPOINTMENT OF HEALTH CARE AGENT

I appoint _____ to be my health care agent.
                          (name)

If my attending physician determines that I am unable to understand and appreciate the nature and consequences of health care decisions and to reach and communicate an informed decision regarding treatment, my health care agent is authorized to:

(1) Convey to my physician my wishes concerning the withholding or removal of life support systems.
(2) Take whatever actions are necessary to ensure that my wishes are given effect.

If this person is unwilling or unable to serve as my health care agent, I appoint_____

_____ to be my alternative health care agent.
                          (name)

This request is made, after careful reflection, while I am of sound mind.

_____
(Signature)

_____
(Date)

This document was signed in our presence, by the above-named_____

_____ , who appeared to be eighteen years of age or older, of
                          (name)
sound mind and able to understand the nature and consequences of health care decisions at the time the document was signed.

Witness _____

Address _____

Witness _____

Address _____

QUESTIONS AND ANSWERS ABOUT THE CONNECTICUT DOCUMENTS

This form contains two sections. The first section, called the document concerning withholding or withdrawal of life support systems, is a living will document that lets you express your wishes about medical care in the event of a terminal condition or permanent unconsciousness. The second section, called the document concerning the appointment of a health care agent, lets you appoint someone to make medical decisions for you if you should lose the ability to make those decisions yourself, and you have a terminal condition or are permanently unconscious. It is a good idea to complete both sections, if you have someone you trust to act as your health care agent. Because Connecticut law **requires** that your agent and alternate agent (if any) know what your wishes are, we strongly suggest that if you appoint someone, you also complete the first (living will) section.

Who may complete a form?

Any adult (18 years of age or older) of sound mind may complete one or both sections of this form.

$\boxed{3}$

When does the form take effect?

The form goes into effect when the following conditions are met:
- you are incapacitated (that is, unable to make your own medical decisions), **and**
- your attending physician has received a copy of the form, **and**
- your attending physician determines that you are in a terminal condition, or determines, together with a neurologist who has examined you, that you are permanently unconscious.

Who may serve as your health care agent?

Any adult may serve as agent **except:**

1) A physician may not act as both agent and attending physician for the patient.
2) Unless related to the principal by blood, marriage, or adoption, the following persons may not serve as agent:

   a) an operator, administrator, or employee of a hospital, home for the aged, rest home with nursing supervision, or chronic and convalescent nursing home, if the principal at the time of the appointment is a patient or resident of or has applied for admission to any of those facilities.
   b) an administrator or employee of a government agency who is financially responsible for the principal's medical care.

What are the witnessing requirements?

Each of the two sections of the form must be signed by **two** witnesses.

1) Any adult can serve as a witness for the first section of the form. (If you appoint a health care agent, however, we advise you not to use that person as a witness to the living will portion of the form.)
2) Witnesses to the second section (the document concerning the appointment of health care agent) must meet the following conditions:

- Anyone you appoint as your agent or as an alternative agent may not serve as a witness.
- If you live in a facility operated or licensed by the department of mental health, you must have at least one witness who is not affiliated with the facility and at least one witness who is a physician or clinical psychologist with specialized training in mental illness.
- If you live in a facility operated or licensed by the department of mental retardation, you must have at least one witness who is not affiliated with the facility and at least one of your witnesses must be a physician or clinical psychologist with specialized training in developmental disabilities.

You have the option of asking any or all of your witnesses to sign an affidavit, in the presence of an officer who is authorized to administer oaths, swearing that they saw you sign the form, that you did so of your own free will, and that you were of sound mind; such affidavits would support the validity of your document in case of a dispute. Please contact the office of the Connecticut Attorney General (203) 566-6027, if you would like more information on this option.

What if a physician or health care provider refuses to comply with the terms of the form?

Any physician or health care provider who is unwilling to comply must take all reasonable steps to transfer you to the care of a physician or health care provider who is willing to comply.

How can a living will or appointment of health care agent be revoked?

You may revoke your living will or appointment of health care agent at any time and in any manner (for example, by destroying the document), regardless of your mental or physical condition.

Your attending physician or other health care provider must make the revocation a part of your medical record.

The appointment of your spouse as health care agent will automatically be revoked if your marriage ends, unless you specify otherwise.

What if I complete both a living will (the first section) and an appointment of a health care agent (the second section)?

If you complete both a living will and an appointment of a health care agent, your physician will look first to your living will as the source of your wishes.

Courtesy of **Choice in Dying**, *200 Varick Street, New York, NY 10014   (212) 366-5540*   LWCT-3/3   2/92

V

PLANNING FOR LARGER ESTATES

Chapter Twelve

The High Cost of Dying: What You Need to Know

G overnments have taxed their citizens since the dawn of time. Tax collecting may not be the world's oldest profession, but it's a close second. Historians have traced the taxation of estates back to the early Greeks and Romans. The Emperor Augustus imposed an estate tax 2,000 years ago. He needed to raise funds to finance his campaigns of conquest and reasoned that the right to transfer property at death was a right granted by the government, and thus it could be taxed. Like it or not, the doctrine of estate taxation has been handed down over the centuries, and it continues to form the basis for our system of gift and estate taxation today.

Before you get too angry at those early Greeks and Romans, however, keep in mind that our system could be worse. One of Augustus' successors, the infamous Emperor Caligula, was cruel, irrational, and very greedy. Some of Rome's wealthiest citizens attempted to curry favor with him by publicly announcing that they had named the Emperor in their wills. Caligula was delighted. He sent these loyal citizens cakes from the Imperial bakery to show his gratitude. As it turned out, the cakes were poisoned, so that Caligula could collect his inheritance as soon as possible. Eventually, the madman was assassinated by his own generals. Fortunately, this particular estate planning tradition died with him, at least as official policy.

ESTATE TAXATION IN THE UNITED STATES

Estate taxation in America is similar to the Roman system in a number of respects. Death taxes and gift taxes are used to raise revenue for the government—federal or state. These taxes are also part of a broader social agenda: the redistribution of wealth.

In exercising the right to tax property transfers at death or during your lifetime, the government, primarily the federal government, can startle citizens who were unaware of how voracious the government's appetite can be.

We had a client a few years back who simply couldn't grasp the basic concept. This was a fairly wealthy but very unsophisticated man, the owner of a plumbing company and several parcels of very valuable land. Let's call him Sal. As many times as we tried to broach the subject of tax planning, Sal would always take a pugnacious stance. "I've paid my taxes all along," Sal would mutter, "so why would I owe anything when I die?" At the time, we didn't think of mentioning Caligula and his Roman colleagues; perhaps that would have helped. Finally, we explained to Sal that when he and his wife Theresa died, their three kids were going to have to pay $4.6 million dollars in federal and state taxes. No doubt, they'd have to sell the company, even though two of them work for it. That got through to Sal, and we were able to start planning.

We didn't try to teach Sal how our American estate tax system has evolved. But it's a useful thing to understand. Prior to 1981, when the most recent major revisions in U.S. estate taxation were enacted, the system was somewhat different. The federal government unified its system of estate and gift taxation in 1976. No longer was it as easy to give something to your heirs during your lifetime and owe less tax than if you held the property until death. That's a concept that many people have trouble understanding. The fact is that the government no longer imposes "death taxes," but rather "transfer taxes." It doesn't matter whether you give property away or leave it to your heirs, you still must pay taxes if the amount of your gifts or estate is large enough.

One problem with the approach taken in 1976 had to do with transfers between husbands and wives. In the eyes of the law, a married couple represents a sacred union. You may not have thought of it that way, but the government does. For example, "married filing jointly" is a unified tax status reserved for married couples. In terms of estate planning the concept began to emerge that a husband and wife team is one unit, not two separate people. The 1976 law also expanded the scope of what had been an existing marital deduction. The first $250,000 of your property, or half your estate, whichever was greater, could pass to your spouse free of estate tax. In addition, a personal exemption of $30,000 was allowed against the balance of your property.

This still left a sizable number of situations in which the surviving spouse was on the hook for some pretty serious estate taxes. One of the least popular aspects of that law was a new capital gains tax, which was imposed on the growth of property held by the deceased. In other words, if you bought a piece of property for $10,000 and it grew in value to $15,000 by the time of your death, your family would owe an estate tax on the $15,000, plus a capital gains tax on the $5,000 increase. The concept didn't have too many fans. Luckily, the law was also very complicated and expensive to administer, and it was repealed as part of the 1981 Economic Recovery Tax Act (ERTA).

Like its predecessor, ERTA is a unified transfer tax on both lifetime gifts and estates. It brought a measure of relief to the middle class (how's that for a switch?) by creating an unlimited marital deduction and increasing the amount of property that could be transferred free of tax. The unlimited marital deduction provides that any assets you give your spouse during your lifetime or leave to your spouse at your death are exempt from federal taxation. Obviously, you have to be married to take advantage of the marital deduction. However, whether you are married or not, the law also provides every person with a tax credit of $192,800, which can be used to offset taxes owed on gifts you make during your lifetime or upon the legacy you leave after your death. The credit equates to $600,000 of property that you can pass along free of federal tax.

What it all means is that if the total value of all your assets (including your life insurance) is less than $600,000, your estate will be exempt from federal tax. Depending upon the state in which you live, there may be some local estate or inheritance taxes due, in addition to the legal and administrative costs of settling your affairs. If you are married, none of the assets you give your spouse will be taxed by the federal government, although again, there may be some state taxes due. Keep in mind that the marital deduction is merely a deferral of the tax. When a surviving spouse dies, the tax will be imposed on the full value of the property that he or she owns at that time, including the property inherited when the first spouse died.

Through proper planning, it is possible to take advantage of the combined benefits of the unlimited marital deduction and the $192,800 credit that exempts $600,000 worth of property from taxation. By leaving some of your property directly to your spouse and placing the balance in trust for your spouse's lifetime, it is possible to pass an estate as large as $1.2 million totally free of federal tax. This does not happen automatically, however. In Chapter 13 we will present a step-by-step guide to this planning technique.

Now for a word to our procrastinating readers who have not updated their wills since ERTA was passed in 1981. Depending on how the will was worded, your heirs could be in for a real shock. If your will states that you leave your spouse the maximum marital deduction, the courts will hold that you meant the maximum marital deduction *at the time you signed your will.* You will recall that prior to 1981, the marital deduction was the greater of $250,000 or half your estate. This means that your estate will owe taxes on everything over and above the old marital deduction. If you update your will, you can defer all federal estate taxes until both you and your spouse have died.

A note to anyone who is married to a foreign citizen: Under a recent revision to the estate tax statutes, foreign citizens are not eligible for the marital deduction unless special trust arrangements are set up. If this applies to you, ask your attorney about a qualified domestic trust (QDT) for noncitizen spouses.

WHAT GETS TAXED?

Almost everything. In Appendix B, we have reproduced Form 706, the Federal Estate Tax Return. Your executor will be required to make an inventory of everything you owned at the time of your death. You can see that this includes life insurance, real estate, personal property, savings, investments, and any interests you had in a business. One half of any joint property held with your spouse is deemed to have been yours. If you owned joint property with anybody else, 100 percent is considered to have been yours unless your estate can prove that your co-owner contributed to the asset. You cannot simply retitle assets to joint ownership with someone else and assume that you have removed some of the value from your own estate.

HOW DOES THE GOVERNMENT KNOW WHAT I HAVE?

To some extent, the IRS must rely on what your executor puts down on Form 706. Bear in mind that if your executor were to deliberately omit assets from the return, he or she could go to jail. If the government audits your estate, it can be quite easy to find things your family hoped it wouldn't.

Naturally, the government will know from your income tax returns whether or not you were receiving interest and dividends from banks or brokerage firms. If those assets aren't listed, the revenuers will want to know why. The IRS may send appraisers to your house to check the value of art works, antiques, jewelry, and the like. We recently had an interesting discussion on this subject with one of our clients. This client owns an extremely valuable work of art, worth at least $1 million. He asked how the IRS would know that he had it. He bought it from a dealer for cash many years ago, when it was worth a small fraction of what it is today. What would happen if, after his death, his children simply took that painting down and replaced it with a worthless print by some other artist? Who would be the wiser?

The response was twofold. One, that would be fraud. The penalties for getting caught are severe. We could be talking hard time here. Second, don't ever take the IRS for a fool. We asked our client whether the painting was insured against fire and theft. His face fell. One of the first things the auditor would look for would be insurance records that would list this painting and the amount it was insured for.

The IRS audits a much higher percentage of estate tax returns than it does income tax returns. If you have a large estate or own a business, your family can virtually count on the estate being audited. The explanation lies, perhaps, in the fact that the IRS knows this is their last shot at you. Aside from the fact that honesty is its own reward, it just isn't that easy to cheat and get away with it.

HOW MUCH IS THE TAX?

Once your estate crosses the $600,000 threshold, the taxes grow rapidly. The tax is progressive, meaning that the more you have, the higher the rate of tax. To give you an idea of the magnitude of these taxes see Table 12-1. This chart shows the amount of federal tax plus the minimum amount of state death tax your estate would owe. Some states charge a higher tax, which we will illustrate later in this chapter.

We have also built in a 5 percent factor for the administrative and legal costs of settling an estate. In most cases the expense need not be that high. With proper planning, as discussed in Chapter 9, the costs can be minimized. In some situations, they can be much higher, especially if litigation is involved. In any event, you can use the chart to help you get a rough estimate of the tax burden your heirs could face.

THE STATE GETS ITS SHARE

As we have stated, Uncle Sam wants a big piece of your estate when you die. Alas, it doesn't end there. State governments need revenue, too. Each and every one of our 50 states, along with the District of Columbia, collect some form of death taxes. Some are more ravenous than others, of course, but all collect something if your estate is large enough.

Death taxes vary from state to state, but they tend to fall into three broad types. The most common is the credit estate tax. The federal estate tax tables include a credit, which has the effect of offsetting any local death taxes. The state credit estate tax is assessed by all states to "soak up" this credit. For this reason it is also called a "sponge tax." Quite a few states (including Florida, which we mention because the favorable estate tax environment actually attracts senior citizens) impose no additional death taxes and are considered low-tax states. These state death tax credits are shown in Appendix D.

A number of states have appetites for revenue that are not satisfied by the credit estate tax. Some impose an additional estate tax, which is levied on the value of all assets owned by the deceased.

TABLE 12-1
The High Cost of Dying

Net Taxable Estate*	Federal Estate Taxes†	Administration Expenses @5%‡	Total Estate Costs
$ 225,000	$ 0	$ 11,250	$ 11,250
300,000	0	15,000	15,000
400,000	0	20,000	20,000
500,000	0	25,000	25,000
600,000	0	30,000	30,000
700,000	37,000	35,000	72,000
800,000	75,000	40,000	115,000
900,000	114,000	45,000	159,000
1,000,000	153,000	50,000	203,000
1,500,000	363,000	75,000	438,000
2,000,000	588,000	100,000	688,000
2,500,000	833,000	125,000	958,000
3,000,000	1,098,000	150,000	1,248,000
3,500,000	1,373,000	175,000	1,548,000
4,000,000	1,648,000	200,000	1,848,000
5,000,000	2,198,000	250,000	2,448,000
6,000,000	2,748,000	300,000	3,048,000
8,000,000	3,848,000	400,000	4,248,000
10,000,000	4,948,000	500,000	5,448,000
15,000,000	7,948,000	750,000	8,698,000
20,000,000	10,948,000	1,000,000	11,948,000
30,000,000	16,500,000	1,500,000	18,000,000
40,000,000	22,000,000	2,000,000	24,000,000
50,000,000	27,500,000	2,500,000	30,000,000
100,000,000	55,000,000	5,000,000	60,000,000

* *Net taxable estate* here means the total estate after deducting the marital deduction on any transfers to a surviving spouse, as well as mortgages or other debts. There will typically not be a tax until the surviving spouse dies.

† This chart also includes the amount that will pass to the state as the maximum credit for state death tax paid. Some states will take more than the credit. Rates are scheduled to drop in 1993.

‡ Administration fees, last illness costs, and burial costs are deductible in determining the federal estate tax. As a rule of thumb, many estate planners use a figure of 5 percent for the approximate cost. The actual costs could be more or less than this amount (*administration expenses* include executor's commissions and attorney's fees).

Most states have adopted the federal marital deduction, which allows all assets to pass to your spouse free of this tax. Thus, the state estate taxes will not be due until the death of the second spouse. In some states, local estate taxes may be owed, even though federal taxes are not.

The third form of state death taxation is the inheritance tax. It differs from an estate tax in that the rate of tax varies based on the relationship of the deceased to the heirs.

States that use this system assess a lower tax rate on assets left to parents and children than they do on assets left to other relatives or friends. Again, many states allow for the marital deduction, so taxes are due only upon the death of the second spouse. Check the rules for your own state when doing your planning.

In planning your estate, it is important to take into account not only your state of residence, but also the location of your property. For example, if you live in Ohio but own a home in Florida, you can actually owe death taxes to both states. Florida will tax the value of the home located there. Ohio will tax the value of all your property, but grant a credit for the taxes paid to Florida. The result is that you will pay the higher of the two taxes. In this case, Ohio has higher death taxes than Florida. The amount due Ohio on the Florida property would be based on Ohio's estate tax tables, with a credit allowed for the lower Florida tax.

In the reverse example, if a Florida resident died owning property in Ohio, there would be a tax due based on Ohio's estate tax table. Since this tax exceeds Florida's tax, there would be no tax payable to Florida on the Ohio property.

This raises an interesting question. Why not move to Florida or some other low-tax state to avoid higher local taxes? The real issue is whether you want to move to Florida—or New Mexico, Alaska, Nevada, or any other low-tax state. Remember that the big tax is the federal tax, and that's the same wherever you go. Unless you have a very large estate, in the millions of dollars, there simply isn't enough financial incentive to pull up roots. Of course, if you *want* to move to someplace warm in your retirement, you might want to consider the fact that Florida has a lower tax than does, say, Mississippi.

Human nature being what it is, some people try to have it both ways. Mr. and Mrs. Example lived in Connecticut all their lives. They raised their kids, ran their business, and prospered. Once retired, they spent most of their time in Connecticut, but fled to their beachfront home in Florida for the months of January, February, and March. The Examples reviewed their estate planning and were very concerned about Connecticut's state inheritance tax, which can run as high as 11 percent if you leave property to relatives or friends.

One day the Examples decided to do something about it. On one of their trips they attempted to establish Florida residency. They registered to vote, registered their cars, and got Florida drivers licenses. They filed their income tax returns using the Florida address. However, they still spent most of their time in Connecticut. Their family was there; their friends and roots in the community were there. Sadly, the Examples passed away, as it happened, in Florida. The family was surprised to learn that Connecticut was one step ahead of them. Through utility bills, phone bills, and church records, the Connecticut tax authorities were able to prove that the Examples actually continued to reside in Connecticut more than 183 days out of the year. The tax collector put in his claim for the Connecticut inheritance tax. And he was upheld in the courts.

The moral of the story is that if you want to move, then move. If you want to avoid your original state's death taxes, then you should sever as many ties as you can. By all means, do not continue to live in your original home for most of the year. Otherwise, you too may be made an "Example" of.

By now, we have made it very clear that there is a penalty to be paid for success. The more wealth you amass, the higher the taxes that your state (and heirs) will pay. You can debate the equity of the system. Meanwhile, it's the system we have. To help your heirs cope with it, you need to determine just how serious a problem you have. In the next section we will show you how to come up with a rough estimate of how much it will cost to settle your estate.

ESTIMATING YOUR EXPENSES

In order to arrive at a reasonable estimate of what your estate will owe, you need to know the following:
- *The Value of all your assets.*
- *Whether your estate will qualify for the marital deduction. If you*

are married and not legally separated, your estate will owe no tax on assets left to your spouse. Bear in mind that if you leave assets to anyone other than your spouse, the assets are taxable. If you are divorced, legally separated, single, or widowed, there is no marital deduction available to your estate, and all your assets will be taxed.

• *Whether your estate will be simple or difficult to settle.* If your family gets along well and there is no likelihood of anyone contesting your will, your estate will probably not incur unusual legal and administrative expenses. On the other hand, if there is discord or if you have complex assets such as a business, vast real estate holdings, and the like, it may take longer and cost much more for the executor and attorneys to settle your estate.

• *Where you reside and where your property is located.* In the preceding section, we covered how the states collect their share of your estate.

• *The debts your estate will have to pay.* Some debts, such as mortgages owed jointly with your spouse, may not have to be paid off. Personal debts, notes, credit cards, car loans, and the like will have to be paid.

• *The expenses of your final illness and burial.* Often people don't realize how much of an estate can be consumed by medical expenses in the last months of a long illness or following an accident that ultimately proves fatal. Some of these expenses may be covered by insurance, but many of them may not. In addition, some of us would prefer a very simple burial. In other cases, the family favors a far more elaborate send-off. We realize this is a lot to think about. We also realize that it is not pleasant to contemplate. To make it easier, let's look at a hypothetical example of how these expenses come into play.

Mrs. Willis was a widow whose husband had passed away some years ago. He left her with the following assets:

Residence (no mortgage)	$330,000
Stock portfolio	250,000
Life insurance proceeds (invested in CDs)	200,000
Municipal bonds	200,000
Car	10,000
Furniture, personal effects	30,000
Stamp collection	10,000
	$1,030,000

TABLE 12–2
Worksheet Estate Settlement Cost

Gross estate	$1,030,000	
less: Administrative and legal fees	20,000	
Last illness expenses	5,000	
Burial expenses	5,000	
Adjusted gross estate	1,000,000	
less: Marital deduction	0	(widow)
Net taxable estate	1,000,000	
less: Tentative federal estate tax	345,800	
Federal estate tax credit	− 192,800	
Net federal tax	153,000	
less: Credit for state death tax	− 36,560	
Net federal tax	116,440	
Cost Summary		
Administrative, final expenses	$ 30,000	
Federal estate tax	116,440	
Florida estate tax	36,560	
Total expenses	183,000	
Mrs. Willis' estate	1,030,000	
less: Total expenses	183,000	
Net to heirs	847,000	
Shrinkage	17.8%	

Mrs. Willis left a will, directing that her two adult daughters share her estate equally. She appointed her eldest daughter as executor. The daughters get along well, and there is little chance of anyone contesting the will. Furthermore, Mrs. Willis did not owe anyone anything. She lived in Florida (a ''sponge tax'' state) and all her property was there.

Now let's look at who gets what out of the estate.

Administrative fees, court costs, legal fees, and the cost of burial together run about $30,000, or 3 percent of the estate. This is typical for a simple estate of this size. Complications could certainly have driven up the cost. Examples of complications would include disagreements among her daughters as to who would get what, or perhaps a lawsuit outstanding against Mrs. Willis at the time of her death. Table 12-2 shows how the taxes are calculated.

If you'd like to go through the exercise for your own estate, we have provided the following tables:

- A blank worksheet, Appendix H.
- Federal estate tax rates, Appendix C.
- Credit for state death tax as ("sponge tax") Appendix D.

On the other hand, if you only want to get an idea of how this works, Table 12-1 will help. Simply estimate your estate's total worth, then find the corresponding column of total expenses. This is a rough estimate at best. It assumes that there is no marital deduction (that you are unmarried or widowed). The marital deduction can defer virtually all taxes until your spouse dies, although there may be legal and administrative costs and possibly state death taxes at the death of the first spouse. Of course, the taxes shown here will eventually be paid at the second death.

Chapter Thirteen

Federal Estate Taxes and Credit Shelter Trusts—the "$1.2 Million Miracle"

I t seems to most people that if you can simply leave everything to your spouse with no tax liability, what could be bad? Nothing, if you like the idea of your family losing nearly $250,000 in unnecessary estate taxes!

Here's how it can happen. Suppose Harold and Maude, a loving couple despite a bit of an age difference, simply leave everything to each other, with no thought of the world after their demise. Maudie's a bit older than Harold, so she goes first. He gets the house, which they own together, her jewelry and other personal possessions, her car, and all the money she has in the bank and invested in stocks, bonds, and mutual funds. If you add it all up, Maude probably had a net worth of—let's just pick a figure out of the air—$600,000. A nice round sum.

Now Harold has it all. Harold is a sober, cautious man. So he does not spend all Maude's worldly wealth. For one thing he has substantial assets of his own. Arbitrarily, let's say he also has $600,000. When Maude died, leaving everything to Harold, the tax collector was held at bay by the tax law provision known as the unlimited marital deduction. Any transfer of property between husbands and wives, while they are alive or upon their death, is always free of gift and estate tax. Now, however, Harold is sitting on top of a combined estate of $1.2 million.

Flash forward. It's several years later. Harold becomes ill, and he too goes to meet his Maker. Upon his death, he leaves everything to his daughter, Cindy. To keep the example simple, let's assume that Harold, through his widowerhood, has only spent income, not dipped into principal at all, and that—unrealistically—the principal has not grown any. So the estate he leaves to Cindy consists of Maude's estate plus the $600,000 he owned himself, for a total of $1.2 million. In reality, since Harold outlived Maude by a period of years, the value of their property, especially their real estate and stocks, would no doubt have grown, probably substantially. But we're keeping it simple to make a point.

THE $1.2 MILLION MIRACLE

The point is that by writing what we call "I-love-you" wills, in which they left everything to each other, Harold and Maude cost their daughter a comparatively large amount of money, specifically $235,800.

That is the tax on the second $600,000. Remember, every person has a lifetime exclusion amount of $600,000. But if you don't use it because you leave everything to your spouse or your spouse leaves everything to you, then it disappears. It wasn't always that way. The 1981 Economic Recovery and Tax Act provided for the unlimited marital deduction. However, all the property one spouse leaves to another gets put into one big pot. Upon the death of the second spouse, it is all fully taxed. Thus, the second spouse can leave only $600,000 tax free; the $600,000 exclusion that the first spouse would have had has been wasted.

The dilemma is that, while it may be tax-smart not to leave everything to your spouse, practically speaking, who wants their resources to be diverted to anyone else while their spouse is alive? Divorce notwithstanding, the commitment is to love, honor, and cherish each other above anything else. You may want your children and grandchildren to ultimately receive your estate, but not until your husband or wife is gone. Your mate's welfare comes first.

Philosophically, it may seem as though the $1.2 million joint estate tax exclusion for couples is unrealistic. Few if any would leave $600,000 to someone other than their spouse just to save on taxes, even though the savings amount to well over $200,000.

CREDIT SHELTER TRUSTS

There is, however, a fairly easy way to have it both ways. That's why we called this chapter the "$1.2 million miracle." You don't have to leave your wealth to a *person* in order to qualify for this exclusion. You can leave property to a legal entity. In this case, you would want to establish a trust. It can be set up in your will. As such, it would be called a testamentary trust and wouldn't actually spring to life until you die. It can also be incorporated into a revocable living trust arrangement. Lawyers commonly refer to this sort of vehicle to shelter from estate taxes as a credit shelter trust. ("Credit" refers to the credit each person gets against the federal estate taxes on $600,000. It amounts to $192,800 of actual federal estate tax, under current law.)

Many of our clients have been squeamish about the use of trusts between husbands and wives. In fairness, a trust isn't a totally unmixed blessing. You do need to make certain concessions, though we believe they are small, especially compared with the benefits such trusts confer. We've had clients violently demur, refusing to accept any limitations on their enjoyment of their spouse's assets. In such cases, obviously, we respect our client's views.

One husband and wife we saw not long ago appeared to be strong candidates for this sort of tax planning. Through careful planning and a bit of good luck, Joe and Annette had amassed far more assets than you would have guessed. Before his recent retirement, Joe was a manufacturing supervisor for a large cosmetics company. Annette had never worked outside the home, though raising two boys and a girl wasn't exactly a day at the beach.

The couple had a lifetime habit of prudence, although they never really had to scrimp. They had built up over $250,000 in Joe's 401(k) plan at work; in addition, the corporation let him take his pension in a lump sum, which amounted to another $220,000. Moreover, they'd received an inheritance from Annette's parents and invested the money wisely, mainly in conservative municipal bonds and utility stocks. That now amounted to nearly $200,000. But the centerpiece of their affluence was real estate. Their suburban home, purchased for $18,500 some 28 years ago had appreciated to over $300,000. And a two-family investment property they'd wisely bought for less than $50,000 two decades ago had gone up in value eightfold. Add in a small amount of life insurance on Joe, and you are looking at an excellent balance sheet, over $1.4 million (with no debts)—and a substantial estate-tax problem.

To compound the problem, when they came to us, Joe had recently suffered his second heart attack. Although he recovered, who knows the future? So we counseled the couple to do some sophisticated planning. By dividing their assets as evenly as possible between them and then including credit shelter trust provisions in their wills, we estimated that they could save some $250,000 in federal estate taxes currently. With appreciation, we figured that their children and grandchildren might eventually receive several times that much, money that otherwise would go to Washington, D.C.

We suggested that their home and investment accounts be put into Annette's name, but that the duplex be retitled to Joe's name alone. Moreover, we advised changing the beneficiary designation on the 401(k) rollover account to a trust created in his will. This way, if he died first—statistically probable, since men tend to have shorter life expectancies than women and Joe is older than Annette and has coronary artery disease—ultimate tax savings could be dramatic. Looking only at the rental property, it would gain what's called a step-up in its basis for capital gains purposes if Joe dies. And Annette could still enjoy income from it, whether it was owned by a trust or she received it outright. If it seemed appropriate, the place could be sold and the proceeds reinvested, also producing income for Annette's benefit.

Try as we might, though, we could not convince Annette that such a strategy would not be burdensome to her. She worried that she would not have complete control over her finances if something happened to Joe. Even the reassurance that one or more of her children could be co-trustees with her failed to convince her. Finally, Joe told us privately not to pursue the matter, and when the attorney drafted the couple's wills, trust provisions were conspicuously absent.

Trusts intended to utilize the estate-tax exclusion on the death of the first spouse can be written in a number of ways. You could identify specific property that would be placed in trust. Few attorneys recommend that approach, and we don't either. When we talked with Joe and Annette about their rental property being a logical asset to go into trust, should Joe die before Annette, we were talking strategy. We never suggested that it be stipulated in Joe's will. You don't want to name specific assets in your will because that would mean you'd have to rewrite your will if your assets changed.

In fact, most attorneys don't even recommend specifying the $600,000 figure in your will, because Congress could change the amount. Generally, an attorney will simply refer to an amount sheltered by the unified credit in existence at the time you die. Then, it's up to your spouse, assuming she or he is your executor, and a trustee or co-trustee to select the appropriate assets to be placed in trust.

DISCLAIMER TRUSTS

For more anxious clients, we suggest what's called a disclaimer trust. This allows the surviving husband or wife to decide after the spouse's death whether to use the trust. That allows for postmortem planning: your surviving spouse can choose to "disclaim" some of your assets. There's no guarantee that the tax strategy will ever be employed, of course. But, it can give people a comfort level of not having to be locked into a course of action. Moreover, it provides flexibility so that if a family's circumstances have changed dramatically since their estate plan was drawn up, they are not committed to a course of action that may no longer be appropriate.

Our clients Helene and Howard are a good example. A number of years ago, when we originally did their planning, both of them balked at using a credit shelter trust. They felt that the greater flexibility of the disclaimer approach was less constricting. Probably they were not emotionally committed to having *any* trust provisions in their wills. But they consented to disclaimer provisions, bowing to the combined urging of their attorney and financial planner.

As it turned out, that was just as well. When they drew up their estate plan, the couple arguably had sufficient assets to justify the use of trust provisions. Between the two of them, their assets totaled something over $900,000.

Then Helene took sick. In her late 70s and frail, she suffered with a persistent flu that turned into pneumonia. Hospital bills mounted. Finally, she was well enough to leave the hospital, but was not strong enough to come home. She was admitted to a nursing home and convalesced there for over a year, her stay prolonged by a fall, which broke her hip. Finally, she was able to come home, but she died less than a year later. In the meantime, the deteriorating real estate market of the late 1980s and early 1990s reduced the value of the couple's home from $350,000 to around $275,000.

Between the money that Helene and Howard needed to spend on her care and the loss of property value, by the time of Helene's death their resources had shrunk to just over $700,000, less than half of it in Helene's name. Of course, Howard could have disclaimed his inheritance, and from a purely estate-tax standpoint that might not have been a terrible idea. In the long run, their children may have saved some tax dollars as a result. Yet, we had to agree with Howard that for the sake of some savings—which might not even materialize if he were to need nursing home care later on and thereby deplete his assets still further—putting assets into trust might be too much cure for too little disease.

Granted, there is much suspicion and misunderstanding about the hindrance that a trust places on a surviving spouse's use of assets that a deceased spouse leaves. A common view is that the money or property placed in trust are locked away, perhaps in a musty bank vault.

Not true. Most of the credit shelter trusts our clients establish involve no financial institutions. The surviving spouse is invariably one of the trustees. The trust can't be so loosely drawn that the surviving spouse could simply spend all the assets in the trust at whim, however. In that case the IRS would take the position that such a trust was a tax-inspired sham. You can come closer to such total discretion than you might think, though.

THE PRACTICALITIES OF TRUSTS

Particularly with small trusts, making them work is probably much simpler than you think. Forget the bank vault. Banish the notion that it will be painful or impossible to have access to assets held in trust. Wipe out the preconception that administering a trust will be expensive or unwieldy. These stereotypes are left over from an earlier age, when only the wealthy used trusts, and then generally to *prevent* someone (typically a wife or child or black-sheep offspring) from having more than a meager allowance. These days, tax-inspired trusts are becoming widespread because of the way the federal estate tax law is constructed. If you can save the next generation hundreds of thousands of dollars, why not, especially if doing so requires only minor inconveniences?

As we have said, when you set up such trusts in your will, most commonly you name your spouse as a trustee. A companion trustee can be one of your grown children, a trusted family member or friend, or even your attorney or financial planner.

It's best to have at least two trustees, not only for the sake of a second viewpoint on how the assets in trust should be invested, but also because an independent trustee will give the IRS a much greater feeling of comfort. All else being equal, we strongly recommend doing whatever it takes to make the revenuers as comfortable as possible.

As co-trustee, a surviving spouse has the right—in fact, the responsibility—to help determine how trust assets should be invested. It's not always possible or appropriate to invest the trust assets so as to produce income for the surviving spouse. But if that is appropriate, the survivor may get an emotional benefit. In fact, unless your estate is very large and the surviving spouse has no foreseeable need for any additional income, we suggest investing trust assets so as to produce regular checks.

Income need not be all that the surviving spouse receives, however. Generally, tax-inspired trusts contain language allowing for invasion of principal under certain specified conditions. For example, expenses relating to the survivor's health or maintenance of lifestyle would justify withdrawals of principal. One attorney we admire and work with regularly is fond of telling our clients that the surviving spouse could take money out of a trust to go on an around-the-world trip if she or he wanted to because that could be considered maintenance. This attorney may be more aggressive in his tax advice than most, but not much more.

What you cannot do, as a surviving spouse who is trustee, is simply loot the trust of all its assets. If that were to happen, the

IRS might very well challenge the trust's tax status, and such a challenge might not come until after the second spouse had died, thus defeating the whole purpose of the planning and giving the children a nasty surprise. Moreover, in this and other trust activities, a surviving spouse who acts as co-trustee alongside someone else is likely to be on much firmer ground with the IRS.

THE "FIVE-AND-FIVE" POWER

One further privilege your attorney can write into the trust is known as the "five-and-five" power. That allows an income beneficiary to withdraw 5 percent of a trust's balance, or $5,000, whichever is greater, every year. (One note: this so-called five-and-five power is not available if you choose the disclaimer approach.) If a credit shelter trust started out at the maximum $600,000, then 5 percent would be $30,000. Together with the income that a $600,000 nest egg could generate, the five-and-five power would provide a surviving spouse with quite a lot of annual income.

Too much, perhaps. Don't forget, the idea of the trust is to keep assets out of the survivor's ultimate estate and, of course, depletion of principal can spell eventual financial disaster.

Lawyers have mixed feelings about the five-and-five power. Some believe that it makes for a too-aggressive stance, courting potential trouble with the IRS. We don't pretend to be legal experts, but we take a different view. In our opinion, this privilege is superfluous. If the planning has been done properly and the trust provision has been correctly drawn, we believe that a credit shelter trust can provide sufficient ability to let a survivor get at needed assets without taking an additional $5,000 or 5 percent per year.

WHICH ASSETS SHOULD FUND A TRUST?

There's really no right or wrong answer. For very large estates, experts recommend using those assets that have the most growth potential, since all future appreciation is removed from the surviving spouse's estate. In contrast, assets that have less growth potential but produce high levels of current income could be placed in the spouse's name. This would allow the spouse to use the income to meet current needs. Going back to Joe and Annette's situation, an ideal asset to fund a credit shelter trust were Joe to die would have been the two-family investment property the couple owned. Annette probably wouldn't have needed to sell the place in order to have income to live on, and if she didn't sell, all future appreciation would have been removed from the estate tax collector's clutches—though not necessarily from *income tax* liability, specifically capital gains tax. (Putting income-generating assets into the trust can be just as appropriate, though, depending on a family's circumstances.)

If all goes well, the growth occurs free of estate taxes for the benefit of your ultimate beneficiaries—your kids. A surviving spouse's assets, which will be taxed upon her or his death, will either grow more slowly or be depleted as they are consumed for day-to-day living expenses or medical or nursing home care.

When you think about it for a second, one asset would seem to be the top candidate for the trust: your home. Real estate is definitely an appreciating asset (or so we always thought), and your house provides no income. On the other hand, do you really want the home that your widow or widower lives in to be owned partially by a trust? Wouldn't that cause some potential conflicts between the survivor and the next generation, your kids? Suppose your spouse wants to sell the house and move? Would she or he feel constrained by not owning the property outright? We're not saying categorically that your home should not be used to fund a credit shelter or disclaimer trust. But if that's what you have in mind, first have a long, careful conversation with your attorney.

When properly used, a credit shelter trust can indeed seem like a $1.2 million miracle. We are reminded of our pal Vito. He's one of our oldest clients—both in age and tenure. We've been working with him for years, in fact since his wife Theresa was alive. When they came in, in the mid-1980s, both were in their 80s. Believe it or not, they didn't even have wills, although they had accumulated a number of rental properties and were worth more than $2 million. Their son, a friend of ours, brought his parents to see us.

A trusting couple who spoke thickly accented English, Vito and Theresa were unduly deferential. Considering that they had come to the United States at a young age early in this century, raised five children, worked hard all their lives, and amassed what any reasonable person would call a fortune, it is *we* who should have been deferential. But Vito and Theresa were painfully unassuming.

Anyway, when we and an attorney whom we recommended tried to explain the estate-tax laws and suggest appropriate defensive strategies, the old couple pretended to understand. Their son and one of his sisters, who attended all meetings with their parents, tried repeatedly to get the concepts across. We were never sure whether the couple understood or were simply being accommodating. Whichever it was, they readily agreed with our advice that they use credit shelter trusts.

Less than a year after they had executed their wills, Theresa died suddenly. That triggered use of the credit shelter trust that had been created in her will. In speaking with Vito and his children, the attorney proposed that a commercial building that had been put into Theresa's name be used to fund the trust. It was not worth quite $600,000, but close enough. The mechanics of executing this suggestion were not difficult. The lawyer drew up a quitclaim deed, and Vito, as executor of his wife's estate, signed the document. He became one of the trustees, his son Peter a co-trustee, and the attorney a third trustee.

From time to time we ask Peter how his dad, now in his 90s, is faring. A little hard of hearing, but otherwise in good spirits is the unvarying reply. And the little office building? It's quietly growing in value, continuing to throw off as much income as ever. Vito still wanders over to it practically every day to make sure his tenants are well taken care of—though in reality his presence is mostly ceremonial. The fact that it is owned by a trust created by his late wife has had no practical consequences. Yet.

It's just that when Vito dies, his kids will have about a quarter-million dollars less to pay Uncle Sam in estate taxes.

Chapter Fourteen

The Irrevocable Life Insurance Trust

I f you are a person who hates paying taxes, this is your chapter. As you have progressed through this book, we've told you several times about the $1.2 million miracle. How would you like to be able to pass several—or even many—times that amount totally tax free? You can easily do so. There are no hidden catches. The up-front cost is not inordinate. And there are few drawbacks.

The irrevocable life insurance trust is one of life's few no-brainers. Anyone who has substantial assets and a significant amount of life insurance coverage would be foolish not to consider using a trust. A lawyer friend of ours likes to call it a loophole in the estate-tax code. We don't consider it that, but we would say it is the greatest and perhaps most underutilized of all estate planning tools.

The premise is quite simple. It starts with the idea that you can give away up to $10,000 per year to anyone, $20,000 annually if two spouses are doing the giving, and owe no gift tax.

So it follows that if you make gifts to a trust, the same exemption applies as if you were giving to a living soul—well, almost. Suppose you were to establish a trust and, give it the right, but not the obligation, to own one or more insurance policies on your life. And suppose further that the annual premiums on policies owned by the trust were, say, $5,000. Conceptually, is there any reason why you couldn't give the trust $5,000 each year, from which gift the trustee of the trust would pay the insurance premium?

Here's where the "almost" comes in. In order for your gift to qualify for the annual exemption, it must be a gift of what's called a present interest. When you make a gift to an irrevocable trust, the beneficiaries don't have a present interest in the gift. Therefore,

FIGURE 14–1
Owning Your Insurance versus the Irrevocable Life Insurance Trust

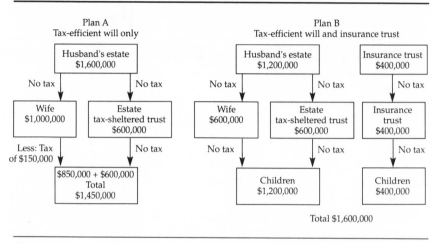

Plan A
The husband's estate includes a $400,000 life insurance policy that he owns. At his death, his will and trust arrangement divides his property into two parts. The first part—to a maximum $600,000—goes into the credit shelter trust. The balance, including the $400,000 of life insurance, goes outright to his wife. Her estate, which totals $1 million would be taxed upon her death. If it remained at $1 million when she died and the federal estate-tax laws had not changed, approximately $150,000 would be due in federal taxes, leaving the children with $850,000. With the $600,000 from the credit shelter trust, they would receive a combined total of $1.45 million.

Plan B
The husband transfers his $400,000 policy to an irrevocable life insurance trust. (If an existing policy were transferred, the husband must live for three years for the gift to be complete. A policy newly issued in the name of the trust would immediately be out of his estate.) Upon death, the $400,000 proceeds are paid to the trustee of the insurance trust, and no estate tax is due then—or ever! The wife receives income from the trust, but it is never part of her estate. Moreover, $600,000 that the husband left to his credit shelter trust is also out of the wife's estate. When she dies, the *$600,000* that *is* part of her estate is sheltered by her uniform credit amount. Thus, the entire estate gets to the children untaxed, saving them at least $150,000.

it doesn't qualify for the gift tax annual exclusion of up to $10,000 per person per year. So, the beneficiaries of the insurance must receive the right to withdraw the amount of each gift, as it is made, up to that annual exclusion amount. Consequently, attorneys build into life insurance trusts so-called Crummey powers, which permit the beneficiaries to make withdrawals as gifts are made to the trust. To visualize the concept, see Figure 14-1.

Not only in concept but also in fact, there is no reason at all why that strategy wouldn't work. In reality, the benefit is even more generous. We have clients, call them Ted and Sally, who have several million dollars of assets. They decided to purchase a $1 million life insurance policy. The idea was to give their children sufficient resources to pay the bulk of their estate taxes after the two of them are gone.

Since the tax liability doesn't really begin until both spouses have died (because you can leave everything to your mate tax free), Ted and Sally bought what's called a second-to-die (or survivorship) policy. That type of life insurance pays a death benefit only upon the death of the second spouse. It is typically purchased in order to assist with an estate-tax liability. But to do that effectively, the insurance should not be part of your taxable estate. If it were, it would only drive your estate into a still higher tax bracket. The way to make the life insurance part of the solution instead of part of the problem is by using a trust.

Ted and Sally, with our assistance, asked an attorney to draft the document establishing the trust. When the trust was created, they appointed a trustee. Then the trustee applied for the second-to-die policy. Ted and Sally were approaching retirement age, so they wanted to pay all the premiums for the policy in just four years. That way, they'd have no large financial obligation after retirement. Even so, they faced $30,000 in premiums for each of the next four years.

Ted and Sally's three children are the ultimate beneficiaries of the $1 million policy. Consequently premiums up to $30,000 per year ($5,000 each for Ted and Sally times three children) qualify for the annual gift tax exclusion because of their respective $5,000 Crummey withdrawal powers. Simply put, that means the entire $1 million death benefit will be *estate-tax free* when the insurance company makes the payment after Ted and Sally both have died.

Among other things, their children could then use the proceeds to defray estate taxes caused by the couple's other assets. In other words, the family may very well have most or all of their estate tax burden paid for—now!

Could all this have happened without using an irrevocable life insurance trust? Yes. But this is the only way to keep the spouse as an eligible beneficiary. Purchasing a $1 million policy outside the trust would make the death benefit part of the taxable estate of the second spouse to die. Because federal estate taxes can gobble up to 50 percent of your assets at the highest level, potentially Ted and Sally's $1 million policy might eventually yield just $500,000 to their children, not terrible but a far cry from a million bucks.

So, have we got your attention? Not to oversell the concept, but anyone with substantial resources and large life insurance policies is definitely missing a bet by not using an irrevocable insurance trust.

Before describing in detail how to create and manage such a trust, we should concede that many people don't need it. As a rule, if you are starting out and don't have much in the way of assets, an insurance trust may be unnecessary; and if you have very little life insurance, creating a trust could be a waste of the money it costs to set one up. A general guideline is that if your total assets, including life insurance, are less than $600,000, you don't need to go to the trouble and expense of creating a trust.

Similarly, if your insurance coverage is less than $100,000—the admittedly oversimplified rule of thumb we use in our office—there's probably no need to bother with a trust. However, if you have large life insurance policies, significantly over $100,000 in death benefit, or if you are in the process of purchasing such substantial coverage, you should probably consider using an insurance trust regardless of your other assets, because your resources are bound to grow.

Frequently we're asked by clients why, given our boundless enthusiasm for this estate planning tool, anyone wouldn't use an irrevocable life insurance trust. There are several reasons. You can understand them most easily by concentrating on the phrase *irrevocable life insurance trust.*

AN IRREVOCABLE. . .

In order to qualify the death benefit proceeds for exclusion from your estate, you must finally, completely, and once and for all give your life insurance policies away. The stilted legalism is that you must have "no incidence of ownership" in policies on your life. You cannot own them. You cannot pay the premiums on them directly. You cannot have the power to designate the beneficiaries. You cannot have the power to borrow or withdraw any cash value that may build up. You have no control over the way any dividends generated by a policy are to be used. You can't even control whether or not any particular policy remains in force (although you *could* refuse to allow a new policy to be written on your life by not cooperating in the application process).

In short, you must give up all control. Moreover, if you want your spouse to have unfettered use of the life insurance proceeds upon your death, you should not put such policies into a trust. In the trust, he or she will have limitations on their enjoyment of the money.

On the other hand, who are you giving control to? Not to the knucklehead next door or some stranger. Typically, you are relinquishing control over the insurance policies to your spouse, albeit within the constraints of a formal legal entity, the trust.

At worst, if you want to be conservative or if both husband and wife are covered by the insurance (with a second-to-die policy), then you select a trusted family member or friend. Several of our clients have asked us to be their trustee, which we agreed to. Others have chosen a brother or sister of one of the spouses, or a cousin.

Naming a friendly trustee means that you have considerable input as to the operation of the trust. You can discuss how the insurance will be treated. And, of course, you exert influence because you undoubtedly will be the one making the premium payments. Not directly, to be sure. Doing that would undermine the trust. Rather, you make gifts to the trust of amounts that can be used to pay the premiums.

Granted you exercise considerable influence. But make no mistake: You cannot treat insurance in a trust as your personal domain, the way you would policies that you owned yourself.

. . . LIFE INSURANCE TRUST

As we've been alluding to, working with a trust is a lot more formal than simply controlling your insurance coverage personally. First, you must pay an attorney to create the trust for you. We prefer to work with lawyers who specialize in estate, trust, and tax law.

There's no question that hiring a specialist costs more. In our area, a top estate attorney charges $1,000 to $1,500 to draft an irrevocable insurance trust. The cost can be less if the attorney is doing the complete job: wills with credit shelter trusts, powers of attorney, living wills, the works.

A nonspecialist may charge about half as much. The only problem is this: What if an unskilled attorney makes a technical goof in your trust? We are not expert enough to catch a subtle miscue and, we daresay, neither are you. So you are taking a chance with an attorney who doesn't draft estate documents for a living. Probably the mistake would not come to light until it is too late. Your savings of a few hundred dollars could cost your heirs many thousands—or even hundreds of thousands—of dollars.

CREATING A TRUST

The cost of birthing a trust is one disadvantage. Another is its care and feeding. To grasp the complexities of using an insurance trust, it may help you to walk through the creation and maintenance of one.

Step one, obviously, is to retain a lawyer to compose the trust agreement. A good attorney will discuss in detail with you the type of insurance you have or are considering buying, your needs, and your family situation. If your children are still young, that suggests one approach: making provision for holding the insurance proceeds in the trust should you die before they are old enough to manage large sums wisely. If your children are older, or if someone else is the beneficiary, such precaution is unnecessary.

The attorney will also help you choose a trustee. Your spouse is the obvious choice, assuming that you have a good relationship and that the same insurance policy does not cover both of you. Let's not skate over the first point too quickly. Since such a high percentage of marriages end in divorce, give this possibility some hard thought. We can say for certain, both of us having been divorced, that the thought of an ex-wife or ex-husband controlling your life insurance is less than enchanting.

Assuming yours is a marriage that is likely to survive and the life insurance policy is on your life only, the lawyer will craft the trust so your spouse can be trustee in the short run as well as a beneficiary in the long run. This need is one reason for choosing an attorney who is a specialist. Otherwise, you risk either having the insurance proceeds brought back into your estate or restricting your spouse's right to utilize them.

When the trust document has been prepared and executed (the lawyerly term for signing it), a new entity has sprung into existence. The lawyers call it a "grantor trust." Attorneys have differing opinions as to whether your trust must have a tax identification number, which is similar to a social security number. Most feel that if your life insurance trust is set up as a grantor trust, a tax I.D. number is unnecessary.

CARE AND FEEDING

Now comes the part where you and your spouse need to get involved. The lawyer has taken you as far as he or she can. It is now your turn.

Existing policies can be transferred to the trust. Figures 14-2 and 14-3 reproduce typical forms you might use to change the ownership and beneficiary designation of a policy to the insurance trust. Each company has its own specific forms, so you must call the insurance company and ask for the appropriate transfer documents.

In our experience, the most difficult insurance to deal with is group term. For some reason, corporate benefits officers seem unfamiliar and unsympathetic to the concept of changing the beneficiary of your group life insurance to a trust. You cannot, of course, change the owner; your company will continue to own the policy. But that's fine, because as long as you give up the right to change the beneficiary—and your estate is not the beneficiary—the death benefit won't be included in your taxable estate. Group term coverage, by the way, is the ideal type of insurance to put in trust, because you are giving away an asset that has absolutely no value to you while you are alive and that in many cases doesn't even cost you anything to carry.

FIGURE 14-2
A Typical Change of Ownership Form

Connecticut Mutual CM Life   **Ownership Designation**

POLICY NO.(S) | INSURED

The COMPANY is directed to change the Owner of the Policy or Policies numbered above to the Owner or Owners designated below. The Company shall be defined as the Company that issued the policy. They are Connecticut Mutual Life Insurance Company or C.M. Life Insurance Company.

INSTRUCTIONS: ONE of the following ownership designations should be selected by inserting a **CHECK MARK** or "**X**" in the box preceding the desired designation. The full name (first name, middle initial and last name) and relationship of the *new* Owner to the Insured or other requested information should also be inserted in the space provided.

The Insured

[ ]   The Insured.

One Owner—Reversion to Insured

[ ]   .... of the Insured, if living, otherwise the Insured.

One Owner—Estate of Owner

[ ]   .... of the Insured.

One Owner—One Contingent Owner—Reversion to Insured

[ ]   .... of the Insured, if living, otherwise
      .... of the Insured, if living, otherwise the Insured.

Two Owners Jointly—Reversion to Insured

[ ]   .... and ....
      .... of the Insured, jointly, or the survivor of them, or if neither be living, the Insured.

Corporate Owner

[ ]   ...., its successors or assigns.
          Name   City and State

Partnership

[ ]   ...., a partnership, or its assigns.
          Name   City and State

If none of the preceding selections are suitable, please refer to the Specimen Ownership Designations set out on the reverse side of the Instruction Sheet. A **CHECK MARK** or "**X**" should then be inserted in the box entitled "Other" and the applicable designation entered in the space provided. Consult your agent or the Home Office for proper wording if the change desired is not covered above or by the specimen designations.

Other

[ ]

Gift Transfer—Additional Provision

[ ]   The change of ownership in this Policy effected by the elected designation is without valuable consideration and is intended to be an outright gift. *(If the change of ownership is intended as a gift, a CHECK MARK or "X" should also be inserted in the box preceding this provision.)*

THIS CHANGE SHALL BE SUBJECT TO THE PROVISIONS ON THE REVERSE HEREOF.
*Plan Trustee/Administrator, see reverse side before signing

Please show correct name and address for future premium or dividend notices. [ ] Check here if no change of address.	• New Owner's Social Security or Employer Identification Number . . .
NAME	(Please include all hyphens)
STREET	Under penalties of perjury, I certify that the above is my correct Tax Identification Number. I also certify that the Internal Revenue Service has not notified me that I am subject to backup withholding.
CITY, STATE & ZIP NO.	• New Policyowner's signature Date

Signed at .... on ....
              City and State   Date

....
          Witness   Signature of Policyowner(s)

This form should be dated and signed in the presence of a witness by the present Policyowner. The witness's signature should be legible. If it is not legible, please type the witness's name under the signature. The witness should not be a designated beneficiary.	For Home Office Use – Date Recorded
	Registrar

F1502C 3-91

Members of the **CM Alliance**   Connecticut Mutual Life Insurance Company
                                        C.M. Life Insurance Company
                                        140 Garden Street, Hartford, CT 06154

The trust should apply for any new insurance coverage on you. The law states that if you fund an insurance trust with existing policies, you must live for at least three years. Otherwise the death

FIGURE 14–3
A Typical Change of Beneficiary Form

Connecticut Mutual
CM Life

Notice of Change of Beneficiary

For use with all annuity contracts and all life insurance policies except family policies.

POLICY NO.(S)   INSURED

The Company is directed to change the payee of any death benefit of the Policy or Policies numbered above to the beneficiary or beneficiaries designated below. The Company shall be defined as the Company who issued the Policy. They are Connecticut Mutual Life Insurance Company or C.M. Life Insurance Company.

INSTRUCTIONS: ONE of the following beneficiary designations should be selected by inserting a **CHECK MARK** or "**X**" in the box preceding the desired designation. The full name (first name, middle initial and last name) and relationship of the beneficiary to the Insured or other requested information should also be inserted in the space provided. If none of the designations are suitable, Form 102 for Connecticut Mutual or F102B for C.M. Life should be used.

Insured's Estate

☐   The Executors or Administrators of the Insured.

One Beneficiary

☐   .... of the Insured.

One Beneficiary—One Second Beneficiary

☐   .... of the Insured, if such beneficiary

survives the Insured, otherwise to.. of the Insured.

One Beneficiary—Two or More Second Beneficiaries

☐   .... of the Insured, if such beneficiary

survives the Insured, otherwise in equal shares to such of ....

.... of the Insured, as may survive the Insured.

One Beneficiary—Unnamed Children of Insured as Second Beneficiaries

☐   .... of the Insured, if such beneficiary

survives the Insured, otherwise in equal shares to the surviving children of the Insured.

One Beneficiary—Unnamed Children of Insured and Their Children as Second Beneficiaries

☐   .... of the Insured, if such beneficiary

survives the Insured, otherwise in equal shares to the surviving children of the Insured and to the surviving children of any deceased children of the Insured, per stirpes.

One Beneficiary (Spouse)—Unnamed Children Born of the Marriage as Second Beneficiaries

☐   ...., Spouse of the Insured, if such beneficiary survives the Insured, otherwise in equal shares to the surviving children born of the marriage of the Insured and said Spouse.

Two or More Beneficiaries

☐   In equal shares to such of ....

.... of the Insured, as may survive the Insured.

Trustee—Revocable or Irrevocable Trust

☐   ...., trustee,

                     NAME(s) OF TRUSTEE(s)

or any successors or successor in trust under Trust Agreement dated ....,
or if such Trust be terminated, to the Executors or Administrators of the Insured.
(Certification of Trust Agreement Provisions Form 918 or copy of trust agreement should be submitted.)

Testamentary Trustee

☐   Such trustee under the last Will and Testament of the Insured as may be qualified to receive such amount, or if there be no such trust, to the Executors or Administrators of the Insured.

THIS CHANGE SHALL BE SUBJECT TO THE PROVISIONS ON THE REVERSE HEREOF.

Signed at .... on ....

            CITY AND STATE   DATE

....
         WITNESS   SIGNATURE OF PERSON ENTITLED TO CHANGE THE BENEFICIARY

PLEASE LIST THE NAMES AND ADDRESSES OF ALL BENEFICIARY(S) IN THE SPACE PROVIDED ON THE REVERSE SIDE OF THIS FORM.

For Home Office Use - Date Recorded

This form should be dated and signed in the presence of a witness by the person entitled to change the beneficiary. The witness's signature should be legible. If it is not legible, please type the witness's name under the signature. The witness should not be a designated beneficiary.

F102C   7-86   REGISTRAR

Connecticut Mutual Life Insurance Company
C.M. Life Insurance Company
Members of the **CM Alliance**   140 Garden Street, Hartford, CT 06154
Client Services Department

benefit proceeds will be includable in your taxable estate. However, if your trust applies for a policy and owns it from the start, then the eventual proceeds are out of your estate, even if you die within that three-year period. Following a recent court decision, the latest in a long succession upholding this concept, the IRS announced that it is finally giving up trying to invoke the three-year waiting period for policies purchased by trusts.

You don't necessarily have to wait until a trust has been executed to apply for a policy. Many insurance companies will allow the creation of a trust and underwriting of a life insurance contract to proceed on parallel tracks. We've even had policies issued to clients, then sent back to be reissued once a trust was in place. As the phrase goes, don't try this at home. A seasoned planner or veteran insurance agent should handle such a touchy transaction for you. You need to be certain ahead of time that your insurance company will be sympathetic. Then, when the time comes, you must get the trustee to sign the new application and be sure to date it *after* the date the trust came into existence.

It used to be that fairly early in the process, your spouse or whoever was trustee would open a bank account in the name of the trust. Not every banker is either familiar with or sympathetic to such an account. Let's face it, this is not going to be a big money-maker for the bank. Our clients Ted and Sally, for instance, endowed the trust account about a month before each annual premium was due on their $1 million policy. Once they put the money in the bank, it remained on deposit for only 30 days, the time during which their children had the right to withdraw their parents' gift. Then the trustee wrote a check for the premium. Thereafter, a minimal $100 or $200 stayed in the bank—just enough to keep the account open. Under current case law, which changed in 1992, it isn't strictly necessary to open a separate bank account for the insurance premiums as long as the trust was the original applicant and owner of the policy(ies).

CRUMMEY LETTERS

This oddly named instrument is a serious annual responsibility—not to mention a chore—for the trustee. The idea is that, in order to qualify for the $10,000 per person annual gift/estate tax exclusion, a gift has to be what's called a present interest. That means that the recipient has to have an immediate right to enjoy the gift. Thus an insurance trust provides that the beneficiary or beneficiaries of the life insurance actually could withdraw and spend the money you deposit into the trust bank account to pay premiums.

Look at your own situation. Suppose you set up an insurance trust. Your husband or wife is trustee. The policy the trust purchases necessitates, say, a $6,000 annual premium payment. After that money has been deposited into the trust bank account, the trustee must write a letter to each of the *ultimate* beneficiaries of the trust. The letter informs each one of his or her right to withdraw the premium payment money and spend it. (These letters are known as Crummey letters after a family that years ago was involved in a court battle with the IRS; that case initiated this strategy.)

For the uninitiated, this can be a daunting concept to grasp. But it is imperative. In its memo to trustees, one large law firm that we work with says: *"It is essential that the trust beneficiaries know of their right to make a withdrawal in the year in which the gift is made."* The emphasis is theirs.

Who, you may be wondering, *are* the beneficiaries? Usually they are your children. Why? It's because the trust is likely to say that if you die, the life insurance proceeds become the property of the trust. While he or she is alive, your spouse is entitled to all income from the money and principal as needed to maintain his or her lifestyle. But upon your spouse's death, the remaining money is to be distributed to the ultimate beneficiaries. This is what prevents the proceeds from being included in your spouse's estate.

As we noted earlier, if your children are not old enough to handle the money when it is to be distributed at the death of the second spouse, a provision of the trust document can prevent distribution until they are. You determine beforehand what age you think is appropriate. As the ultimate beneficiaries, then, your children—or whoever the ultimate beneficiaries are—must be given the right to withdraw money given to the trust.

Do you mean to say that my kids could frustrate this whole thing by spending the money I deposit to pay the insurance premiums? From the incredulous tone of your question, dear reader, it's clear

FIGURE 14–4
Sample Crummey Letter

December 16, 1992

Mr. John Q. Smith
Ms. Jane I. Smith
Mr. Robert W. Smith

Dear Niece and Nephews:

I am writing to you as Trustee of the Philip W. Smith Irrevocable Life
Insurance Trust Number Two established by your father on December 16,
1992. Under Article 4 of the Trust Agreement, you have the right to withdraw
from the trust your pro-rata portion of the gifts made to the trust during the
year, which for 1992 is approximately $5,000.00. The amount subject to
withdrawal will decrease by $5,000.00 on December 31 unless you advise me
of your desire to exercise your withdrawal right before then. Please
acknowledge your receipt of this notice by signing and returning the enclosed
copy of this letter in the envelope provided.

Sincerely yours,

William C. Smith

WCS:CEC:es
9589E

---

you're getting this. The answer, which many of our clients have
tumbled to, is simple: In a pig's eye they will!

When you stop to think about it, are your children really going
to exercise their right? If they're young, you'll threaten to break
their darling little fingers if they try; when they're older, you'll
reason with them. (They'll have to be *much* older.) A couple of
things would happen if they withdrew the money. One, without
its annual feeding of dollars, your life insurance policy would
soon collapse from financial starvation. Thus, there would be no
death benefit for anyone, least of all the kids. Spending an annual
premium at the forfeit of a much larger eventual death benefit
would be shortsighted, to say the least. Two, the immediate
beneficiary is generally Mom; sometimes it's Dad. By depriving

their parent of a major element of financial security, the children could be ensuring that they must take care of Mom or Dad themselves later on.

We won't beat it to death, but there is one small controversy in the legal world regarding Crummey letters. Some lawyers maintain that you can write each beneficiary once, inform them of their rights, and then forget about it. We take the more conservative view, which is the majority opinion among estate planners. We advise our clients to send out the letters every year, and give the beneficiaries 30 days notice. We also suggest asking the beneficiaries to sign a copy of the letter and return it to the trustee. That way, if an IRS audit ever raised the question, documentary evidence would exist in the trust file proving that the necessary opportunity had been given for withdrawal. Figure 14–4 provides a sample of the annual letter a trustee could use.

RIGHTS AND RESPONSIBILITIES OF TRUSTEES

As the word implies, a trustee occupies a position of trust. You must have complete confidence that the person you select will act in the best interest of all concerned. Whether you are the grantor of the trust, a beneficiary, or the trustee, you should realize that the trustee does have some discretion. Depending on how the trust was drawn, the trustee could maintain a particular policy or not, apply for additional insurance, pay premiums, or withdraw a policy's cash value. Whatever the trustee does, though, is always in the context of the trust. There's a word that perfectly describes a trustee's withdrawing money from the trust for his or her own benefit: *embezzlement.* Short of acting illegally, however, trustees have wide latitude.

One responsibility that trustees have is filing tax returns. Whether or not the trust has to file a return depends on the nature of the trust. In any case, if the trust has less than $600 per year of taxable income—as is the case with most life insurance trusts because of the tax-free buildup of life insurance cash values—then the trustee doesn't need to worry about filing an annual tax return.

NEW TRUSTEES

A trustee may be unable or unwilling to continue in that capacity. Thus, a trust agreement is usually written to allow the trustee to appoint a successor. Such a power is desirable. It is better still, however, to name the successor or successors in the document. That way, if a trustee dies or is incapacitated without exercising the prerogative, the trust continues uninterrupted. Otherwise, a court must appoint a successor.

When the grantor of the trust—the insured person—dies, the spouse who has been sole trustee needs a co-trustee. That's because the spouse is almost invariably one of the beneficiaries. Usually the spouse is entitled to receive income from the invested proceeds of the life insurance payment and can often dip into principal as well. If he or she were the sole trustee as well as a beneficiary, the IRS would question the legitimacy of the trust. In that case, it could appear to be a sham. A second trustee, especially an independent trustee who has no stake in the trust, helps insulate it from an IRS challenge.

You should name the additional trustee ahead of time. Since a life insurance trust could easily be in force for decades before you die, you ought to consider one or more alternates to the additional trustee, successors who would act when the time comes if your first choice can't. The person you prefer may have died, moved away, or had a change of circumstances. The thought is unpleasant, but you could also have a change in your relationship with the additional trustee, a falling out. So most trust agreements provide for the primary trustee to change the cast of characters at will.

AFTER DEATH

The nature of the trust changes dramatically following the death of the grantor(s), the person (or people) whose life was insured. As soon after death as possible, the trustee has to notify the insurance company or companies that have issued policies owned by the trust. In short order, usually within a couple of weeks, the death benefit proceeds will be paid.

That's when the responsibilities of a trustee multiply. First, there's the issue of taxation. Even though policies in the trust will most likely be tax free, the executor of the deceased person's estate must report them along with other estate assets. When a trustee files a claim with an insurance company, it's best to ask the company to send Treasury Department Form 712 to the executor, who files it for informational purposes with the estate tax return.

Throughout this discussion of the irrevocable insurance trust, we have assumed that in most cases the trustee is a spouse. So the trustee may well be executor of the deceased person's estate, too. That makes coordination of settling the estate and taking the trust to the next stage easier than if different people occupied the two roles.

As we've observed, the spouse was the lone trustee while the insured person was alive. That is not advisable after death. One of the first tasks a spouse/trustee needs to attend to is taking on the additional trustee(s) named in the trust agreement.

Our clients Joe and Sara are a textbook example of how this can work smoothly. Joe owned a prosperous delicatessen business, while Sara taught briefly before staying home to raise their two children. To protect Sara and assure the kids' college educations, Joe purchased substantial insurance over the years—three policies totaling $950,000. At our suggestion several years back Joe turned the policies over to a trust with Sara the trustee. Just shy of his 52nd birthday, Joe suddenly collapsed grasping his chest. Before an assistant could reach him, Joe was dead. Shortly after his funeral, we helped Sara file claims with the insurance companies, and within weeks she had received large checks from each.

In our earlier deliberations with the couple and a good estate attorney, we had suggested naming an additional trustee in the trust agreement to assist Sara after Joe's death. Joe's brother Hal, an accountant a few years younger than Joe, agreed to serve as co-trustee. We felt it advisable to name a successor in case Hal was not able to take that responsibility when the time came, but because Joe died so young, Hal was very much up to the task.

Hal's presence had a salutary effect on Sara. She had little investment experience. Her husband had handled their financial affairs and regrettably had included her only to a very limited extent. So having a more worldly co-trustee gave Sara confidence that the large sum of money from the insurance policies would be carefully managed. She was involved in the decision making, but she did not have the entire responsibility thrust upon her.

The disinterested co-trustee also shielded Sara from any potentially compromising conflicts of interest. After all, she was not only trustee but also the first beneficiary. The life insurance proceeds were intended mainly for her use during her lifetime. Joe had put most of his earnings back into his business. So the life insurance was Sara's main source of financial security. Once the dollars were invested, Sara lived off the income, occasionally tapping principal for a major expense. With her brother-in-law as independent co-trustee, she had no worry that her children would ever accuse her of looting their birthright.

To defend herself still further—as well as to protect herself against inflation—we advised Sara to invest in a balanced portfolio within the trust. She could generate more income if she invested everything in fixed-return assets, primarily bonds. But we recommended a strong component of stocks, especially high-dividend utility stocks, in order to give the portfolio growth potential. That way, 30 years from now when Sara dies, the portfolio should have kept up with inflation. Nobody would benefit, neither Sara nor her children and grandchildren, from a portfolio that lost purchasing power.

WHY USE A TRUST?

Occasionally, clients have asked us why they need to go to all the fuss and bother of creating a trust. Couldn't we achieve the same result, they wonder, by making our grown children the owners and beneficiaries of the life insurance? The question has most relevance for a second-to-die insurance policy, which is intended to benefit the next generation anyway.

Years ago, husbands and wives often owned policies on each other's lives. That was before the law was changed to allow an unlimited marital deduction. In those days, husbands and wives had to protect themselves from potential estate taxes upon the death of their mate. That's no longer the case, so no purpose is served by owning an insurance policy on your spouse.

However, if your children were to own a policy and you gave

them the money each year to make premium payments, always keeping in mind the $10,000 per person annual exclusion, the concept could work. Consider the practical issues, though. Suppose the purpose of your life insurance is to assure your husband's or wife's permanent financial security. Surely, you would not want your spouse to be dependent on your children for his or her welfare—not to mention that if your kids are, say, under 30, their ability to manage money is probably suspect. Speaking for ourselves, we both have grown children in their 20s, and we shudder at the thought that these delightful young people might be compelled by circumstance to manage wisely hundreds of thousands of dollars.

This is a serious consideration even in the case of a second-to-die life insurance policy, where the death benefit won't be paid until both husband and wife have passed away. At that point, the insurance proceeds are for the children's benefit, especially to help them pay estate taxes. Even so, who knows what the circumstances will be at the time of your death? What if you and your spouse went down in a plane crash next week? Suppose your children were, say, 18 and 23. How would they react to such a sudden major financial responsibility?

A final question concerns maintenance of the insurance coverage. Would you really want to entrust to your kids such a large responsibility as keeping your life insurance policies in force?

You'd send them a check once, twice, or four times a year. Then you'd pray that they didn't forget to send the premiums in on time. All the while, you'd be having nightmares about your son, who perpetually complained about not having enough money. Would he be tempted to try to find a way to ''borrow'' the money—just temporarily, of course?

The irrevocable life insurance trust is a far more certain and reliable course. It's one of the few times in life when the more you give away, the more your family has.

Chapter Fifteen

A Case Study

J ack and Elaine Washington, two of the most gracious clients we've ever worked with, are textbook examples of middle Americans. Their income is higher than average, but in deeper terms they embody American values, hold deeply to middle-class aspirations, and grapple with Everyman's crises. Jack is an elder in his Presbyterian church; Elaine, who quit work as an accountant to have children, now is active in the PTA as well as other volunteer work. The Washingtons cherish their family life and dote on their offspring.

If you met them in any middle-class suburb in America, you'd recognize them. Jack would be the guy leaning on the lawn mower, mopping his brow and chatting amiably with his next-door neighbor. In his early 40s, he'd better be careful or he'll soon resemble the Pillsbury doughboy. He has a grand sense of humor and a gentle way about him that is very endearing.

Elaine would never qualify as a sergeant in the Marines—a corporal in the Army, maybe. As Jack lounges, she eyes him through the window, frowning good-naturedly. Then, hearing ''Mommy!, Mommy!'' she turns her attention to the latest minor domestic crisis. Elaine feigns constant exasperation at her husband's casual approach to life. To be truthful, though, she was scarcely more organized than he was before the two came to us.

The Washingtons were referred to our firm four or five years ago by another client, Sal. Both Sal and Jack are marketing executives of a large pharmaceutical manufacturer. At the time, the two of them—as well as others in top and middle management—were about to be rewarded with stock options as part of a defensive maneuver the company was taking to ward off a hostile takeover attempt against the corporation. Jack and Elaine were not certain what a financial planner was or whether they needed the assistance of one. They did realize that they'd spent virtually no effort on the financial side of their lives. In fact, they weren't entirely certain just what that was. During our very first meeting, we began asking some questions to get an idea of their situation, and their answers were revealing.

Estate planning? Well, we have wills, but they're pretty old. We wrote them just after we were married, long before Catherine was born.

Investments? We just save what we can and put it into CDs.

College planning? Uh . . .

Property and casualty coverage? What's an umbrella, anyway, except something that protects you against the rain?

Life insurance? We have lots of that (brightening). Plenty, right?

We did a thorough analysis of the Washingtons' financial life and presented our findings in a document we call a financial plan. It covered all the above areas and more, ending in a series of recommendations. Write new wills. Begin investing $200 a month for Catherine's education. Make maximum use of Jack's 401(k) plan at work. Reposition the CDs to achieve growth. Purchase a $1 million excess liability (umbrella) policy to more fully protect you in the event you are involved in a catastrophic auto accident or an accident occurs at your home.

Regarding life insurance, we performed what's called a capital needs analysis (described in Chapter 5). That's the evaluation that determines how your current assets plus life insurance compare to your needs. For most people, the Washingtons included, the largest need by far is retirement security. Amassing enough money by the time you are 60 or 65 so you and your spouse can live comfortably to the end of your days requires accumulating a large nest egg.

In addition, like most folks, Jack and Elaine wanted to be certain that no matter what might happen to them, Catherine would not be deprived of a college education for lack of funds. The couple also felt that Elaine should not have to worry about their mortgage and other debts if Jack were to die.

The appraisal came out something like this:

Elaine Survives Jack

Needs

Capital needed for Elaine's retirement security	$950,000
Estate settlement and final expenses	25,000
College education for Catherine	48,000
Paying off mortgage and car loan	120,000
Emergency readjustment fund	25,000
Total Needed	$1,168,000

Available resources

Investments	$175,000
Existing Life Insurance:	385,000*
Total available	$560,000
Unfunded Need:	$608,000

*Group term of 3 times salary, or $285,000, plus $100,000 private policy.

True, Jack you do have quite a bit of life insurance. False, Jack, it's not exactly "plenty."

As with most clients, the Washingtons greeted this news without shock, outrage, or disbelief. They didn't storm around the office or glare at us or even challenge or deny the reality. Rather, they greeted the $600,000 deficit with a figurative yawn and proceeded to forget about it entirely. We were equally to blame. With so many other pressing priorities in their financial life, we let the life insurance issue slide. By far the most interesting issue to the vast majority of clients is their investment portfolio. Most clients *love* to discuss investments. After that, the majority realize that certain issues, while about as pleasant as getting root canal surgery done, need to be addressed. Tax planning. Updating their wills. Evaluating their cash flow. Putting money into a college education fund. Life insurance is such a distasteful topic to most that *we* are the ones who quake when it finally can be put off no longer. It's almost as if we're breeching some unwritten social taboo—discussing AIDS at a cocktail party, for example.

For months we worked with Jack and Elaine on the other aspects of their financial life, growing increasingly fond of them as we progressed. Ultimately, as we worked through our checklist of issues in need of attention, it became embarrassingly clear to all of us that the life insurance discussion was in the middle of the road straight ahead.

Much hemming and hawing ensued. First came some tentative questions from Jack.

"Let me see if I understand this—we need lots of insurance on me because I earn $95,000 a year and am due for a raise and a bonus, whereas we don't need insurance on Elaine because she isn't earning any money now?" Almost right, Jack. She would suffer by far a more serious financial loss if you died than you would if she died. But if something happened to Elaine, who would care for Catherine? You'd need to pay someone. That's a financial issue, and it's why you have the $50,000 policy on Elaine, remember?

"We don't need more than that, though, do we?" Not according to our calculations, Jack, no.

"But you really feel that we need to have another $600,000 on me?" It's not that we feel that way, Jack. That's what our analysis shows regarding what Elaine would need to live comfortably and educate Catherine.

Jack went up many notches in our esteem when, at this point, he did not casually dismiss his responsibility to his loved ones. Far too often in our practice we have heard men insensitively dismiss their obligations, saying "Oh, she'll be taken care of; as soon as I'm cold, she'll be remarried." Or, more savagely, "I'm not going to spend money just so she can be well off when I'm gone!"

Desperately trying to deny the reality, Jack's next approach was to cite his current insurance. *"Look, I get three times my salary in group coverage at work, and that's $285,000, and we have that old $100,000 whole life policy that I bought right after we were married. My gosh, isn't almost $400,000 enough?"* Not to assure the financial well-being of your family, Jack. Face it, if you were to die now, your wife and child would miss a quarter-century of your paychecks.

At this point, we've found, many a demure, self-effacing wife will pipe up helpfully: "I'll go back to work and support us if something happens to you," they will say, or "I'll sell the house and we'll live in a cottage; we don't need to live so luxuriously. I'll go back to Idaho (or Alabama, or Iowa). We could live with Mother and Daddy. They'd love to have the kids around."

Elaine said nothing.

The reality eventually sank in, though the dialogue rambled on and off for several meetings with the Washingtons, over a period of months. Finally, coming to grips with the reality, Jack asked with vague interest, *"Well, what's all this going to cost?"* That provoked another long period of intermittent conversations. We commissioned endless illustrations from the various brokerage firms and insurance companies that we work with.

Throughout the deliberations, a recurring refrain was Jack's query about his group plan at work. *"Why can't I just increase that insurance?"* he would ask, *"it's cheap."* You can, Jack, but don't forget, the maximum you can buy is $500,000 (only $215,000 more than you have now). And if you put so much reliance on group term, then leave the group—because you go to work for another company, for example—you lose the insurance. *"Okay, I'll buy coverage at my new company!"* Fine, but what if they don't offer it? What if the maximum you're entitled to is much less? What if, like we did, you decide to start your own company? *"Fine, I'll buy it then."* What if your health has changed? Your blood pressure is elevated, your cholesterol is high, your weight is up? And in any case, you'll be older, so the premiums will be higher.

Gradually logic won out. Or perhaps it was because Elaine entered the fray at a strategic moment. Maybe it was self-interest, or maybe she was simply weary of the prolonged fencing. Whatever the reason, at one point Elaine wondered aloud whether we shouldn't just get on with it. We were then zeroing in on a package that combined a $350,000 universal life contract from one company with a $250,000 term policy from another. As the conversations headed toward a plan of attack, an event occurred to clinch the strategy and give it a sense of urgency. Elaine became pregnant. Since the Washingtons had married late and had Catherine still later, and since Elaine by now was 38, this was a blessed development, greeted with much joy by husband and wife.

It also changed everyone's thinking. No longer was there any illusion that Elaine would return to work anytime soon. So Jack now bore the weight of fatherly responsibility more soberly. Now there would be three mouths to feed if anything happened to him, twice as many college educations to finance, much less flexibility in planning the future.

Long before little Tyler was born nine months later, the Washingtons' attitude toward planning in general altered noticeably. They made mutual fund investments for college funding. They finally executed their estate plan. They completed household projects long delayed. They swapped Jack's old heap of a car for a new heap of a station wagon. Regarding life insurance, Jack's view now was, ''we gotta get this done.'' We scarcely had the heart to tell him that the ante had gone up now, with a second college education to pay for.

As the application process began, we reminded the Washingtons of a conversation we'd had months before. Rather than buy more life insurance outright, we suggested, you should purchase it in an irrevocable life insurance trust. When you add up all your resources, we mentioned to Jack and Elaine, you'll have well over $1 million in assets. By using a trust, we observed, you can remove the $650,000 (now become $700,000) of new insurance coverage from your taxable estate immediately. The existing insurance can be gifted to the trust; but, we told Jack, you'll need to live another three years for it to be out of your estate.

Altogether, we could reduce the Washingtons' potentially taxable estate from around $1.5 million to less than $500,000 by subtracting the life insurance, since it would be in an irrevocable trust. In an absolutely worst-case catastrophe, in which Jack and Elaine dropped from the sky in a plane crash, little Catherine and Tyler would be spared something like $400,000 to $500,000 in federal estate taxes. That's small solace to kids who'd suddenly become orphans. But the Washingtons agreed that they'd rather their children's emotional tragedy not be compounded by financial disaster.

We called back into session the same gathering we'd convened when we revised the Washingtons' wills months earlier. The group was chaired by an attorney in our community who we consider one of the ablest estate specialists we know. She reiterated to Jack and Elaine most of what we'd told them about insurance trusts and included a wealth of additional detail.

Jack seemed relieved to be able to deputize Elaine to handle all life insurance matters. She was exhilarated to be gaining a title so exalted as trustee. On a more practical level, she and Jack both recognized that she is more temperamentally suited to the detailed formalities of the position than is Jack.

The first draft of the trust document, a 20-page opus written in dense legalese, was prepared and circulated. It might as well have been Senegalese to Jack and Elaine the first time they read it. But, as we have found to be usual, the actual execution of the agreement was not held up while the Washingtons struggled to digest every detail in the document. Rather, it was delayed so the couple could decide whom to name as a co-trustee with Elaine after Jack died or a successor to her if she herself died. We've observed elsewhere in this book that choosing guardians and trustees seems to cause our clients more difficulties than all other estate issues combined.

A month or more passed before the couple finally decided that their dear friends of many years, George and Betty Altschuh, could act on Elaine's behalf if she couldn't (or wouldn't) and would join her as co-trustees if Jack died. Elaine's sister Marsha was chosen to be the backup, in case the Altschuhs couldn't fulfill their commitment. It's questionable how much effort Jack and Elaine put into briefing George and Betty or Marsha. We recommended that they talk this over seriously, since it involves a major commitment eventually. But who knows if they did.

The signing ceremony was something of an anticlimax. The attorney was out of town so she sent her understudy, a young woman who looked as though she'd been out of law school at least two hours. But she was very efficient and polite, and execution of the agreement took possibly 15 minutes.

The main provisions of the trust

Spelled out its purpose: to hold life insurance policies on Jack's life;

Named the trustee: Elaine;

Discussed distribution of funds after Jack's death: Elaine would receive all net income and any part of the principal needed for her "maintenance in health and reasonable comfort, education or support in her accustomed manner of living . . ."

Designated co-, additional, and successor trustees: the Altschuhs to replace Elaine if she died or became incapacitated and to assist her if Jack died; Marsha if the Altschuhs were unable to act.

Properly drawn, a life insurance trust must perform many other functions, and the Washingtons' covered much other ground. There has to be something on those 20 pages, after all. For example, the trust needs to cover the contingency that the couple's children may still be young when they die in what the lawyers term a "family disaster." In that case, the Altschuhs would invest the money and could use it to help the children's guardians pay for their care. The discretion would belong to the Altschuhs.

Ultimately, when the children turned 30, they would each be entitled to one half of their portion of the remaining funds; they'd get the rest of their entitlement at age 35. You can set the ages however your judgment dictates. One lawyer friend of ours likes to joke that the older he gets, the older he thinks kids should be before they receive their inheritance. Pity the poor children of his clients if he's still practicing law into his 70s or 80s.

Another essential provision allows beneficiaries to withdraw money given to the trust to pay the insurance premiums. Elaine, as trustee, is supposed to notify all beneficiaries when money has been deposited into the trust bank account; they then have 30 days to take the money and run, if they want. Legally, the insurance premiums are considered gifts to the beneficiaries rather than to the trust. That way they are eligible for the $10,000 per person per year annual gift tax exclusion. In Elaine's case, the notification obligation is rather perfunctory, since only she and her small children are beneficiaries.

The remainder of the document spells out Elaine's powers. She has wide latitude to determine what insurance to own, how to pay for it, whether to borrow against it, and what other investments to make. This last power would be used after Jack's death. She can close down the trust if that seems appropriate, for example many years in the future if there is no longer a need to maintain life insurance on Jack. She may fire co-trustees or replace successor trustees.

Did all this authority inspire Elaine? "Right," she shrugged sarcastically. "Seems like the only power I really have is to do more work!"

Initially, the work was annoying. Applying for the two new policies that we all agreed on was not such a big deal. In fact, as fate would have it, much of that landed back on Jack. He finished the paperwork and took his insurance physical during the week that Elaine was in the hospital giving birth to Tyler.

Making sure that the existing policies got signed over to the trust was another matter. The private policy they owned did not present much difficulty. Elaine simply called the insurance company and requested a change of ownership form, completed it, and returned it along with copies of pertinent pages from the trust agreement.

Executing the change in Jack's group coverage at work was much more time-consuming. Typically, the appropriate clerk in the company's benefits office was a rookie and had no idea how to fulfill Jack's request. Rather dolefully, he suggested calling the company's insurance agent, who proved as elusive as Batman. It took two more reminder calls over a six-week period to extract the proper form from him. In all, marching the existing life insurance into the trust took more than two months, several weeks longer than having the new policies issued.

To fund the trust, we decided to use some of the Washingtons' new investments. As we apportioned the portfolio, some money went into income-oriented investments—bonds, Ginny Maes, and dividend-paying stocks. Getting sufficient income into the trust bank account to pay the insurance premiums meant instructing the various investment companies, primarily mutual funds, to send their distributions directly to the bank. It took more than the snap of her fingers, Elaine can tell you.

Life, Elaine grumbled later, should be half as complicated and twice as much fun! She did prove to be a model trustee, though, being not only intense when necessary but doggedly thorough about details and relentless at making sure each step was completed.

Administration is perhaps the biggest drawback to a life insurance trust. As Elaine's experience illustrates, from the very outset it's fraught with tedium. The cost was not inconsiderable, either. The Washingtons' legal bill came to $961.50.

Other law firms in our area, and no doubt in yours, charge less. The justification for using this particular large firm is the comfort of knowing that the trust agreement would be perfectly drafted. Our rationale is that saving a few hundred dollars at the potential future jeopardy of a *few hundred thousand dollars* if the trust were defective just doesn't make sense.

Our planning with the Washingtons began in the early summer of the year in which their daughter Catherine celebrated her fifth birthday. It concluded two autumns later, when she was the proud big sister to a new baby brother. To us, the satisfaction of helping Jack and Elaine has a lot to do with those youngsters. As parents ourselves, we are only too aware that the world can be a difficult and dangerous place for our offspring. We know they're bound to get beaten up out there, just as we all have. So we ought to fix the things we can for them.

Catherine and Tyler, here's what your Mom and Dad have done for you. They've

- Written new wills, so God forbid if something happens to them, you'll be taken care of by your Aunt Lilly and Uncle Pete.
- Purchased an excess liability umbrella policy, so a lawsuit can't wipe your family out financially.
- Begun investments to help pay for your education if you want to go to college.
- Changed their other investments so your family's life savings can stay a beat or two ahead of inflation.
- Bought enough life insurance to ensure that if anything were to happen to your Dad, you kids and your Mom will be financially secure.
- Put the insurance in a trust, so it can always be properly handled for your benefit and your Mom's and will not ever be depleted by estate taxes.

Now, as far as doing your homework and cleaning your rooms, eating your spinach and brushing your teeth, that's your responsibility. And will you kids please stop fighting!

Chapter Sixteen

The Most Effective
Strategy: Giving It Away

H ow would you like to be the most unusual person on your
block? How would you like to do something ingenious and
enormously positive? How would you like to leave a lasting monu-
ment to yourself, something that would make your children and
maybe their children's children feel proud that you were their
ancestor? We know how hard it is to be a hero these days, but
we're about to give you an easy, relatively inexpensive prescription.

Psst. Listen up. This is a little tricky, but the technique we're
about to describe may just pay for this book—many times over—
not only financially, but also in terms of personal satisfaction.

Step 1. Choose a charity or cause or institution you would
like to assist, your church or synagogue, for example, or sending
worthy students from poor families through college. Underwrite
the glad sound of music in your community, by endowing the
second trombone in your local symphony orchestra; health and
happiness, by assisting a shelter for battered women or pregnant
teenagers or a soup kitchen or an AIDS shelter; medical research,
by helping the American Cancer Society or Heart Association. As
long as it's a genuine charity, it doesn't matter which—and you're
not limited to one. But let's not get too ambitious too soon.

Step 2. Establish a private foundation, which you immod-
estly name after yourself. Of course, you don't have to name it at
all. But let's say you want to become a legend. This will cost you
a few bucks up front. Depending on the lawyer who sets it up for
you, establishing your foundation may cost you $1,000, give or

take. (It could cost you nothing, if you are partial to an existing institution that can provide you with legal assistance.) Of course, you'll need trustees. Probably you'll want to be one yourself. And you may want to name your husband, or wife, or brother, or daughter. You may want to ask your attorney or financial planner. Mind you, we're not talking a lot of money here. So far, you've spent maybe $1,000, and you're not going to spend much more. The responsibilities of the trustees while you are alive are nominal to nonexistent. As you get older, though, you'll want to start adding younger trustees to the group.

Step 3.   Take out a $1 million life insurance policy, naming the _____ (your name goes here) Foundation as irrevocable beneficiary. If you are 35, the insurance is likely to cost you in the vicinity of $2,000 a year. At 55, it will cost maybe $5,000 if you're in good health. And if you are 70, you may need to spend $10,000. It's nowhere near that costly, though, because you will receive a full income tax deduction for your annual premium payments—unless your income is extremely low. (The actual rule is that you can't deduct more than 20 percent of your adjusted gross income per year for gifts you make to a private foundation.) So, if you are in the 28 percent bracket and spend $5,000 each year, you'd really only be spending $3,600; Uncle Sam would contribute the other $1,400.

Except for the quiet thrill of knowing how much good you're going to accomplish, *you* won't enjoy the money at all. Its' a gift— no strings attached, but very savvy and sophisticated. You get tax breaks all along the way, and the whole $1 million (or however much you choose) goes to your foundation estate-tax free upon your death.

So what's the catch? There isn't any. It will work perfectly. You will make modest annual contributions, completely tax-deductible. You will have established a long-term force for good. After you die, whether it's 10 years from now or way into the 21st century, some folks who perhaps aren't even born yet will be grateful to you.

If you're like us, a little worried about what you're going to say when you meet your Maker in the hereafter, this could be a little conversation starter.

Are you beginning to see what this is all about? Go back to the first page of the chapter. This is the chapter on *giving.*

Face it, we're all living on borrowed time. We're here on earth for just the briefest instant. While we're here, not just time but everything we have is borrowed. Some of us, your authors included, have been fortunate enough to have borrowed way more than our fair share. Others are equally fortunate to have borrowed way less. In either case, we have to give it all back when we go. In this chapter, we're going to offer suggestions for giving some back while you're still here.

We opened the chapter so unusually because we wanted to start you thinking. Normally, when we talk about giving in the context of estate planning, the first thing that comes to mind is passing your assets to your heirs. And don't worry, we have plenty to say on that score. We'll coach you on how to leave your resources to your children, grandchildren, nieces, nephews, or whoever most effectively.

But giving is a much larger issue, and before we start to map out strategies, it's not a bad idea to take the broad view. Most people, including the large majority of our clients, think of giving away worldly wealth purely in terms of writing a will that leaves everything to husband or wife (using strategies to minimize the eventual estate-tax obligation), then on to the kids when both parents are gone.

A few people deviate from the norm. They do some gifting while they are alive, again, trying if possible to take the tax laws into consideration. We certainly don't suggest that there's anything wrong with that approach. Far from it. But the possibilities are much wider.

Some of our clients are charitably inclined, though generally that comes second. We're reminded of a dear couple who we've been working with for years. Some time back, we helped them write new wills in which they made a $100,000 bequest to their church. They were beaming with pride. Their two children, they reckoned, will receive the balance of their estate, whatever that turns out to be. They expected it to be several times that $100,000. Then the couple suffered a serious financial reversal. Through no fault of theirs, just as they reached retirement they were cheated out of almost all their life savings. They will be lucky to live out their days without having to reduce their standard of living.

When their misfortune became irretrievable, these folks rewrote their wills. They removed the bequest to the church and left everything to their offspring. And they don't even get along that well with the children, who are both grown now but unmarried.

Several other elderly clients are childless. In almost every case, they designate family members as their heirs: nieces, stepsons, cousins. Of course, it doesn't have to be that way. For one thing, you could use it all up. A woman we know jokes that her Uncle Pasquale for years has told everyone how he intends that his last nickel be spent at the instant of his passing. In a way, you could argue that he earned it, so he's entitled to spend it. But an attitude like that provokes nervous laughter in our society. You're considered odd if you deviate from the accepted course: Build your nest egg as large as you can, and in retirement spend only the interest, then leave your capital to your kids and their kids. If you don't have children, pick some other favorite family members.

We're not anthropologists. For all we know, maybe every society is like that. Maybe it's as natural a human instinct as propagating. Perhaps it has something to do with the desire to leave a lasting legacy, to have your life on earth mean something. Throughout most of this book we've talked about how best to leave your estate. In this chapter we'll deal with giving your assets away while you're still around.

GIVING TO YOUR CHILDREN

Over the years, we have watched the constant struggle between parents and children with growing fascination. When we were young, we gave unquestioning allegiance to the notions we've just recited. Mom and Dad spend a lifetime building their nest egg. Then you get it when they die. You try to be a good steward to your birthright. Depending on your age, mostly, and experience, you either handle the money wisely or you don't.

So as not to sound too pompous on the subject, we'll tell you a story about ourselves. *Both* of your authors received small- to moderate-sized inheritances in our 20s. They weren't huge—low five figures. Ask us where the money is now. It was wisely invested in stocks and bonds and has tripled in size. Not! It was used to purchase an investment property, which is now worth twice what it originally cost. Not! It was put in the bank, hardly grew at all but at least is now helping finance the kids' college educations. Not! Instead, it just disappeared. We don't know where it went. It's just gone! Spent.

We've thought about this and talked about it for years. What would have made a difference? Receiving the money in our 50s or 60s, we believe. Here's a radical idea: If you die before your children turn, say, 55, leave your assets to a trust that they have no access to at least until then; then see if your money isn't wisely managed! Oh, don't raise such a ruckus. We know no one's going to do that. But we're half-serious; it would be better for a lot of reasons, not least that your offspring would be compelled to make their own way in the world.

A better solution, perhaps, involves gifting. Neither of us had parents who were unusually sophisticated in dealing with money. But they weren't terrible, either. They were prudent, cautious, and half-sophisticated. What if, while they lived, they'd started on a regular program of giving their children financial gifts, with the stipulation that the money be invested? What if our parents had coached us? On the other hand, would we have listened?

Giving money to your children provides you with a number of advantages. Properly handled, the gift will aid both giver and recipient. Starting with the homeliest example, we'll work up to some fairly sophisticated concepts.

At the most basic level, you write out a check once a year. Depending on your resources, you can give up to $10,000 per year per recipient. You and your spouse combined could give away $20,000—or $40,000 annually if your child is married, or $80,000 if your daughter and son-in-law have two kids. You get the idea.

A number of our clients actually have embarked on such regular gifting programs. It gives their children a boost and removes assets from their estate that otherwise could be taxed at their deaths. On a less coldly calculating level, the gifts make our clients feel good, especially those who are endowing their grandchildren's education. In only one case, however, has a donor gone the next step.

You may not be at a stage of financial development at which you can give your children and their families $80,000 regularly. Who knows what the future may bring, and what if you needed the money later on? One of our clients has worked out a solution. Her dad, who has been retired for several years, sends her a $10,000 check each January. The unwritten agreement is that she will invest the money, using her name and social security number. Presumably her dad won't ever need the money. But if he does, she will make it available. To qualify for the $10,000 annual gift tax exclusion, of course, Dad can have no hope of ever getting the money back. It has to be a no-strings-attached gift. But we're talking about family, about love and complete trust between father and daughter. The IRS doesn't monitor those long talks sitting by the Christmas tree after everyone else has gone to bed or strolling the neighborhood on a hot summer night. Not to mention that technically you can give someone $10,000 and they can give it right back to you and both of you have stayed well within the federal estate and gift tax laws.

By now, this particular client has built up quite a tidy account with the money her father has given her. With our help, the dollars have grown reasonably well. If he dies without needing the funds back, both of them intend that the money will help pay for his grandchildren's education. But it intentionally has not been put into accounts in their names, because little Eddie and Matthew may not be as sympathetic to Grandpa's needs as their mom is.

GIVING TO MINORS

UGMA accounts are wonderful tools. The acronym stands for Uniform Gift to Minors Act. The *uniform* means that all 50 states now recognize the device. Virtually every financial institution will open an UGMA account, with lesser or greater restrictions on the minimum amount of your initial investment. Many of our clients use such accounts, typically investing in mutual funds, because they are so mercifully simple. There are no costs or fees or charges. You just title the account jointly between parent and child, using the child's social security number.

That accomplishes two objectives: the money has been given

irrevocably to the child, and within certain limitations, income that the investments generate are taxed to the child.

The 1986 Tax Reform Act restricted the advantages of income shifting. If your child is younger than 14, the first $600 of investment income that he or she receives each year is tax free, and the next $600 is taxed at the rate for his or her bracket, which is 15 percent. If there's more income than $1,200, it's taxed at the parents' rates until the child turns 14 and experiences the joy of having a personal tax bracket. We suggest making investments that pay little or no income, but instead rely on growth of capital.

Especially in accounts for very young children, the most appropriate investments are stocks, which provide excellent long-term growth potential and very little income, which the children don't need and would have to reinvest, and which would be taxable at their parents' higher rate at a certain point.

Clients often fret about the irrevocability of an UGMA gift. A refrain we frequently hear goes like this: What if little Jamie decides not to go to college? Are we going to have to hand over a big check from his mutual fund account at his 18th (or 21st) birthday? Which would you prefer—the legal or the practical answer? Legally, yes. Unequivocally, children are entitled to their money upon reaching adulthood. But practically, we know of few people who will blithely turn thousands or tens of thousands of dollars over to their 18- or 21-year-olds. Could they really manage $23,467 wisely?

What's the alternative? Legally, none. Practically, quite a few of our clients have carefully picked the moment when they tell their kids about the money. Quietly, they manage the money until they feel the children are ready for it. Legally, they have no justification. Morally, that's another story.

Where do you cross the admittedly fine line between protection and control? Hard to say. You have to use your judgment. We tend to advise our clients to deal with the issue by metering money out over a period of time, all the while gently coaching their kids on the value of a buck.

One thing is certain. If you spend the money on yourself, or even on your kids, you have not only broken the law, you've betrayed your trust. A friend of ours, a vivacious young woman from an affluent family, learned only in her late 20s that her father and stepmother had financed their lavish lifestyle during her youth largely by spending her brother's and her inheritance. Granted some of the money benefited the two children, who attended private schools and grew up in a beautiful home in San Francisco's posh Pacific Heights neighborhood after their mother died. But that wasn't the deal. Their mother had intended that the money be theirs, and at 25 they were entitled to many times what they actually received. It's tough to sue your family, and after all this came to light (following some hints dropped by an uncle) it was quietly settled. Our friend believes she ultimately received dimes on her dollars, though.

Trusts for minors have changed dramatically over the past few years. Before the 1986 Tax Reform Act, these devices were very popular. A trust called the Clifford trust allowed you to give substantial sums to your kids, have income taxed to them, and in 10 years and one day get all your money back. Such reversionary trusts were done away with by the Tax Reform Act of 1986.

Another common vehicle was called the 2503(c) trust, named for the empowering IRS code section. Its advantages have greatly diminished, since you can no longer effectively shift income to your children if they are under 14. Nor do you really need to. The progressive income tax was scrapped by the Tax Reform Act of 1986 in favor of a system in which there were only three brackets: 15 percent, 28 percent, and (for now) 31 percent. Most Americans now pay as much or more in Social Security (FICA) taxes as they do in income taxes. As a result, there's no longer as much reason to try to put money into your children's names. The income tax savings would not be that great.

Nor would a 2503(c) minor's trust allow you total discretion as to when your child could receive the proceeds. The law says that at 21 the trust terminates, but it could be extended if the child is given a withdrawal right. Effectively, the child can get everything anytime he or she wants to.

The UGMA, then, is probably a superior approach for most people. It costs nothing to set up, whereas a trust is expensive to establish—figure $500 to $1,000 in legal fees most places in the United States. It is a slightly more relaxed vehicle. And, unlike a 2503(c) trust, you get to be custodian; with a trust, the person who gives the property cannot be the trustee.

If you—or your children's grandparents or aunts or uncles—

want to make sizable gifts to the kids, it's undoubtedly advisable to tailor a trust for that purpose in the trust agreement. You can spell out what ages the children have to be in order to receive distributions. One client recently established trusts for this three young grandsons. He and his wife set the trusts up to receive $40,000 each—$20,000 contributed in December and another $20,000 in January. They intend to add $20,000 a year to each for the foreseeable future. Such a gifting program helps with their ultimate estate tax liability. But they don't want the money to spoil the boys.

So they have provided in the trusts that each boy receive one third of the trust principal at age 21, half of the remainder at age 30, and the balance when they reach 40. Meanwhile, they are entitled to income, but the trusts state that the income cannot be used to defray any obligations the parents have to support their kids. In other words, you can't go out and buy groceries with the kids' money or use it to finance a family trip to Disney World.

DON'T SEND CASH

Throughout this discussion, we've implied that you or Grandma and Grandpa write out a check to your offspring or theirs. That's not necessarily always the best strategy.

Many people own assets that would be very costly to sell. The most common are real estate and stock purchased years ago that has a very low cost basis. Our clients Archie and Lilly, for example, have been putting their youngest daughter through college using Coca-Cola stock that Archie received from his father Rex years ago. If Archie and Lilly were to sell the shares, they'd pay a punishing capital gains tax. The cost basis of the stock is almost nothing. So selling it to raise the money to pay for college would mean giving Uncle Sam nearly 28 cents of every dollar of the proceeds. Instead, by giving it to Tammy and letting her sell it, they are able to realize 85 cents, since she is in the minimum 15 percent tax bracket.

Obviously, you need to think carefully about the income tax implications of any gift you make. At the time of your life when death seems far off, the income tax issues may seem paramount.

But bear in mind that the ravages of estate taxes, if you qualify for them, are far worse.

At a maximum, the highest federal income tax bracket is currently 31 percent (though for some very high income people it can get to nearly 34 percent because of some recent technical changes that deprive upper income taxpayers of the benefit of personal exemptions and itemized deductions). The federal estate tax, however, *starts* at a 37 percent level above $600,000 of assets, and it goes all the way up to 50 percent if you are fortunate enough to leave an estate of more than $2 million.

Sometimes, the two taxes work at cross-purposes. In other circumstances, you can foil both at once. A scenario that we frequently encounter is this: Your church or synagogue or Elks Club or what have you is undertaking, say, a building drive. You are an active member and would like to make a sizable pledge—$1,000, $5,000, or whatever. Rather than writing a check, you instead donate stock (or mutual fund shares) with a current market value equaling your pledge. You choose among your investments those with the lowest cost basis in comparison to their current value and the greatest probability of future increases in value. You escape the capital gains liability because the nonprofit institution pays no income tax. So if it sells your shares, Uncle Sam is deprived of his due. Moreover, with the stock or mutual funds out of your possession, you've reduced your estate tax exposure. If the shares are worth $1,000 now, what if they were worth $10,000 by the time you die? By giving them away, you have saved your estate not just, for example, 37 percent of $1,000 but that much or an even higher percentage of $10,000.

USING UP YOUR $600,000

Few people are willing to do it, we've found, but many affluent folks should consider giving their families $600,000—$1.2 million per couple—while they are alive. Three compelling advantages make the strategy tempting.

We've just described the first. You can potentially remove far more than $600,000 from your estate. (For the sake of simplicity, let's agree that in this discussion we'll use $600,000 as each person's unified estate/gift tax exclusion amount. Understand that for married couples it's more logical to think in terms of $1.2 million.) Say, for example, that you recently purchased a small commercial building for $600,000. You don't anticipate ever needing to sell this property to maintain your lifestyle. By giving it away you will remove all future appreciation from your estate. One drawback is that the recipient, let's say your son, would have to pay capital gains tax in the future if he sells the building at a profit. If you kept the property, he would avoid capital gains tax because of a quirk in the law. When someone dies, their heirs receive a step-up in the cost basis of assets, which are allowed to be valued as of the date of death or six months later. The executor is allowed to choose whichever is most advantageous to the estate.

Of course, if you kept the building, your estate might have to pay federal estate taxes, assuming that your assets totaled more than $600,000. The income tax advantage of keeping the property until death has to be weighed against the potential estate-tax savings on the appreciation of the property that accrues following the transfer. Typically, an estate tax obligation is larger than the capital gains burden.

USE IT OR LOSE IT

We call the second benefit "use it or lose it." By that we mean that the current $600,000 exclusion amount is not likely to increase (it was phased in from a much smaller amount starting in 1982), and it may be reduced. There hasn't been much ferment in Congress lately, but several members of Congress have proposed reducing the estate/gift tax exclusion. Were you to use up your $600,000 now, of course, you would presumably be immune to any Congressional machinations. Let them lower the exclusion; you've already gotten yours!

The ideal vehicle for making a $600,000 gift is a trust. You probably don't want to suddenly settle a large amount of money on your children or grandchildren. But more to the point, you may want to wait until both you and your spouse have passed away before letting your offspring have the money.

Make no mistake, we're not talking about attaching strings. You can't do that. To be a bona fide gift, you must make it irrevocably, and you may not retain any control. You cannot, for instance, be a trustee.

You can, however, establish a trust. In the trust agreement you can specify that all income from trust investments be for the benefit of your husband or wife while he or she is alive. You need to be extremely careful about allowing any access to the principal, and you need to discuss this with your attorney. You can even name your spouse as a trustee, though you are much better advised to include an independent co-trustee who is not a beneficiary—your lawyer or financial planner, for instance. But you must step out of the picture entirely yourself. Otherwise the IRS can disallow the transaction as a sham.

Just because you've set up the trust does not imply that you must fund it. The trust agreement can lie dormant for a time. We've had clients spend several years working up the courage to give away $600,000—even though the assets would stay in the family. One reason they delayed funding the trust was their indecision as to which assets would be most appropriate.

It rarely works out this way, but the most effective assets would be those that are illiquid (meaning they'd be difficult for you to sell, hence ideal to gift), have a comparatively high cost basis (so you wouldn't be concerned about losing the after-death step-up to escape capital gains tax), great prospects for future appreciation (all of which would be out of your estate), and little in the way of income (so your spouse wouldn't have to worry about the trust).

Of all the assets that might meet these tests, the best would be recently purchased real estate or stocks that weren't doing too well, either because of a sluggish market or because the companies or industries were in a lull.

FOR THE CHARITABLY MINDED

Two things always amaze us about charitable contributions: There are some strings attached if you give your assets away while you're alive, and there are virtually *none* after you die. Ours is a nation of charitably minded folks. We Americans are more self-critical than most other peoples, but we are also more inclined to help our fellow citizens than most. We do so as a nation and as individuals in our own neighborhoods. Woe betide anyone who challenges our charitable inclinations.

So it's a little surprising that there are *any* limitations on the tax deductibility of gifts. But there are, and you should understand them first, before deciding whether to give while you're alive or bequeath upon your death.

THE 30 PERCENT SOLUTION—OR IS IT 50 PERCENT? OR 20 PERCENT?

The rest of the IRS code is dense with complexities. So why should the laws governing charitable deductions be any different? Starting with the easiest first, keep in mind that we're mainly addressing contributions to recognized, approved charitable institutions. As our example at the start of this chapter noted, you are not limited to organized charities. However, if you contribute to the Homer Simpson Foundation for Indigent Rap Musicians—presumably a genuine, but not a recognized charity—you can take an income tax deduction of not more each year than 20 percent of your adjusted gross income. Thus, if you earn $50,000 (and have no adjustments), your $10,000 contribution to the good old Homer Fund would be fully deductible. But if you mail off a check for $12,000, the extra $2,000 is entirely on you. Uncle Sam won't assist you in any way. You can't postpone your deductions for the other $2,000 until next year—unless you delay contributing it until next year. Generally, when you give to a publicly recognized charity, you have the right to chose whether you'd like to take a deduction of up to 30 percent or 50 percent of your adjusted gross income.

Our friends Gerald and Patsy decided to sell their house. It was an expensive home, but sort of a white elephant, and it took forever to sell. In the meantime, they got the idea of donating an acre of land they owned adjacent to the house. It was marshland and would have been difficult to build on, so they chose to give the property to a nature conservancy, ever after to be preserved as a bird sanctuary.

Getting the property appraised proved difficult. One appraiser, taking the position that the land was unbuildable, gave a very low figure. A second appraiser was much more generous, reckoning that the property was worth $150,000.

When they met with their trusty accountant the following spring he informed the couple that they had two choices. They could take a tax deduction of up to 30 percent of their adjusted gross income (AGI) no questions asked. Okay, they wondered, how much would that amount to? A little quick arithmetic: their AGI was $120,000 (we're rounding it off) for the prior year; so they could deduct $36,000 (30 percent of $120,000). "Ouch," they cried—"our land was worth $150,000!" "Not to worry," their soothing accountant purred, "you have up to five years to write off the balance."

The couple did some mental math: $150,000 minus $36,000 equals $114,000. Divided by five, that equals $22,800 per year. Does the $22,800 change if our income drops, they wondered. Indeed it does, the accountant informed them. If their AGI in any year of the subsequent five falls below $90,000, then $22,800 would be more than 30 percent of it, but 30 percent is the maximum tax deduction allowed.

Gulp. "What's the other approach you spoke of," the couple asked.

The other alternative—and it's always your choice—is to use the 50 percent rule. If you were giving cash, then you could deduct up to 50 percent of your AGI in a given year and carry the unused balance over for up to five years. In this family, however, it would make no sense to think in terms of cash donations equivalent to the property donation to the nature conservancy. For one thing, they were donating the property because they wanted it specifically to benefit the conservancy. Then, too, the donation was largely inspired by the difficulty they were having selling their property. Perhaps the most important disadvantage, though, had to do with taxes. If they were to sell the property in order to donate cash, they'd potentially owe a capital gains tax on the difference between what they originally paid for the land and what they sold it for.

So, scratch that idea. However, as their accountant told them, the 50 percent-of-AGI approach also has a downside, namely that you must make a capital gains computation. So they had to subtract the original cost basis of the land from the donation value (current market value). After much figuring, the accountant concluded that they'd originally paid about $30,000 for the parcel, which now carried a $150,000 price tag, according to the appraiser. Thus, $150,000 minus $30,000 equals $120,000. The law requires you to reduce your tax deductions by 40 percent of the gain—in this case, $48,000 ($120,000 times 40 percent)—meaning that the couple could take a total deduction of only $102,000.

In short, they had two options: at the 50 percent limitation, based on their $120,000 income they could deduct $60,000 the first year, and they would have $42,000 left to deduct in up to five future years. If their income was just as high the following year, they could subtract the entire remainder. Or, under the 30 percent of AGI option they could deduct $36,000 the first year and save $114,000 to deduct in later years.

These folks faced a predicament—to take big deductions the first two years, but risk losing some if they retired in the near future and had a large permanent drop in their income.

These decisions are perplexing, and they sometimes make you want to throw your arms up in despair and forget the whole thing. The best planning, obviously, is done well in advance. Had Gerald and Patsy considered the donation several years earlier, the outcome would have been easier to determine. If they had made the gift before the 1986 tax law change, they would have gotten a still bigger kick. Since the maximum tax bracket then was 50 percent, tax deductions of all sorts brought more potent relief.

This discussion is already complex enough, and we hesitate to make it still more abstruse. But we must confess to having oversimplified slightly. When you give away appreciated assets, depending on the amount of appreciation and your own tax picture, it is possible that you may trigger what's called an alternative minimum tax (AMT). Your accountant will tell you if you have an AMT income tax problem, which in any case may not be so bad in the long run because you can recapture on future tax returns the deductions you didn't get to take in the current year.

You also need to take into account the type of property you're donating and how it relates to the purpose of the charity. Suppose you give your tabernacle a large mural; beautiful as it is, the painting will not further the religious work of the organization. So, you are allowed a deduction of the artwork's original cost plus 60 percent of the growth in its value. In the case of Gerald and Patsy's deduction, since the property furthers the nature conservancy's specific work, no such limitation is imposed.

TO GIVE NOW OR LATER?

As we said, you face all these income limitations on gifts you make while you are alive, but no restrictions at all if you leave the same property upon your death. The IRS cares not the slightest what the cost basis is of land you will to PTA for a leadership center or stock that you give to the Alzheimer's foundation to further research. For one simple reason: There is no capital gains tax after death. Whether you leave property to charity or to your cousin Ludlow, the tax basis gets stepped up to its market value on the day you die (or six months later; it's your executor's choice).

When I give my property away, is it gone? You might wonder about that. There is a way to give it away, but still use it while you and your spouse are alive. In the next chapter, we will explore a variety of trust planning techniques that allow you to do exactly that.

Chapter Seventeen

Trust Planning for Larger Estates

A re you a self-made millionaire (or do you hope to be)? Did you inherit money from your family? Regardless of how you gained your wealth, chances are you want to hang onto it. Furthermore, you'd like to see to it that your family has the ongoing opportunity to enjoy the benefits of wealth after you are gone.

This chapter is for those readers who have arrived—or who are at least on the way. You are in the top 5 percent of all Americans in terms of income and wealth. Congratulations!

Now for the bad news. You know about income taxes. We've already covered estate and gift taxes, along with the basic ways to minimize them. But if you are very wealthy, Uncle Sam is going to grab as much as he can from you during your lifetime, and even more when you die. We won't debate the social, fiscal, and ethical issues surrounding our tax system. As financial planners, our job is to help you use the laws to your and your family's best advantage.

As this book is written in 1993, federal estate tax rates go as high as 50 percent. Prior to 1993 for estates in excess of $10 million, there was a phaseout of the graduated tax rates leading up to 55 percent and the unified credit. The result: an effective rate of 60 percent.) Don't be too surprised if Congress raises the rates right back up again in the near future.

It's difficult to grasp the impact that taxation can have on us. Let's look at a simplified example for someone in the maximum estate tax bracket. You earn a dollar. Considering only federal income taxes, you shell out 31 cents, leaving you with 69 cents. For simplicity's sake, assume that there is no growth in the value of that 69 cents. At your death, you left the 69 cents to your children. Then 55 percent of it went to federal tax, and we'll assume another

5 percent to state tax. Sixty percent of 69 cents is 41 cents in taxes, which leaves just 28 cents of the original $1.00 you earned. If you had instead decided to leave your 69 cents to your grandkids, something called the generation skipping transfer tax kicks in at the rate of an additional 55 percent. Your grandchildren would net just 12 cents of that original $1.00 you earned!

Fortunately, there are some ways you can ease the pain. In this chapter, we will show you some of the more sophisticated techniques, using trusts, to help save both income taxes and estate taxes.

THE CHARITABLE REMAINDER TRUST

They say you can't have your cake and eat it too. But, if there is a charitable institution you care about, you can come close. You will have to share some of your cake with the charity of course, but the law provides significant incentives for you to do so.

We should clarify the term *charity*. Certain institutions, including universities, colleges, hospitals, foundations, and organizations like the United Way, American Cancer Society, and so on have a special tax status granted by the IRS. Their operations are tax exempt and money donated to them may be deductible by the donor from ordinary income. If you have any doubt about whether or not a particular institution qualifies, you can check up on it through your local IRS office.

"Great," you might say. "I'd love to endow a fellowship at my alma mater, but frankly I don't want to part with that much capital during my lifetime." That's perfectly understandable. However, you may find that the charitable remainder trust is the perfect vehicle for accomplishing your objective. The CRT is a trust in which both an "income interest" and a "remainder interest" are created. In this arrangement, you give property in trust to a charity. However, you retain a right to receive income from the trust for a term of years or for as long as you live. If you are married, this income can be payable over both lives. The right to receive income is the so-called income interest. At the death of the last beneficiary, the charity gets full control of the assets in the trust. This is the remainder interest.

The beauty of this arrangement is that you get a current income tax deduction based on the value of the remainder interest. Even so, you will continue to receive income for life. All you have given up is the right to pass the asset on to your family. There are two basic variations of the charitable remainder trust: the annuity trust (CRAT) and the unitrust (CRUT). We will start with CRATs because they are the simplest.

Charitable Remainder Annuity Trust (CRAT)

Under this variation, the income payable to you must be set at a flat rate of at least 5 percent of the initial value of the assets you place in the trust. By law, payable income can be more than 5 percent, but not less. For example, if you put $100,000 worth of property into a 5 percent CRAT, you and your spouse would be guaranteed annuity payments of $5,000 per year. If you choose a higher rate, that will lower the value of the remainder interest. The IRS publishes a table that determines the value of your income interest and the remainder interest based on your ages, life expectancies, the term of the trust, and current interest rates. For now, it's enough to understand that the higher the rate of interest you receive during your lifetime, the greater the value of the life interest you are retaining. The greater the value of your life interest, the smaller the value of the remainder interest you are giving away. Thus, the lower your tax deduction.

The other key factors are your age and the number of beneficiaries of the trust. The older you are when you set up your trust, the sooner the charity is likely to get full control of the money. This increases the value of the remainder of interest and hence your tax deduction. If you choose a trust term shorter than your life expectancy, that will also increase the value of the remainder interest. You will get a bigger current tax deduction, but you must accept the fact that the trust, and your annuity payments, will terminate after the number of years specified in the trust agreement.

The charitable remainder annuity trust is the most conservative approach from your standpoint. If the trust earns less than the amount needed to pay you out, the trustee must make the difference up from principal. On the other hand, if the trust earns more than is needed, this excess is plowed back into the trust, which will ultimately benefit the charity but will do nothing to increase your income.

Charitable Remainder Unitrust (CRUT)

If you are a bit more adventurous or if you are concerned about inflation, a CRUT could be a good alternative. This is similar to the annuity trust. The only difference is in how your income is computed and paid out.

Instead of paying out a fixed percentage of at least 5 percent on the initial value of the property placed in trust, the CRUT pays out a rate of at least 5 percent of the *current* value of the assets in the trust. Thus, if the value of the trust assets goes up, so does your income. But, if the asset values go down, you will be getting 5 percent of a lower number, and hence a smaller annuity payment.

Because the potential is there to receive more income, a CRUT will generally provide a lower current tax deduction than a CRAT.

Which is better? That really depends on you. You will need to evaluate your expectations for inflation and prospects for appreciation in the value of the property that you place in trust. If you are confident that it will grow in value over time, a unitrust may pay you more income. But if you are nervous about the prospects for appreciation or prefer to play it safe, then an annuity trust will allow you to sleep better at night.

We should also mention that the assets you give to the trust may not be the assets that remain there. The charity may decide to sell the property and reinvest the proceeds in its own accounts. If you are choosing a unitrust, you will need to know what the performance history has been for the various accounts managed by the charity. You should also stick to well-known, well-established charities. If for some reason the charity were to go bankrupt you could lose your payments.

What type of property should you place in the trust? You can give cash. Or you can donate property. If you donate appreciated property, you gain an additional income tax advantage. You can convert a nonincome-producing asset, which has grown in value, to an income-producing asset (your charitable remainder trust), without actually selling it and paying a fat capital gains tax.

For example, say that 20 years ago you bought stock in XYZ Corporation. You paid $10 per share and bought 1,000 shares. Although it pays no dividend, XYZ shares have grown in value and are now worth $100. Your investment has grown from $10,000 to $100,000. But now you need income. If you sell the stock you will have to pay a capital gains tax on the $90,000 of growth that you have gained. Between federal and state taxes you could be looking at a $30,000 tax bite. So, you will really only have $70,000 to invest for income. If you invested the $70,000 in tax free bonds at 6 percent, that would produce $4,200 per year. Now let's look at an alternative, using a charitable remainder annuity trust.

Assumptions
Date of gift Jan. 1992
Your age: 60
Adjusted gross income: $100,000/year
Contribution to CRAT: $100,000 in XYZ stock
Constant annuity factor: 7.4491 (from IRS table)
Annual annuity income:
  7% ($7,000 per year)
$7,000 × 7.4491 = $52,143 life interest
$100,000 − $52,143 = $47,857 allowable charitable deduction
Annual income = $7,000 for life
Current tax savings* 1992 $ 9,300 ($30,000 × 31%)
                     1993 $ 5,535 ($17,857 × 31%)

                Total $14,835

* The tax savings are payable over two years because the law limits your tax deduction for the gift of the remainder interest to 30 percent of your adjusted gross income if you give appreciated property. The balance can be carried forward for up to five years. In this example all the remaining tax benefits will be realized in the following year. If you give cash, you may take deductions for up to 50 percent of your adjusted gross income, again carrying forward any balance for five years. Obviously it is better to give appreciated property and spread out your tax benefits than it is to pay capital gains tax and then use the cash to fund the trust.

To sum up, you now have $7,000 of income from the CRAT, which can even be tax free if invested in municipal bonds. (The yield you actually get will obviously vary with prevailing interest rates at the time you set up your CRAT or CRUT).

Had you sold your XYZ stock and invested what was left after capital gains taxes, you would have only $4,200 of income. So you are ahead by $2,800 per year. In addition, you also have tax deductions that will save you almost $15,000 in taxes over the next two years. If you invest that at 7 percent, you have another $1,050 per year of income. In some cases, the alternative minimum tax may deprive you of some of these tax savings. Your accountant should be a key advisor in this decision.

But, you may ask, what about my kids? Well, if you were planning on leaving $100,000 to charity in your will anyway, the point is moot. If that was more than you had anticipated, there is a nifty way to make sure your kids are not shortchanged. You can use some of the extra cash flow and tax savings the CRAT provides to buy a life insurance policy on yourself (or a second-to-die policy if you are married). By placing that policy in an irrevocable life insurance trust you can make your kids whole and still have more spendable income than you would have had without the CRAT.

This doesn't work in every case. A lot depends on your age, your current tax bracket, and your state of health. If your prognosis for at least a normal life expectancy is not good, you may wish to explore other alternatives. However, the potential tax savings and income benefits make it worth a look. Virtually every large charity has a planned giving department staffed by professionals familiar with the CRATs and CRUTs. Together with your attorney, planner, accountant, and insurance agent, they can help you determine whether this strategy can work for you.

CHARITABLE LEAD TRUST

Very affluent families may find themselves with "superfluous" assets. To most of us, that's a bizarre notion, sort of akin to being too smart or too thin.

But there are people who have more resources than they know what to do with. Our clients Samantha and Gerald are quite well-to-do. His family was wealthy and she made herself rich by building a very successful property management business. Likewise, their three children are all prosperous professionals. One is heir apparent in his mother's firm, another is a dentist, and the third married a landscape architect. None of them have any need for additional income; all are in the top tax bracket.

Sam and Gerry, meanwhile, are active members of a very large church, and they would like to do something for it. They have been thinking in terms of making a sizable donation, but they don't want to take the money away from their children and grandchildren. Moveover, neither of them is very healthy, even though they are only in their early 60s. Samantha has had two heart attacks, and Gerald is a diabetic. So purchasing life insurance would not be easy.

A charitable lead trust may provide a solution for the couple. In general, it would work this way. They would put, say, $500,000 into the trust. The contributions would generate income that would be paid to the church—perhaps $40,000 a year (at 8 percent). The trust can be structured so that the $500,000 principal does not revert to Samantha and Gerald's family until after they are gone and their children are in lower tax brackets, for instance when they themselves are retired. For that matter, they could structure it so that the principal would go to their grandchildren at particular ages—25 or 30 or 35.

It can become as complicated as they want to make it. From an estate point of view, though, they would have accomplished several objectives. They've removed income they don't need for themselves; they've given their favorite charity a predictable, continuing income stream for a long period; they've secured a small estate-tax saving (the value of the annuity interest to the church reduces their potential estate-tax liability); and they've done all this without permanently giving up their property.

One word of caution regrading the grandchildren. Before 1976, you could easily pass assets to your grandchildren, effectively sidestepping estate taxes at the intermediate level. Your estate would meet its tax obligations, of course, but leaving property directly to your grandchildren would eliminate a tax at your children's death.

The 1976 tax act initiated a new concept: the generation-skipping tax. The 1986 Tax Reform Act broadened the notion. Now, there's a $1 million exemption for legacies that skip a generation.

Think of it this way: Suppose you could set up a trust in which successive generations of your heirs could benefit from your money, but only face estate taxes at the first pass (from you to your children). Sound attractive? Well it was, but now it's basically gone, at least for the very wealthy. For the rest of us, being able to carve out a $1 million exemption for assets we leave directly to our grandchildren is probably sufficient!

GRANTOR RETAINED ANNUITY TRUSTS (GRATS) AND GRANTOR RETAINED UNITRUSTS (GRUTS)

We were sitting down with one of our better-heeled clients in the affluent town of New Canaan, Connecticut. We had been discussing the concept of charitable remainder unitrusts. "That's all very well and good," he harumphed, "but I've always believed that charity begins in the home." In other words, he felt he had already done everything for charity that he cared to and now he wanted to focus on himself and his family.

GRATs and GRUTs are ways for you to transfer assets to heirs at reduced estate and gift tax costs. They are similar to their charitable cousins in some respects. Both an income interest and remainder interest are created. You retain the income interest and give the remainder interest to an irrevocable trust for the benefit of your heirs. Because a charity is not involved, however, the tax consequences are much different. Naturally, you get no tax deduction for the gift to your heirs. In fact, that will be a taxable event under our gift tax rules. In addition, all the income of the trust will be taxable to you unless invested by the trust in municipal bonds.

Despite the lack of income tax benefits, the estate-tax results can be very rewarding. Let's look at an example.

Jim, age 65, creates a GRAT for his two children, funded with $1 million in mutual fund investments. The trust agreement sets the annuity payout at 8 percent, or $80,000, for 10 years. After 10 years, the trust terminates and the trust property is distributed to his kids. The IRS tables place the value of Jim's retained income interest at $491,568. This means that the transfer of the remainder interest of $508,432 is a taxable gift. Jim will not have to pay any tax, however, because it will be covered by using most of his unified credit, which would shelter up to $600,000 worth of taxable transfers. Jim will not be able to also use the $10,000 annual exclusion because this is a gift of future interest: The kids won't get the use of the money for 10 years. The annual exclusion only applies to gifts of present interest, which can be enjoyed in the here and now.

Now suppose that Jim lives the 10 years, and during that time the fund has grown in value to $1.5 million. His children will receive $1.5 million. Yet Jim was only charged with a gift of a little over $500,000 for estate-tax purposes. Had Jim held these assets until his death, his family would have paid hundreds of thousands of dollars in additional estate taxes. On the downside, Jim paid tax on the $80,000 each year, plus any other income generated by the trust. But coordinated income tax and investment planning could be used to help improve on that result, for example, by investing in municipal bonds.

Another drawback to the GRAT is the fact that the income coming back to Jim stays in his estate. So he should plan on spending it all. Poor Jim! Seriously, though, this technique makes sense only if the asset placed in the trust appreciates during his lifetime.

Why did Jim choose a 10-year term, instead of retaining an income interest for his entire lifetime? If Jim died before the end of the term of his income interest, some portion of the original $1 million trust principal would be brought back into his estate. The computation of the amount taxed in Jim's estate is too complex to be covered here. In most cases, there will still be some benefits accruing to the family, even if the donor dies prematurely. Still, it is better planning to use a trust term that is well within Jim's life expectancy.

Grantor retained unitrusts (GRUTs) work in similar fashion. The primary difference is that the payout will rise and fall with the value of the trust. If Jim had chosen an 8 percent GRUT, he would have received the same $80,000 per year as he would have with an 8 percent GRAT. However, if the trust grew in value to $1.5 million, the GRUT would pay out $120,000 per year. On the other hand, if the assets fell in value to $750,000, Jim's income would go down to $60,000 per year. In contrast, the GRAT would pay a flat $80,000 regardless of fluctuations in the value of trust assets.

The choice of GRAT or GRUT is a complex topic. The amount of annual income retained by the grantor, current interest factors published by the IRS, and your assumptions for growth of the trust assets are all key factors in deciding which variation will produce the greatest estate and gift tax benefit.

The objective is generally to value the remainder interest as low as possible in order to minimize the value of the gift to the trust. If the value of the income payments retained by the grantor is greater than the income and appreciation (total return) of the trust assets, the GRAT will produce a smaller remainder interest. This is because the payment of the income to the donor will require the trustees to dip into the principal of the trust.

It is even possible to manipulate the remainder interest down to zero by a combination of a large income payment and a long annuity term. The downside to all this is that all the trust assets could conceivably be paid back to the donor over her or his lifetime. This is one of many strategies that need to be carefully thought through before implementation.

A GRUT will produce a lower remainder interest in the opposite situation, in which the total return of the trust exceeds the income payout back to the grantor. This is because the annuity payments from the GRUT will increase as the value of the assets increases. This produces a lower value for the value of the remainder interest.

To sum up, GRATs and GRUTs both are useful tools for transferring property that will greatly appreciate in value. This is especially true if retaining the right to income from the property is important to you. Properly used, large amounts of estate and gift taxes can be legally avoided. However, you will need the input of skilled estate planning practitioners to execute this transaction successfully. These trusts are irrevocable, so correcting mistakes will not be easy.

GRANTOR RETAINED INCOME TRUST (GRIT)

What's better than a GRAT or a GRUT? What else? A GRIT! In many cases, the retained income feature of a GRAT or GRUT is not a plus. Often, the income simply isn't needed. In addition, the income comes back into the estate of the donor, which is what we were trying to avoid in the first place. GRITs are an allowable alternative, but only for certain types of property. Most of the time, GRITs are used for a personal residence owned by an older person. However, you are also permitted to fund a GRIT with other tangible personal assets, such as antiques and artwork.

As with a GRAT or GRUT, the grantor of a grantor retained income trust is entitled to be paid income from the trust. However, the income she or he receives is limited to the income actually produced. Thus, if the GRIT earns no income, the grantor receives nothing. In contrast, grantors of GRATs and GRUTs *must* receive a fixed payment from the trustee, even if the trust does not generate enough income. For someone who has no need or desire to receive income from the assets being transferred into trust, GRITs are a powerful alternative. Furthermore, the remainder interest calculations are performed differently, which can result in a lower value being assigned to the gift. The reason for this is that there is a risk that the GRIT will not serve its purpose. If the grantor dies during the term of the trust, the entire value of the asset comes back into the grantor's estate.

Take the case of Lucy Smith, a 65-year-old widow who lives in the same home she and her husband purchased 30 years ago. The home is now worth $1 million and she just sent in her last mortgage payment. The rest of her assets, savings, and investments also total about $1 million. She is very concerned about the high taxes her family will have to pay when she dies.

Enter the grantor retained income trust. The GRIT allows her to set up a trust for her children (or other heirs) who will now own the house. However, she will retain the right to live in the house for at least 10 years. (Ten years is the minimum allowable). She could also retain the right for a longer term, but as we shall see, she may not wish to do so. What has she accomplished? If she gave the house outright to her kids, there would be a number of problems. First of all, the gift would be taxable. The first $600,000 would be sheltered by the unified credit, but the taxes on the next $400,000 would be over $150,000. Ouch! In addition, if she were living there rent free, the IRS could make a case that the kids were making gifts back to her. Ouch! Ouch!

The GRIT solves that problem. By retaining the right to live in the house, Lucy is effectively reducing the value of the gift to her children. After all, they won't have the right to use the property for 10 years. That time element is what makes the gift less valuable. Table 17–1 shows the value that would be assigned to the gift at different ages under different circumstances.

As you can see, with a 10-year GRIT Lucy can transfer the house to her children at age 65 with it valued at only $284,001. These numbers are based on IRS tables, which are readjusted periodically to reflect current interest rates. Lucy will owe no tax on this gift, since the unified credit will totally shelter it. She will have enough

TABLE 17-1
Taxable Gift to GRIT of $1 Million with Reversion on Death of Grantor

Age	No GRIT	10-Year GRIT	20-Year GRIT
55	$1,000,000	$336,489	$95,562
60	$1,000,000	314,263	76,659
65	$1,000,000	284,001	53,902

unified credit left to shelter over $300,000 of other assets in her estate. Better yet, if the real estate market takes off again, which we hope it does, all the future appreciation will accrue to her kids free of estate tax. If she died still owning the house, the full value, including appreciation, would be estate taxable.

As you can also see, if Lucy chose a 20-year GRIT at age 65, the value of the gift goes down to $53,901. Why not do that? If Lucy dies during those 20 years, the full value of the house comes back into her estate. True, the family is no worse off than it was before, but on the other hand, it is no better off either. The trick is to set a GRIT term well within the grantor's life expectancy. Younger, healthier people can try using longer term GRITS. Older and sicker people can use a shorter duration.

Assume that Lucy lives the 10 years. Her kids now own the house. She wants (and they want her) to stay in her home. There is no reason why she couldn't pay her kids rent. In fact, that could be a good estate and income tax planning idea. If she has enough money, she will be reducing her taxable estate by the amount of the rent. Her kids would owe income tax on the rent, but they could shelter that by deducting depreciation, expenses, and real estate taxes. If she couldn't afford to pay the rent, the kids could always gift it back to her. Since each child can gift Lucy up to $10,000 (or $20,000 if married), there should be ample room to deal with this issue.

On the other hand, by age 75, Lucy may be ready to move to a condominium or nursing home or to move in with her children at that point. The kids could either keep or sell the house as they see fit.

This same tool can also be used for certain types of tangible personal property, such as artworks or antiques. If you have a Picasso on the wall you can put it in a GRIT just as you could your home. You can keep it on your wall for the entire term of the GRIT and rest assured that even if it triples in value, your heirs will owe no taxes on it as long as you survive the term of the GRIT.

Unfortunately, recent tax law changes prevent you from using this technique for other types of property such as investments, business interests, or real estate other than your personal residence.

PLANNING FOR THE GENERATION SKIPPING TRANSFER TAX

Chapter 13 (how appropriate!) of the Internal Revenue Code was enacted in 1986 to plug a perceived loophole in the estate and gift tax laws. The law is complex, but the basic strategy is to avoid skipping generations to avoid tax. Take the case of Grandpa Bill, who has, as they say, more money than God. In doing his planning, he realizes that leaving money to his children will not be terribly productive. They are also quite wealthy and don't need the money. Besides, by the time it is taxed in Grandpa Bill's estate, at rates up to 55 percent, and later in his children's estates, again at up to 55 percent, there will be very little left for the darling grandchildren he dearly loves. Grandpa Bill has the brilliant idea to bypass his own children's estates (with their 55 percent estate tax brackets) and give his money directly to his grandchildren. That's where the generation skipping transfer tax (GSTT) comes in. Very simply it imposes an additional 55 percent tax on transfers that skip generations, and that's *in addition* to the regular gift or estate tax.

Happily, there is help. First of all, the law does allow for a $1 million lifetime exemption against the GSTT. This exemption operates in a manner similar to the unified estate and gift tax credit. A husband and wife each have a $1 million GSTT exemption, which means they can "double up" and pass up to $2 million to grandchildren without this penalty tax being imposed.

It is often advisable for wealthy estate owners to use their GSTT exemptions during their lifetimes. If possible, they should look for ways to leverage these exemptions. For example, it may make sense to combine a number of different tax breaks to keep the maximum amount of wealth within the family. For example, our friend Grandpa Bill could use his unified credit to gift $600,000 to his grandchildren. Since this gift is less than $1 million there will be no generation skipping transfer tax, either. Grandpa Bill may even decide to make a taxable gift of the next $400,000. While the gift tax would be almost $160,000, that is far less than paying estate taxes at rates of 55 percent in Grandpa's estate and again in his kids' estates. And, of course, if Grandma is still alive we can double up on these numbers, using her GSTT exemption and unified credit.

There is another intriguing way to leverage generation skipping transfers. Gifts that qualify for the $10,000 annual exclusion are exempt from gift tax, estate tax, and the GSTT. One strategy would be for the grandparents to make a combined gift of $20,000 every year to each of their grandchildren. Another possibility would be to use that money to buy a life insurance policy in an irrevocable life insurance trust.

Let's look at the example of two happy 55-year-olds who just became grandparents. They want to start putting money away for the little fella just as soon as possible. They evaluate three alternatives.

Alternative 1: Keep the money. This assumes that the grandparents set aside $20,000 per year in accounts under their own names, earning 7 percent. They die at the end of 20 years and the accumulated capital is taxed at the maximum rate of 55 percent. Their children then take the money they receive after estate taxes and reinvest it for the next 20 years until their deaths. The grandchildren finally inherit what's left after payment of estate taxes in their parents' estates. Not a great strategy!

Alternative 2: Gift to trust. In this example the grandparents make combined annual gifts of $20,000—exempt from transfer taxes of any kind—to irrevocable trusts for the grandchildren. At their deaths in 20 years the assets accumulated in trust remain

TABLE 17–2
Wealth Transfer Analysis

	1 *Keep the Money*	2 *Trust*	3 *Life Insurance Trust*
First generation:			
20-year accumulation	$ 877,304	$ 877,304	$2,000,000
Less estate tax	(482,518)	0	0
Left to 2nd generation	394,786	877,304	2,000,000
Second generation:			
20-year accumulation	$1,527,696	$3,394,888	$7,739,366
Less estate tax	(840,232)	0	0
Left to 3rd generation	687,732	3,394,888	7,739,366

invested until the death of the second generation 20 years later. The assets then go intact to the grandchildren. Good plan!

Alternative 3: Gift to a life insurance trust. The grandparents set up an irrevocable trust as in alternative 2. However, in this case, the trust uses the $20,000 gifts to purchase a second-to-die life insurance policy. At their age of 55, they are able to buy a $2 million policy. At the death of the second spouse 20 years later, the proceeds are invested for 20 years at 7 percent. Upon the death of the second generation, the grandchildren receive the proceeds. Even better approach!

Table 17–2 contains a synopsis of the three strategies.

As you can see, almost any plan is preferable to keeping the money and having it taxed in successive generations. In many cases, life insurance can be an interesting way to leverage the benefit of using tax breaks such as the annual exclusion, unified credit, and generation skipping transfer exclusion.

VI

ESTATE PLANNING FOR BUSINESS OWNERS

Chapter Eighteen

The Keep-Sell Decision

I f you are a business owner you have many things to consider in planning your estate. Your business may be worth nothing when you die, or it may be worth millions. If you don't plan properly, even a very valuable business can be worth next to nothing by the time it gets dragged through the estate settlement process.

How can this happen? Take the case of Vera, who owned and managed a successful hotel in upstate New York. When she died in 1987, she left the hotel to her husband Ed, a retired advertising executive. He didn't know much about running a hotel, but he decided to give it a try. He even gave their son Joe a job as assistant manager. Joe knew even less about running the hotel. But the two of them struggled on.

Then Ed died, leaving the hotel and property to Joe. The IRS placed a very high value on the establishment, presenting Joe with an estate tax bill for a cool $1 million. After intensive and expensive negotiation, Joe's attorneys and accountants settled with the IRS for $750,000. Joe wanted to keep the hotel, so he borrowed the money to pay the estate taxes. Things went along fine for a few years, but then the economy soured and the hotel business went soft. Joe got squeezed. He had a high fixed overhead, real estate taxes, and the debt to the IRS to pay off, with interest. If he missed payments to the IRS, the revenuers could foreclose. Rather than risk the possibility, he put the hotel up for sale. Sad to say, due to the economy and the fact that he was anxious to sell, Joe didn't get the best price. In fact, he got clobbered. By the time the real estate commissions, legal fees, and remaining IRS debt were paid, Joe was left with very little.

That sad story has been repeated countless times in this country. Only 35 percent of privately held businesses are successfully transferred from one generation to the next. Fewer than 10 percent make it to the third generation. Why? Because business owners are human beings. They don't plan to fail, they fail to plan. So how should a business owner plan his or her estate?

Step one involves making a key decision. In the event of your death, do you want your business to be kept in your family? Do you want to sell as an ongoing enterprise? Or do you want to liquidate?

Before you can answer these questions, you need to consider many factors. First, can the business survive you? Many small enterprises are merely an extension of their owners' unique talents and hard work. In the event that the owner dies, there goes the business. The best a family can hope for in that circumstance is to collect any outstanding receivables, and perhaps a check from a life insurance company, and lock the doors forever.

Our client Fred, a self-employed management consultant, is a good example. He lost his job at a major consulting firm in 1991. Happily, he had a good network of contacts, as well as a great deal of experience and ability. He was able to start his own one-man consulting practice and now earns a very good living. However, if Fred dies there will be no more business. The loss of his personal services and contacts would be irreplaceable. If Fred had groomed an heir to succeed him, the story might be different. Since his children, now 15 and 18, are still young, it could be a long time before they are ready to step into their father's business—assuming they have the talents and inclination to do so. Fred's only choice in preparing for the unlikely event of an untimely death, is to give his executor the power to wind down and liquidate his consulting practice, collecting his receivables, paying any debts, and selling whatever assets the business has.

It is unlikely that the executor would want to go beyond liquidating the business. If he tried to keep it running by entering into new contracts, then he would become personally liable to the family for any losses. So, the only prudent thing to do if Fred were to die is to shut down his management consulting firm.

Many other businesses can survive the death of the owner. Typically, they have a management team that could continue to produce goods or services profitably. While the owner's death might be a serious blow, the new leadership has at least a chance to keep things going. If this is the case for your enterprise, the next question is whether you plan to keep the business for your family or intend your enterprise to be sold after your death.

The remainder of this chapter will deal with helping you answer that question. In Chapter 19, we discuss the planning techniques you should consider if you want your business to be kept in your family. Chapter 20 explains what you need to know if you think your company should be sold.

Let's dream a bit. You have a really nice business. You make a product that fills a steady and profitable niche. You earn a good living. You realize, at this point, that the enterprise has a life and a reputation of its own. Still, you work hard, but frankly you are doing work that someone else could easily learn to do. As you plan ahead, you wonder if it would make sense to keep this business for your family after you are gone. Maybe. But first, you need to answer a few questions.

WHO WILL RUN THE BUSINESS?

Are your children capable of and interested in managing your operation? It is surprising how often we meet the owners of very successful companies whose children simply are not interested in the family business. It is also sad how often we see children who might be interested but simply aren't capable or were never given the opportunity by their parents. Obviously, you need to do some honest soul-searching on this one. A talk with your kids wouldn't hurt either. If one or more of them shows an interest, the sooner you start grooming them the better. If your children are not capable or are too young, you may have nonfamily management who can run the business. In this case you have to consider whether or not the business can pay management enough to keep the managers interested in doing a good job and still be profitable enough to be a good investment for your family. Bear in mind that the business is likely to be somewhat less profitable for at least a while after your death. Other problems arise from human nature. Will your management team resent doing all the work, only to see your family get all the profits? Will children who do come into the business have conflicts with the children who don't?

If you cannot satisfactorily answer the questions regarding the management of your business after your death, you probably should not consider keeping the firm in the family. Even if you have a management team in place, your estate would still have the IRS to contend with.

HOW WILL THE IRS VALUE YOUR COMPANY?

What is your business worth? That depends on who's asking. If you own AT&T stock, you can look up its price in the daily paper. The value of your company obviously cannot be fixed so precisely. The one thing you can count on is that the IRS will attempt to place as high a value as possible on your firm. Even if you are leaving it to your spouse, thus deferring estate taxes because of the marital deduction, the value will determine the taxes when they come due at your spouse's death. In our next chapter, we will go over some ways you can make sure your family will not owe taxes on an IRS-inflated value.

HOW WILL THE TAXES BE PAID?

If you have a successful company that you want kept for your family, you need to face the fact that estate taxes will ultimately have to be paid. As we saw at the beginning of this chapter, these taxes can force a family out of an otherwise good business. In the next chapter, we'll review the potential sources of estate-tax payments. If none is feasible, your family may not be able to retain your business.

WHAT ABOUT YOUR HEIRS WHO ARE NOT IN THE BUSINESS?

In some cases, everything else in the estate has to be sold to raise the money to pay the taxes on the business. If that happens, how do you provide for the inheritance to your children who are not involved in the enterprise? If they become shareholders, would that be fair to those of your children who are working for the business? On the other hand, is it fair for them to get nothing? This is a common problem, and one we'll address at length in our next chapter.

IS THIS REALLY AN APPROPRIATE INVESTMENT FOR MY FAMILY?

Business owners have a lot invested in their companies, both financially and emotionally. However, it is important to take a clear-headed look at whether or not it makes sense for the family to retain it. If the family sold your business and invested the proceeds, would they be better off? How much risk is there in keeping the company compared to owning a quality portfolio of diversified financial investments? Can the business pay them enough to compensate them for the added risk? This is another tough question. However, it is much better if you answer it during your lifetime, rather than forcing your grieving heirs to deal with the problem after your death.

THE SELL DECISION

After mulling over these issues, you may be almost convinced that your heirs should sell your business at your death. Again, a series of questions can help you clarify your thoughts.

TO WHOM?

Unlike owning stocks or bonds, your family can't easily call a broker and instantly sell your company. Finding someone who has the interest, the ability, and the money to buy your business may not be an easy matter. All three are crucial. The need for the interest and the money are obvious. The need for the ability is due to the fact that, chances are, the deal will not be entirely for cash. Typically, your family will have to lend some of the money to the buyer. If the buyer fails in the business and defaults on the note, the family may be stuck. So where do you find a qualified buyer?

If you have a partner or partners, the answer is obvious. If you don't, then you may consider existing key employees, competitors, or even business brokers. If no one is apparent, it may make more sense to sell the business while you are still alive. You will almost certainly be able to negotiate a higher price during your lifetime than your estate could after your death.

For What Price?

Again, the value of your business depends on who is asking. Assuming you have identified a buyer, you must establish a price. This is done according to the terms of a buy-sell agreement, which you must investigate. We discuss business valuation and buy-sell agreements in Chapter 20.

Is It Enough?

Just like anyone else, you need to consider whether the proceeds of the sale, plus your other resources, will be adequate to provide for your family. Chapter 5 on assessing your needs covers this topic. As a business owner, however, you have the advantage of being able to use the business to help provide for your family's needs in this area.

Keep. Sell. Liquidate. There is one other choice. Do nothing. All too often, doing nothing results in the liquidation of a business for pennies on the dollar. Even if a liquidation is the only choice, a planned liquidation is far better than a forced one. If you know the business will not survive you, you can certainly use it to help you buy enough life insurance to take care of your family. You can also use the business to set up your own retirement plan so you will have something to live on after you close up shop. But none of this will happen without planning.

Chapter Nineteen

Keeping Your Business in the Family

I t's not easy to keep a successful business in the family after your death, disability, or retirement. In fact, it's an incredible challenge. Every place you turn, you will find obstacles. The roadblocks may be placed by your customers, your suppliers, the banks, the IRS, even your employees and members of your own family. So why would you want to bother? Our clients who have decided to structure "keep" plans give two main reasons. First, they have worked hard to build their businesses. Their companies have grown into prosperous enterprises, and they view continued family involvement in the business as the best means of providing for their long-term financial well being. That's a tangible benefit. Second and less tangible, but just as meaningful, is the natural desire to leave a legacy.

A businessperson who passes the reins over to the next generation gains a measure of immortality. The continued prosperity of the founder's company and family serves as a lasting tribute to her or his hard work and determination to succeed.

But first, there are obstacles to be overcome. Successor management must be groomed. Will the new management have the experience and strength to deal with the inevitable changes to come? Family discord must be anticipated and planned for. Many an enterprise has been scuttled by family members competing for control of the founder's business. Moreover, the world changes and the family must be able to cope with the changes. Finally, the tax collector must be paid.

Whether the business is sold to the next generation, gifted during lifetime, or bequeathed at death, Uncle Sam will want something. Depending on the value of the company, the tax bill is often enough to cripple the company.

If you are to realize your dream of keeping the enterprise in the family, you must first address the issue of successor management. Here's how things should work.

THE "NEXT-GENERATION" MANAGER

Ken Brooks started Brooks Auto Parts Company in his garage 40 years ago. The business has grown to the point where it now boasts three warehouses and employs more than 50 people. Ken's firm grossed more than $6 million in sales last year, and the numbers are growing. Ken is now in his 60s and though he's still in good health, he's ready to slow down a bit. He probably will never retire completely, however. Most likely he will "work until they carry me out of here," as he insists.

Ken and his wife Sylvia have raised two children. Ralph, 27, just graduated from medical school and is studying to be an orthopedic surgeon. Jane, 34, finished business school 10 years ago. Her first job was with General Motors, where she was involved in the production and procurement of car parts.

Five years ago, Jane joined her dad's company. Her corporate experience was invaluable, and she was able to show Ken how to streamline his operation to become more efficient and profitable. Over the years Jane has developed a good relationship with the company's customers, suppliers, and bankers. It took a little longer for some of the older employees to accept her. They had been comfortable working with Ken, and they felt put out at having to deal with "the boss's daughter." With time, though, and with her father's support, Jane was able to win their respect as a capable person in her own right. When the time came for Ken to do his estate planning, he was confident that Jane would be able to manage the company successfully after he was gone.

Sounds great, doesn't it? Almost like a fairy tale come true. The truth is, it can happen that way, but first, you need a candidate like Jane, someone who is committed, capable, and ready to step into management. Second, you need to make a conscious effort to expose your heir apparent to all the vital aspects of your business.

A successor needs to learn to deal with both the headaches and the opportunities. A "next-generation manager" also needs to work harmoniously with your employees, without whose support and confidence an orderly transition may be impossible.

THE KEY PERSON

What if your situation isn't quite so ideal? Maybe your children are too young, too inexperienced, too immature, or just plain not interested. In that case you need to plan for nonfamily management. Now a whole new set of problems emerges. The foremost is finding and keeping the talent. Anyone good enough to run your company—with the profits going to your family—probably is good enough to run her or his own company with the profits going to her or his family. True, the key person may not have the capital to start a business today. But if the ability and ambition exist, chances are that person will one day find a way to start something. Meanwhile, you may be providing the schooling.

So here we have a Catch-22. The people you would want to run your business will probably one day want to run their own. If you have identified someone who would be suitable, you need to figure out how to keep that person around.

George Baker owns Package X, a company that manufactures cardboard boxes. Like Ken Brooks he has built a successful business over many years. Unfortunately, none of his children is interested in making boxes. His son Dave is a professor of astrophysics at a major university; his daughter, Wilma has a busy law practice specializing in divorce.

Still, George feels the business is worth trying to keep in the family. The corporation has a very good reputation and an extensive and dependable base of customers. The long-term outlook is bright, and the opportunity exists to expand into new markets. George realizes that he needs to find someone who can preserve the value of the enterprise and lead it into the next century.

As luck would have it, George found just the right person several years ago. George hired Jerry Garcia to help him out with his finances. While working for George, Jerry studied nights, eventually passing the exams to qualify as a certified public accountant

(CPA). To George's surprise, Jerry also showed aptitude and interest in the production and sales aspects of the business.

George decided that Jerry could be taught to manage the company. He also realized that he would have to find a way to entice Jerry into staying. One option was money—simply give Jerry a raise. That wouldn't be a long-term solution, however. A bigger company could offer Jerry more money than George could afford to pay. So he would have to find a way to give Jerry a stake in the success of Package X. George decided to let Jerry buy a chunk of the company, giving him very favorable terms. The price was set using commonly accepted valuation methods, and it was all done legally. Let's just say that George and his accountants made sure that Jerry got a good deal. So when Jerry got a bonus, he bought stock. When he had extra money, he bought stock.

He continued to purchase stock until he owned 10 percent of the company. George agreed to sell Jerry up to another 30 percent of his stock at death. To make sure he'd have the money when the time came, Jerry purchased a life insurance policy on George. It guaranteed that he would have sufficient funds to exercise his 30 percent option.

George could rest easy now, knowing that Jerry had a strong stake in staying on in the business after he was gone. He knew too, that the business would stand a good chance of thriving in the future, providing security for his family.

As they say in commercials, this has been a dramatization. Sadly, real life usually doesn't work this way. If your business isn't as stable as Ken's or George's, and if your family isn't as stable either, join the club. If there's no one you trust enough to run your business, you may have to consider selling it or having it sold at your death.

SOWING SEEDS OF CONFLICT

Even so, do you still think you want to keep your company? Here are some other problems. In Ken's case, one of his children, Dr. Ralph, was clearly not interested in the business and was headed toward a career in medicine. His daughter was very interested in the business. If Ken is not careful, seeds of conflict can be sown without anyone realizing it.

In doing his estate planning, Ken learned that he had an estate-tax problem. His car parts company was naturally his single largest asset. If it was to be kept intact for Jane, the estate might have to sell almost all the couple's other assets to pay federal estate taxes. But then, if Jane got the business, what would Ralph receive? True, doctors can earn a lot of money, and Ken paid for Ralph's education. Still, Ken knew his son would feel some resentment if he found that his sister had inherited the multimillion dollar family company while he got nothing.

A number of options are open to Ken. He might, for instance, choose to leave only half the business to Jane and the other half to Ralph. But is that fair? After all, Jane took the risk of leaving a job at GM to come into the family firm; moreover, she is putting in long hours to help make the company successful. Ralph works hard too, but his medical practice does nothing for the family enterprise. Then too, he will eventually be well paid, in all likelihood. Does he really deserve half the profits from Jane's hard work? Suffice it to say, family shareholders who are not active in the business often are at odds with those who are.

Children who pursue other careers tend to look upon the family company as an investment asset. They expect dividends or other benefits to accrue to them as their birthright. Family members involved in day-to-day management of the enterprise may have a different agenda. It is most often to their advantage to reinvest profits in the corporation to help make it grow.

Sometimes family members can work this out. Sometimes they wind up in court. You know your children best. But you can't know how they (or their spouses) will react when presented with this situation.

Thus, business owners often plan for other ways of equalizing their estates. Another possibility for Ken would be to obtain a second-to-die life insurance policy on his life and his wife's. The policy would be held in an irrevocable life insurance trust. At the second death, the policy would pay a tax-free benefit to the trust. The money could be used to help pay estate taxes, freeing up other assets for Ralph.

Must inheritances be equal? Again, there is no definitive answer.

Equal and equitable are not always the same. If Ralph receives assets less than the value of the business that's being passed along to Jane, is that necessarily unfair? Ralph's inheritance can be in cash, which he can invest any way he likes—with little or no risk, if that's what he chooses. Jane has to work 16-hour days to keep the family company moving ahead, and there's always the risk that the value of the firm will decline or evaporate as a result of factors beyond her control.

This is one time when the wisdom of Solomon would come in handy. In planning your own estate you need to decide what is fair to your children who decide to be active in the business as well as to those who are not.

POWER HUNGRY

Another pitfall is a rivalry between two or more of your children who are interested in one day taking control of the family business. Some siblings are good at sharing power, some aren't. Situations tend to become more complicated when your children marry. Jealousy and resentment can grow among brothers, sisters, and spouses. Add money and the quest for control of a substantial company, and you have a roiling caldron of emotions—the ingredients for the mother of all family feuds. What can you do about it? If you think the situation is hopeless, see Chapter 20; you can fix those kids of yours by selling your business. On the other hand, you can help avoid these problems by being open and precise in your planning.

If one sibling is the obvious heir apparent, you need to make it clear that it is your wish. It may be best to disassociate your other children from the business and provide for them separately in your estate. If that is not practical, then you need to do all you can to help your children resolve their differences. We're not talking about legal agreements or insurance policies at this stage. No attorney, CPA, insurance agent, or financial planner can take the place of you as a parent and founder of your company. You must sit down with your family and talk through the issues.

If the children can be taught to act as equal partners, that's fine. Perhaps one is good at finance, another at sales and marketing. If you can help them find their respective niches, things may work out. On the other hand, if all of them want to be Number 1, you have a problem. You can let them fight it out and hope for the best. You can fire the bunch of them and hire new management. Or you can sell the company. Once again, we come back to planning. While you are still vigorous, exert your authority over the situation. If you don't exercise that control during your lifetime, you may be leaving a terrible mess behind when you die.

THE TAX COLLECTOR COMETH

You still want to keep your business? Fine, but now you must deal with the tax collector. How much tax you pay will depend on two things: what your estate is worth and how you decide to dispose of it.

Baker Auto Parts can serve as a model. Ken and Sylvia have a net estate that totals $5 million. Of that sum, the business comprises $3 million. When Ken and Sylvia are both gone, Uncle Sam and their home state will present the estate with tax bills of roughly $2.5 million. Where will the money to pay the bills come from? Even if their children, Jane and Ralph, sell everything the Bakers own except for the company, they will be $500,000 short. And, as we have already mentioned, that would leave no assets to give to Ralph, unless he got a share of the family business, which Jane is managing.

Not only that, but selling the property can be expensive. Much of the business property is real estate and other illiquid investments. Of course, Uncle Sam doesn't care how inconvenient it is for your estate. Your favorite uncle wants any taxes due to be paid within nine months of your death. Many homes and other pieces of property have been sold at heartbreaking prices by estates desperate to raise cash. (In fact, if you want to make a smart purchase, watch for an estate sale the next time you are looking for a house).

Even if the sale goes well, Ken's estate is still $500,000 short. Jane could try to sell a minority interest in the business. Minority interests in small companies are not hot items in the marketplace, however. Or, she could try to borrow the money. A bank may or may not agree to a loan, though. What if money is tight just at the time Jane and Ralph need to borrow? Or what if Brooks Auto Parts has already taken on substantial debt for expansion? If the bank does agree, it will certainly make it harder for the company to borrow money for routine business uses. And if Brooks Auto Parks experiences cash flow problems, that $500,000 debt to pay taxes, plus restrictions on further borrowing, could imperil a fine company.

UNCLE SAM, YOUR FRIENDLY LENDER?

There is another option: You may be able to borrow the tax money from the federal government. Section 6166 of the Internal Revenue Code provides for deferred payment of the federal estate tax under certain circumstances.

To qualify, a business must comprise at least 35 percent of a person's adjusted gross estate. If you own more than one company, they can be lumped together as long as you own at least 20 percent of each one.

The amount of tax that can be deferred is only that amount attributed to the business itself, minus the unified credit. For example, if the adjusted gross estate equals $4 million and the value of the business equals $2 million, this estate would qualify for Section 6166 deferral because the business is more than 35 percent of the adjusted gross estate.

Total federal tax due	
Federal tax due on $4,000,000	$1,775,800
Minus owner's unified credit	192,800
Net tax obligation	1,583,000
Amount attributable to business	
Federal tax due on $2,000,000	$780,800
Minus unified credit	192,800
Amount to be deferred	588,000
Balance due within nine months of death	
Total federal tax	$1,583,000
Amount qualifying for deferral	588,000
Balance due	995,000

In addition, there may well be state death taxes, legal fees, and other estate settlement costs.

As you can see, Section 6166 deferral is not a total answer for most estates. Even the amount eligible to be deferred carries problems. The debt can be carried for four years at interest-only; then it must be paid over the next 10 years. By law, the interest rate on the first $153,000 that is tax deferred is 4 percent. However, the remainder is carried at the IRS's regular rate for deficiencies, which can be pretty high (as you know if you've ever owed the IRS money).

While it has some appeal, Section 6166 is one of those things that people often talk about, but seldom do. There are just too many drawbacks. The loan has to be paid back. Where does the estate get the money? If it comes from the business, will that cause a terrible drain on the company's cash flow for many years? This is especially dangerous in the days and years immediately after the death of the head honcho. Furthermore, the IRS has a lien on the business until all the money is paid back with interest. That makes it harder for the company to borrow money for other purposes.

Perhaps the most frightening aspect of Section 6166 is the IRS's right to call the note if the heirs fall behind in their payments or if the heirs sell more than 50 percent of their interest. This almost always results in a forced sale of the company, and no matter how little the business is sold for, the remaining principal of the note is still due to the IRS. The tax collectors really don't care how much the business dropped in value following the original owner's death.

THE INSURANCE OPTION

For all these reasons, most of our clients look to other techniques to fund their estate-tax liabilities. Other than selling assets, the only viable option is to purchase life insurance. Billions of dollars of coverage are being sold these days for the purpose of funding the estate tax. The most common scenario involves the so-called second-to-die policy, with both husband and wife being insured. That's because if one spouse dies, all assets can be left to the surviving estate-tax free. Of course, that causes other problems, but that's another chapter.

It is not unusual to see such insurance policies written when the insureds are in their 60s, 70s, or even 80s. The premiums are quite low compared to the cost of insurance on either the husband's or wife's life alone. Furthermore, coverage frequently can be obtained even when one of the spouses is in poor health.

Yes, the insurance does cost money. But with a policy owned by an irrevocable life insurance trust, the tax-free death benefit can provide the dollars needed to pay estate taxes and keep the business alive.

"But, wait a minute," you say. "Aren't there other ways to transfer my business or otherwise reduce my estate taxes?" Sure there are, and we'll review them. But often a tax liability will remain, and it needs to be planned for.

SOME OTHER TACTICS

A key objective for a business owner planning his estate is to make sure that the estate-tax obligation is kept as low as possible. Using both a marital bypass trust and an irrevocable life insurance trust is as vital to a business owner as to anyone else. You should also examine ways to get control over the growth of the business. A successful company tends to increase in value year after year and so, consequently, does the estate-tax burden. Ultimately the tax liability may become so large that it's impossible to pay, with or without insurance.

Gifting

One obvious strategy is gifting, which we covered in Chapter 16. You will recall that you can give up to $10,000 to any person each year. If your spouse joins with you in giving the gift, the limit is $20,000. There is no reason you can't make a gift of stock in your business. Just be careful not to underestimate the value too drastically. The IRS would be very upset to learn that you gave away stock worth $1 million yet only declared a value of $10,000.

Now, $20,000 per year may be only a drop in the bucket. If your business is large and growing, such a sum seems almost a pittance. Still, it's a start, and it will at least help hold down the growth. If you have children who are not involved in the business, consider giving them something other than stock. As we mentioned, things

can get messy when children not active in the business own significant portions of company stock.

Beyond the $10,000 or $20,000 annual gift limitation, you can
also use your lifetime unified credit amount and give away up to
$600,000 worth of corporate stock to your heirs. Again your spouse
can join, bringing the total to $1.2 million. Bear in mind that the
original value of this gift comes back into your estate at death.
What you have gained is that the growth on the value of the stock
you gave away occurs outside of the estate, which can be very
useful if the company is rapidly increasing in value.

To make these gifts, you will have to value your business. Techniques for doing this are discussed in Chapter 20. One consequence
of gifting more than the $10,000 or $20,000 annual exclusion is that
the IRS will have a chance to accept or challenge your valuation.
Obviously, that can be good or bad. If done properly, a gifting
program can help peg a value for the business that will hold up
later on when it is time to settle the estate.

We should mention that most of our clients don't do this. It's
not that they don't love their kids or don't trust them. They just
don't want to give their business away while they are alive. Typically, they have too much invested, both emotionally and financially, to give it up so meekly. Another problem is that some states
will impose local gift taxes without regard to the Federal Unified
Credit.

Some of our clients have resisted gifting because they are concerned about giving up their security; others worry about the consequences of giving their children something for nothing. For a
few of these clients, selling all or part of the business to their
children is a possible alternative.

Selling in Installments

The estate tax benefits of an installment sale are often overlooked.
If our client Chuck sells his business to his son Eric, for example
for $1 million, to be paid in 10 equal installments of $100,000 plus
interest, Chuck's interest in the business is frozen at the value of
the note. If the business appreciates from then on, all that growth
escapes estate taxation. Furthermore, Chuck gets favorable capital
gains tax treatment, paying taxes spread out over the 10-year pay-

out. As with gifting, the IRS will be checking to see that the business is being fairly valued.

There are limitations. Eric has to be able to generate enough cash from the business to support himself and pay his father back. At 9 percent, this comes to more than $155,000 per year. If he falls behind, what does his father do? As you can see, it won't work in all situations.

An attractive variation is the use of what's called a private annuity. Though seldom used, it can be a terrific way to transfer the business given the right situation. Rather than receiving cash, Chuck gets Eric's promise to make fixed payments to him for the rest of his life. In other words, the seller gets the guarantee of an annuity from the purchaser. So in return for his $1 million business, Chuck would get payments of roughly $130,000 per year for the rest of his life. They cease at death, even if that is after only one payment. This amount is determined using Chuck's age (which is 65) and current IRS tables, which factor in prevailing life expectancy and interest rate assumptions.

As in an installment sale, a private annuity gets the stock, as well as future growth in its value, out of Chuck's estate. In addition, tax on the gain in the stock's value is prorated over Chuck's life expectancy. Chuck will also owe tax on the interest portion of each payment, obtained from IRS tables.

All this works out nicely for Chuck, and Eric may make out okay too, especially if Chuck doesn't live for long. For this reason Chuck needs to make sure there are enough other assets to take care of his wife if he dies early and the payments stop. On the other hand, if Chuck lives a long time, Eric is stuck making the payments, which can add up to more than it would have cost to buy the business using an installment sale. As with an installment sale, a private annuity requires that Eric have sufficient cash flow to make the payments. Of course, nothing would prevent Chuck and his wife from giving Eric back $20,000 per year tax free to help ease the burden.

The ESOP

Another method, available to larger businesses (those with at least $10 million in sales), is the employee stock ownership plan (ESOP). An ESOP entails selling a portion of your business (at least 35 percent) to a special retirement plan set up for your employees. You first set up a form of profit sharing for the employees. Then you sell your stock to this ESOP. The ESOP borrows money from a bank to buy your stock. Each year your company contributes money to the ESOP so it can pay back the loan. Your employees become part-owners of the company through the retirement plan. As trustee of the plan, you can still vote the stock.

The benefit to you is that you get cash for your stock. You won't even owe capital gains tax if you invest the sale proceeds in what are called *qualified domestic securities*, basically the stocks and/or bonds of U.S. corporations. This increases the liquidity of your estate, a big advantage. It also removes from your estate the growth in the value of the stock. Best of all, you can retain control of your company and pass it along to your heirs. ESOPs are expensive to set up and maintain. They require that a professional valuation of your business be made each year, since stock in the company is now a retirement plan asset. Furthermore, the company must make ongoing contributions of cash to the ESOP so it can pay back the bank. On the other hand, many companies report gains in employee morale and productivity when workers have a stake in the firm through an ESOP. In the right situation it can be a valuable planning tool.

Many other planning techniques have been eliminated by changes in the law. For example, such methods as preferred stock recapitalizations and other "estate freeze" techniques are now gone. Congress and the IRS are not making it easier for you to keep your business in the family. Never mind that family businesses employ a *huge* percentage of the work force. We could debate the merits of our government's fiscal needs and social agenda. But we won't. Like it or not, it's the system.

Fortunately, there are steps you can take to protect yourself, your family, and your business. It will take a well-thought-out plan, involving your financial planner, your insurance agent, your accountant, and your attorney. Using the techniques discussed here, you can keep your business in the family, despite the tax policies that our leaders have given us.

Chapter Twenty

Cashing in Your Chips: Planning for the Sale of Your Business

T he sale of your business may be your most practical choice. Let's examine some of the most common issues.

YOU HAVE A PARTNER OR PARTNERS IN THE BUSINESS

In most cases, two or more partners in a business have compatible objectives in running the enterprise. Over the years they become comfortable working together, and they learn how to draw upon each other's unique talents to make the company go. What differences they may have get ironed out in ways that are unique to each company. This give and take is vital to the ongoing success of the firm. When the harmony breaks down, very often the business fails. It should come as no surprise then, that the last thing the partners want is for outsiders to become involved.

The term *outsider* describes anyone not currently involved in the ownership and management of the company, including the partners' families.

YOU HAVE A PROFESSIONAL PRACTICE OR A SPECIALIZED SKILL

If you are a doctor, lawyer, CPA, engineer, or other licensed professional, it may not be possible or practical to keep your business in the family. Naturally, if your spouse is a professional with similar credentials, that is an exception. Likewise, if your children have followed in your footsteps, you may wish to bring them into your operation with the intent of having them eventually take over.

In most cases, however, you will want to sell out to your partners, if you have any, or to outsiders. This also applies to a non-professional business driven by the unique talents or abilities of the owner. If the owner's family does not possess the same skills and desire needed to work the business, then selling may be the only option.

Even when the possibility of bringing the next generation into the business exists, you must consider the prudence of such a move. Most companies are like people: They have a natural life span. As conditions change, once-dynamic enterprises can falter. Some businesses adapt and continue to prosper; others fall by the wayside. This risk must be taken into account. You should ask yourself, "Where is my business today? Will my family be able to deal with the loss of my leadership and continue to compete in the years ahead? What changes and problems are on the horizon? Is the potential reward worth the risk?" In many cases the answers, sadly, are no. If that's your conclusion, selling may be the best solution.

CASHING OUT

Businesses with more than one owner present special challenges. They can be partners—co-owners of unincorporated businesses—or co-shareholders—co-owners of corporations. However, co-shareholders in privately held companies think of themselves as partners, act like partners, and look, smell, and feel like partners. So, we'll call them partners, too.

The cornerstone of estate planning for partners in a business is what's called the buy-sell agreement. A written contract between the partners, it stipulates what will happen to their respective interests if one of them should die, become disabled, or want to leave the business.

The buy-sell agreement is vital for several reasons. First and foremost, it addresses the need to preserve the harmony between the owners of the company. Let's look at an example of what can happen when one of the partners dies. Joe and Bill ran a highly successful painting company in New York's Westchester county. Childhood friends, they decided to start the business after graduating from high school. They began by painting the houses of friends and neighbors, worked hard, and gained a good reputation.

In the mid–1970s, their business really took off. Westchester County experienced a boom in both residential and commercial construction. Joe and Bill hired more people, bought trucks and equipment, even purchased a building so they could keep up with the demand. More and more of their time was consumed managing the firm. Joe became adept at bidding on jobs and hobnobbing with the real estate developers who brought them work. Bill supervised the workers, bought the supplies, and kept track of the work schedule.

Joe and Bill were in their early 30s and highly successful. Planning for death was the last thing on their minds. Both were married and had young children. The two families were friendly and often socialized together. Then, on a rainy night in November 1984, disaster struck. Joe was driving back from a meeting of local real estate developers when his car was hit head-on by a drunk driver. Joe's seat belt was not enough to save his life—though the drunk driver wobbled away from the accident.

The tragedy of Joe's death is obvious. A young man's life was cut short, leaving a widow and two small children. But because Joe was a business owner and because he and his partner had done no planning, the tragedy became worse.

While both Joe and Bill were alive, their business thrived. Both men gave everything they had to the enterprise. They agreed on how much of the profits should be plowed back into the operation and how much they could prudently draw out. The company was dependent on each partner's unique contributions. Now, everything was changed. Joe had little life insurance. He felt that his business was, in effect, his life insurance policy. So when Joe died, his widow naturally looked toward the business for security for her family.

Things had changed. Bill became a partner with Joe's widow. However, she had absolutely no experience in doing the things Joe did. In fact, between raising the children and working at her own part-time job, she had very little time and energy left to contribute to the painting business. Bill now faced a dilemma. First of all, somebody had to do Joe's work. Bill was a great production guy. But frankly, schmoozing with customers was not his forte. Until Bill could find somebody to replace Joe, he would have to struggle along the best he could. Meanwhile, Joe's widow was in need of cash from the business. So here's Bill, working harder to make up for Joe's loss, fearful of a drop in revenue, and in need of cash to hire a replacement for Joe.

To make matters worse, by the mid-1980s business started to get soft. New construction slowed, and bidding on the remaining jobs became much more competitive. Bill was unable to find a workable replacement for Joe. After several costly attempts, Bill became resigned to doing everything himself. As business fell, profits did too. Joe and Bill had always been loyal to their employees, and Bill was reluctant to lay any workers off. Finally, he approached Joe's widow with the hard facts. Times were tough, and he would have to cut back on the monthly payment he was making to her.

Joe's widow was furious. She demanded that her income continue unabated. Bill tried to explain that it was necessary to conserve cash to allow the business to survive the slowdown intact. This was in direct conflict with Joe's family's need for cash. The relationship quickly deteriorated, and both sides hired attorneys. Because Joe's widow was a 50 percent shareholder, she could effectively block any management decision Bill wished to make. Neither party had firm control. In exasperation, Bill offered to buy Joe's family's share of the firm for what he felt was a reasonable price based on current profits. Joe's widow refused. She felt the business was worth far more. The standoff continued for several years, with lawsuits filed by both sides.

While the personal situation was deteriorating, so was the business. By 1990 the recession had a firm hold on the Northeast, including once-booming Westchester County. New construction virtually stopped. Bill was distracted from his business by the conflicts with Joe's family.

He was finally forced to lay off workers and sell equipment. By early 1991 he gave up and the business was liquidated. Bill and Joe's widow divided a mere fraction of what the company had once been worth. Bill took a job as an employee of a larger painting company, and Joe's widow returned to work full-time, leaving her children to fend for themselves after school.

It didn't have to end that way. A properly designed and funded buy-sell agreement would have left Bill in full control of the painting company, and it would have provided Joe's family with enough money to compensate them for the true worth of Joe's investment and hard work.

WRITING A BUY-SELL AGREEMENT

An agreement, first of all, must be in writing. It should be drafted by an attorney familiar with business law. It should contain a valuation clause. Fair value is, of course, critical. If an agreement is "arm's length," meaning it represents a price that would be agreed upon by a willing buyer and a willing seller, then it will be binding upon both the partners and their estates. The price specified in the agreement should be the same whether a sale is made at death or during the lifetime of the owners. This makes the price binding upon the IRS as well. If you don't make an arm's length evaluation, the IRS could later claim a higher value for the business than the agreement calls for, which would create a potential tax liability. The IRS could argue that the difference between the real value of the business and the sale price was a gift, with the selling party responsible for any gift tax.

The valuation issue is also crucial in other terms. Sometimes partners attempt to underrate the value of the business because they want to avoid taxes or to avoid having to burden each other and the business with the cost of funding the buyout. We generally do not recommend such underestimating. In attempting to dissuade our clients, we ask them several simple questions. Say your interest in the business was truly worth $500,000. How would you feel knowing that your partner bought your family out for, say, $300,000? How do you think your family would feel?

Businesses can be valued in several different ways. Choosing the proper one depends on the type of business. It often makes sense to use a formula that takes into account changing profit and business conditions. A stated price may be fair when it is agreed upon. However, all too often, business owners neglect to update their agreements, and the stated price no longer reflects the business's worth. The agreement remains binding, however, which could be unfair to one of the parties depending on whether the value has gone up or down. A formula approach to pegging the value can avoid this problem.

CHOOSING THE TYPE OF AGREEMENT

Once you've decided on the need for an agreement and the correct way to value your company, you must decide on how the agreement should work.

There are two basic types of agreements. The simplest and most common is called a stock redemption agreement, which applies to corporations. In the case of partnerships it's called an entity purchase agreement.

This type of agreement is between the individual owners and the corporation or partnership. We illustrate the agreement in Figure 20–1. The agreement stipulates the price to be paid upon the death of a partner. The price is also used if a partner wants to sell out during his or her lifetime. Before offering the stock or partnership interest to an outsider, he or she must offer the ownership interest back to the corporation or partnership entity at the same price, which is called a right of first refusal. If the business is unwilling or unable to exercise its option to buy within a stated period of time (often 60 days) the existing partner is free to offer the interest to someone else.

Upon the death of the partner, the agreement becomes binding. The corporation or partnership must buy back the deceased partner's interest, and the deceased partner's estate must sell that interest for the agreed-upon price.

CROSS-PURCHASE AGREEMENT

In some situations, a different type of agreement can make sense. A cross-purchase agreement exists only between the partners themselves and does not involve the corporation or partnership directly. A cross-purchase agreement is illustrated in Figure 20–2.

FIGURE 20-1

The Stock Redemption Agreement (Entity Purchase for Partnerships)

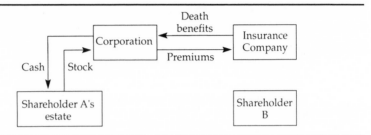

1. A dies.

2. Insurance company pays death benefit to corporation.

3. A's estate sells stock to corporation (if insurance is not used, corporation uses cash and notes for purchase). A's stock is retired by the corporation.

4. Shareholder B is now 100% owner of the remaining oustanding stock.

Note: This transaction would be similar for an unincorporated partnership. It would be called an entity purchase arrangement instead of a stock redemption. The end results would be similar.

FIGURE 20-2

The Cross Purchase Agreement

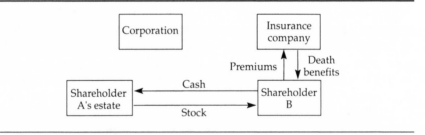

1. A dies.

2. Insurance company pays the benefits to B.

3. B uses proceeds to buy stock from A's estate. (Again, if insurance is not used, cash and notes are used for purchase.)

4. B now owns A's shares, with 100% control of the business. B's basis in A's shares is equal to the full amount paid for them at A's death.

Take an example of two partners, April and Beth. If April dies, Beth buys her stock from April's estate. By contrast, with a stock redemption or entity purchase agreement, the corporation or partnership buys the deceased's interest. What's the difference? First, there is the question of liability. If a corporation fails to perform under a stock redemption agreement, the deceased's estate can sue the corporation, but not the other shareholders. If the surviving shareholders decide to walk away and close the business, the deceased shareholder's family—along with the other creditors—may be left with nothing. In a cross-purchase, the individual shareholders are liable personally to perform under the terms of the agreement. Thus, there is more incentive for the agreement to be honored.

There is also an income tax incentive for a surviving partner or shareholder to elect a cross-purchase agreement. If a C corporation (tax-paying) redeems the stock of a deceased shareholder, there is no increase in the cost basis of the stock for the surviving shareholders. If they later decide to sell the company to someone else, their capital gains taxes will be much higher than if they had chosen to use a cross-purchase agreement. Under a cross-purchase agreement the surviving shareholders buy the stock, so that purchase price does add to their cost basis. This would result in a lower capital gains tax upon their selling the business. For example, let's get back to April and Beth. When they started the business, they each scraped together $1,000 to get started. This became their cost basis in the company. By the time April passed away, the company had grown to a total value of $200,000. If Beth and April had signed a stock redemption agreement, their corporation would have purchased April's stock for $100,000. If Beth later gets a great offer and decides to sell the business for that same $200,000, she will be in for a rude surprise. The $100,000 the corporation paid for April's stock did nothing to raise Beth's original basis of $1,000 in her stock. When she sells the company for $200,000 she will owe a capital gains tax on $199,000. Depending on what state she lives in, that could come to well over $60,000!

By choosing a cross-purchase instead, Beth will obtain a far more favorable result. By purchasing April's stock herself, Beth is increasing her basis in the company's stock by the full amount she paid for it, in this case $100,000. So when she sells the company for $200,000 she will owe capital gains tax only on the excess over her new basis of $101,000. Thus her taxable gain is reduced to $99,000. You don't have to be a Wharton grad to figure out that Beth will save almost $30,000 in taxes simply because she and April had drawn up the proper type of buy-sell agreement.

So why doesn't everyone use a cross-purchase? There are several reasons. Partnerships and S corporations are taxed differently from C corporations. Properly drafted redemption or entity purchase agreements can provide at least a partial step up in basis for partnerships and S corporations.

A cross-purchase agreement also puts the responsibility for buying the stock on the individual rather than the corporation. As mentioned, this is beneficial to the family of the deceased shareholder. If the surviving shareholder fails to buy the stock, the family has recourse against his or her personal assets. This provides more security than merely being creditors of the corporation, as is the case in a stock redemption.

In a stock redemption, the surviving shareholder could bleed the company and default on the note, and the family would have a claim only against the bankrupt company. This can have the effect of making the cross-purchase agreement somewhat *less* attractive to the shareholders while they are still alive. Businesspeople generally prefer not to make themselves personally liable for anything unless they have no other choice.

Cross-purchase agreements are generally recommended only in cases in which adequate funding is assured to the shareholders. This is usually provided by life insurance policies on each shareholder, which brings up the next drawback of the cross-purchase agreement. If insurance policies are used for funding the agreement, each shareholder or partner must own a policy on the other. That's fine, as long as there are only two shareholders. But what if there are three? In that case you would need a total of six policies. This is because each partner needs two policies, one on each of the other partners. If there are four partners, they will need 12 policies. If there are five partners, there will be 20 policies to be written. As you might imagine, this can rapidly become quite cumbersome.

Some financial planners and accountants recommend that a trust be the owner of just one policy on each life, with each shareholder or partner being a beneficiary of the trust. This approach can work, but it requires careful drafting by an attorney familiar with these agreements.

There is also a new form of life insurance policy on the market designed for multiple life buy-sell situations. It's called a first to die policy. It can cover up to eight lives under one contract and pays a benefit upon the first death. The surviving partners then have the guaranteed right to continue coverage on themselves. The cost of this policy is generally lower than the cost of separate policies on each owner.

TAX IMPLICATIONS

Finally, another issue involves income taxes. In a regular tax-paying corporation (a C corporation), a redemption of stock is made with after-tax dollars. If the corporation is in a lower tax bracket than the shareholders, it will be cheaper to do a redemption than for the individual shareholders to buy the stock personally. In addition, if the purchase is made with cash and a note, the interest is deductible for the corporation. It would not be deductible for an individual.

Furthermore, if life insurance is used to fund the agreement, it is generally preferable to have the corporation pay the premiums, if it is in a lower tax bracket than the individual. Again, the premiums are after-tax dollars, so we want to use the cheapest dollars available. In a stock redemption agreement, the corporation owns the policy and is the beneficiary. It should be noted that while life insurance is generally income tax free, if it's owned by a corporation it may be subject to the corporate alternative minimum tax.

In a cross-purchase, each shareholder owns and is the beneficiary of a policy on the other shareholders. In contrast to the stock redemption agreement, the proceeds would be totally income tax free to the beneficiaries.

There is a method of insurance ownership called split-dollar that allows cheaper corporate dollars to be used for payment of most of the premiums. This removes one of the drawbacks to cross-purchase arrangements.

Partnerships and S corporations do not have tax rates separate from those of their owners, so it makes no difference from an ordinary income tax standpoint whether a redemption or cross-purchase is used.

As you can see, choosing the right type of agreement is a complex decision, requiring input from a full planning team, including a financial planner, attorney, CPA, and insurance agent. You can sometimes take a wait-and-see approach and draft an agreement that gives shareholders the first option to buy out a deceased partner's share. As with a cross-purchase, the shareholders are the owners of the life insurance. If for any reason it is not advantageous for the surviving shareholder or partner to buy the stock, the corporation will then redeem it. The surviving shareholder or partner simply lends the insurance proceeds to the company to fund the buyout.

THE RISK OF DISABILITY

When thinking about buy-sell agreements, don't forget about the risks of disability, which can be up to four times greater than the risk of death prior to age 65. Disability can be just as devastating to a business. For this reason, business owners should deal with the possibility in their agreement. Generally speaking, the buyout would not be triggered for one to two years following the onset of a disability; a stricken partner needs time to recover before being forced to sell out. Insurance policies are available to provide funding for buyouts in the event of disability. They should be considered along with life insurance when you are doing your planning.

Do you really need insurance—whether life or disability—for your buy-sell agreement? No law says that you do, but you may be better off having it. The corporation has just lost a key player to either illness or death. Credit may be tight, sales may be off, and a replacement could be expensive. Banks and suppliers may balk at extending credit to a company that is known to be paying off a big debt to the family of a deceased owner. Usually, it is far more prudent to pay relatively small premiums today, when all partners are alive, well, and productive, than to pay large settlements when one or more partners aren't. In some cases the health of the partners precludes the purchase of more insurance. In that case, an installment payout may be the only option. This makes it all the more vital to insure the healthy partners. Nothing would be worse than a healthy partner dying during the payout phase following the death of an uninsurable partner.

The insurance protects not only the business, but also the families as well. As we mentioned earlier, if a business fails during the installment payout phase, the family may be stuck. Insurance provides the tax-free dollars to honor this obligation, removing the risk to the family of the deceased partner.

SELLING TO OUTSIDERS

What if you have no partner? To whom can you turn to buy your business?

A Key Employee

Perhaps there is a candidate right under your nose. An employee who has shown unusual ambition, loyalty, and ability may be a possible choice. Or there may be a small group of employees that could buy you out. If so, a so-called one-way buy-sell agreement could be crafted to give key employees the right to buy your company at a predetermined price upon your death. Obviously, don't enter into such an agreement lightly. Can your key employees really do the job needed to make the business run? Where would they get the money to buy you out? If they use an installment purchase note and default, your family is left high and dry. For this reason, it would make sense for the buyer or buyers to have a life insurance policy that will provide them with the money when needed. But can they afford the premiums? Perhaps you can help pay the premium, but if you do you are, in effect, giving them the money to buy you out. As unduly generous as that may seem, it can make sense. It helps provide your family with security and a ready, willing, and able buyer for your business. It also helps ensure that your business will live on after you are gone. This may be an intangible benefit, but for many hardworking business owners it has great meaning.

Selling to All of Your Employees

We mentioned the use of ESOPs (employee stock ownership plans) in our previous chapter. The ESOP is a strategy to help keep the business in the family. The same technique can be used by your estate to sell your entire interest. It is far more difficult to accomplish such a sale if the ESOP were not in existence before your death. The red tape and delays of setting up an ESOP, along with the fact that there are plenty of other problems for the estate to deal with, make postmortem ESOPs impractical, unless your business is very large and has competent successor management in place.

Otherwise it is unlikely that the banks or your employees would go along with such a proposal. On the other hand, if an ESOP has already been established and is funded by at least the minimum of 35 percent of your interest in the business, your estate may well be able to raise more cash by selling the balance of your stock to the ESOP.

Going Public

If your business is big, over $30 million in sales, for example, you may consider going public. Investment banking firms specialize in selling stock in new companies. An initial public offering is expensive and time-consuming, but potentially very rewarding. A qualified CPA should be able to tell you whether this is an option. If it is, you may be able to structure an offering that leaves you and your family in control, or one that transfers control to a new management team. Thus, it can play a role in both ''keep'' and ''sell'' strategies.

Competitors and Suppliers

If you belong to an industry association or to the Rotary, Chamber of Commerce, or another business organization, chances are you know other business owners who have operations compatible with yours. There is no reason that you cannot discuss the possibility of a merger in the event one of you dies or becomes disabled. This type of agreement is rare, but it is worth considering if no other candidates are in sight.

A business similar to yours may be right across town. You each have your own customer base and have gotten to know each other over the years. Both of you are concerned about what will happen to your businesses if you die or become disabled. On the other hand, you don't want or need to join forces now. It's at least worth discussing the possibility of forming an agreement to buy each other out upon the death or disability of one of you.

Business Brokers and Venture Capitalists

A number of firms specialize in helping business owners find buyers for their companies. Of course, they receive a commission if they are successful, which is paid by the seller. The price that a broker may help you get for your enterprise may be higher than you can get on your own, but there is no guarantee of that. A lot will depend on what demand there is for your operation.

It will also depend greatly on the current management of your business. If you are dead and the business is in shambles, your family will be lucky to get any more than rock bottom liquidation value. On the other hand, if you died leaving a strong management team and perhaps a little life insurance payable to the company to help keep things going, your family could hang on for a much more favorable price.

PLANNED LIQUIDATION

Some businesses are simply not transferable. Perhaps your talents are too unique to be replaced. Perhaps you are in an industry that is dying or becoming unprofitable. Perhaps your business is in a neighborhood that is changing. If it looks like your business will die when you do, then you need to do some serious thinking about your future and your family's. Our basic recommendation is that you explore every tax-favorable angle allowable to have your business provide disability and retirement benefits for you, as well as life insurance for your family. That's a topic for another book, but it is important enough to warrant mentioning some common techniques.

DISABILITY INSURANCE

Coverage can be paid for by your company. If you pay income taxes on the premiums, then any benefit you receive will be tax free. This is the only choice you have if you are a sole proprietor, a partner in an unincorporated business or the owner of an S corporation. If you are an employee or shareholder of a C corporation you can elect not to pay taxes on the premium paid by your company. However, if you receive disability benefits, they will then be taxable.

RETIREMENT PLANS

The rules governing retirement plans are complex. In general you must include all your employees in a plan, which many business owners find unacceptable. However, a new type of pension called the age-weighted profit-sharing plan allows you to put away a larger amount for older workers than for younger workers. If you are older than the majority of your employees, it is worth asking your advisory team about this approach.

If a retirement plan is not in the cards, you are left with saving as much money on an after-tax basis as you can. The services of a qualified financial planner can be invaluable here. He or she can help you improve your cash flow and establish a budget for saving for your future needs.

LIFE INSURANCE

Finally, your company can help you buy life insurance. In a C corporation you can use what is called a split-dollar policy, which is paid for by the company. The company cannot deduct its premium, but if it is in a lower tax bracket than you are there will be a tax advantage, since it pays less tax on each dollar than you do. You will owe taxes on a tiny fraction of the premium, because all you have is the right to control the death benefit. The cash value remains under the control of your corporation, with the remaining proceeds payable to your beneficiary.

An S corporation or an unincorporated business won't be able to use this approach because the owners' tax brackets are the same as the business's. Still, business earnings can be directed toward the purchase of insurance simply by treating the premiums as income to the policy owner. In reality, you are paying yourself a bonus and using taxable funds to pay your insurance premiums. But often our clients tell us it just feels better to pay those darn premiums with a company check.

METHODS OF VALUING YOUR BUSINESS

One final issue remains: How do you value your business? Now, there's a tough one! Whether you plan to keep or sell your business, you need to have a good idea of what it's worth. Although there are several accepted methods, none of them is perfect. Each business is unique, and coming up with a fair value is more an art than a science. Let's look at some common valuation techniques.

Stated Value

The simplest way to set a price is to "ballpark" it. This may not be as cavalier as it sounds. After you've been in business for a while, you know better than anyone what its tangible (and intangible) assets and liabilities are. You may have seen similar businesses bought and sold. You may even have worked some of the following formulas. After adjusting for the unique aspects of your operation, you can come up with a price very close to your "gut feel" number.

Book Value

This is the simplest of formulas. Look at your balance sheet. Subtract liabilities from assets. That's it. This is not appropriate for many businesses because it ignores intangibles such as goodwill and depth of management. Furthermore, tangible assets are shown at depreciated cost. Thus the market value of an asset such as real estate or equipment may be grossly understated. Business owners are sometimes tempted to undervalue their businesses in setting up a buy-sell agreement. A book value approach can certainly do that. The rationale is that a lower value may save taxes and be easier to deal with in the event of death. Be careful, though. If you are the one who is disabled or dies, it will be your family that gets bought out cheaply—and your partner who gets a great buy.

Straight Capitalization

Many businesses have little or no tangible assets. Their value is in their ability to generate earnings. Most service industry businesses fall into this category. Thus a company that generates $100,000 per year may have a very low book value.

The straight capitalization method puts a value on those earnings by calculating the amount of capital that would have to be invested to produce the same return. Usually an average of the last five years of earnings is used. Without question, a small business is a riskier investment than a bank CD. Thus the interest rate assumption used to capitalize a company's earnings should reflect that higher risk. Generally speaking, a 15 percent rate is appropriate for a business with low risk, and a rate of 20 percent or more would fit a higher risk company. How does this impact valuation? If your company earns $50,000 per year and we use a 15 percent rate, the value of your company would be $333,333. ($333,333 times 15 percent is equal to $50,000.) If your business were riskier, a buyer might want to see a 20 percent return on investment. Thus he or she might pay you only $250,000.

The earnings used in these calculations may have to be adjusted. Many small businesses show little or no actual earnings. However, very often the owner is paying himself or herself a salary and taking other "perks" that far exceed what he or she would have to pay a nonowner to do the job. This excess can be added to earnings.

Capitalization of Earnings

While similar to the straight capitalization approach, capitalization of earnings attempts to take into account both the fair market value of a firm's assets and the value of intangibles, such as management ability and goodwill.

The first step is to adjust the book value of the firm's assets to reflect a truer picture of the assets' market value. So if you have real estate that has been depreciated for tax purposes, you would list that asset at what you feel it is really worth.

You then assume a fair rate of return on those assets, similar to the return used under the straight capitalization method. Any earnings of the firm over this assumed rate are attributed to goodwill and good management and are themselves capitalized at an appropriate rate. The result of these steps is then added to give us the full value. For example:

MNO Corporation

Book value (adjusted)	$300,000
Net earnings (average 5 years)	100,000
Fair return on book value (15%)	45,000
Excess earnings	55,000
Capitalization of excess (at 15%)	.15%
Value of management and goodwill	366,666
Total value	$666,666

None of the preceding methods can assure a precise valuation. There are too many variables in each case. Perhaps the biggest variable is you. The business may be worth one amount with you, and considerably less without you. Thus, a business owner may agree to stay at the helm for a number of years after selling the business. This buys time to break in new management. Obviously, this is not an option at the death of a business owner.

Professional Appraisal

A properly done appraisal is an expensive proposition. However, there's an advantage to being appraised by a trained, impartial expert. For most business transfers, a formal appraisal is necessary. However, if your business is very large and you are contemplating creating an ESOP or selling stock to the public, an appraisal will be required. There are many fine companies that specialize in business valuation. Your accountant or attorney may be able to refer you to one of them.

THE BOTTOM LINE

Keep. Sell. Do nothing. Having read these chapters you can appreciate why so many business owners feel compelled to do nothing. But as we have seen, there is so much to lose by doing nothing, and so much to gain by planning. If your advisory team is not familiar with these techniques, trade it in for a new one. You've worked hard to grow your business and make it succeed. You owe it to yourself and your family to preserve its value.

An Afterword

PERILS AND PITFALLS

As we close this book, we want to give you an overview of some of the more common mistakes you can make in planning your estate. It is our hope that you will use the information from the preceding chapters to avoid these pitfalls in your planning.

PROCRASTINATION

This is where we started, back in Chapter 1, and we come back to it here. Throughout the book, we have pointed out the perils of putting off. We'd like to quote Ben Feldman, who for decades has been one of the country's leading life insurance salesmen: "Nobody has a lease on life." Those six simple words have made Ben an awful lot of money. And they are, of course, nothing but the honest truth. There is never a convenient time to do your estate planning. Family and career worries intrude. We also need to find time to exercise or learn French or just plain take it easy.

None of this cloaks us in a mantle of immunity, however, when it comes to dealing with that most precious of all commodities: time. None of us knows when our time is up. So obviously, the time to start planning is now.

Many of the techniques we have discussed require time to work. Most gifting strategies are only effective if initiated years before death. If life insurance plays a role in your planning, you need to get it while you are healthy. People can and do buy coverage when they are in their 70s, but the odds that you might have a medical impairment that would prevent the purchase obviously increase with age. In any event, the cost certainly does.

Some techniques will permit limited postmortem estate planning. For example, if an owner of a large estate dies before executing a tax-saving credit shelter trust will, his widow could disclaim a portion of her inheritance. In effect, she is saying she doesn't need all the money, and by letting it go to the next in line in her husband's will, she could potentially save on the ultimate estate-tax burden. The next in line, presumably, would be the kids.

If the widow were to disclaim $600,000 worth of property, she would accomplish virtually the same thing as the credit shelter trust would have. There is no guarantee that she would disclaim her inheritance, of course. Understandably, without being compelled to by her husband's will, she might be disinclined to give up her inheritance. Even if she did disclaim, it would be messier and entail extra legal and administrative costs than using the will would have. Leaving the planning to chance may work out—but you can't assume that your family will act sagely if you didn't.

LACK OF COORDINATION

We have also mentioned the need to coordinate all your assets into your comprehensive estate plan. Your estate may include probate assets, jointly titled assets, trust assets, and assets distributed by beneficiary designation. It is absolutely vital that your attorney and other advisers are aware of these assets.

It is equally imperative that you implement their recommendations if changing beneficiary designations or property titling is appropriate. You can easily defeat the most sophisticated plan if you fail to follow through in these areas.

FAILURE TO KEEP YOUR PLAN CURRENT

Tax laws change. Your personal circumstances and objectives change. The values of your assets rise and fall. You may move from one job to another and have a whole new set of benefits that can affect the planning you had previously done. So you ought to revisit your planning whenever a major change occurs in your life.

Some of the changes are gradual, almost imperceptible. In some cases, you may not even be aware of the significant changes taking place around you that can have a major impact on you. This is particularly true of estate-tax law changes.

For these reasons, it's a good idea to sit down with your advisers every few years, just to make sure nothing has gotten ahead of you and your plan is still on track.

To illustrate the importance of keeping current, we'd like to tell you about our client George. In 1989 he constructed a beautiful estate plan. He had a will with a credit shelter trust. His personal and group life insurance were assigned to an irrevocable life insurance trust. He changed the beneficiary of his 401(k) plan to a revocable living trust. He was all set.

Then George lost his job as a senior design engineer with a major defense contractor. A victim of the so-called peace dividend, George was out of work for six months. Finally, he landed a good job in another part of the country. So he packed his family and moved on. Needless to say, these were difficult times for George and his family, and his focus frankly was not on estate planning. It was on keeping his family eating and on finding a new job.

With all the distractions, a number of things fell through the cracks. George received a $120,000 payout from his 401(k) plan and rolled it over into an IRA. He used a local bank in his new community as custodian. The banker, unfamiliar with George's previous planning, assumed George wanted his wife to be the beneficiary of his account. Not remembering his revocable trust, George agreed.

Furthermore, when George signed up for his new corporate benefits package, he automatically listed his wife and children as beneficiaries of the company's life insurance coverage. The assignment of his old employer's group life policy was now history, of course. By not assigning his new policy to the insurance trust he had created, George was exposing his family to exactly the estate taxes that he'd been trying to avoid.

Fortunately for George, these problems were all correctable. He hadn't died, and we were able to rectify the issues. That's because he at least had the good sense to seek out a competent attorney and financial planner once he was settled into his new community—our community. If, like George, you've made changes in your life since you did your estate planning, you should certainly question whether you need to revisit that planning.

POOR COMMUNICATION

We cannot overemphasize the need to prepare your family for life without you. This means much more than simply writing a will. Once you are gone, you will no longer be able to settle disputes or help your loved ones decide what the proper course of action is.

Of course, there's no way to supervise your family from the grave, and that's good when you stop and think about it. What you can do, however, is make sure that your wishes are very clear and ensure that they are carried out through your estate plan. In the final analysis, though, it's people who must enforce your wishes, not documents. If your heirs are in conflict with each other or feel they have been unfairly treated, they may tie your estate up in squabbling for years to come.

Your estate represents your life's work, and that legacy is yours to distribute as you see fit to the next generation. We realize that conflicts and jealousies are a normal part of family life. Your job, tough as it is, must be to make decisions about the distribution of your assets and then communicate those decisions to your loved ones. If you do so while you are alive, you risk having to deal with resentment from those who feel slighted. If you wait and let your will do the talking, you risk the possibility that some disgruntled heir might contest it.

The answer, we feel, is to do your best to resolve these potential conflicts while you are still alive. If you are favoring one beneficiary over another, it will be important for them to know why. With luck, they will understand your reasoning and accept it.

We know that many readers will not do this. And some may even think it's absurd to suggest it. On the other hand, harking back to the Gediman Research Group's study we referred to in Chapter 2, "Inheritance: The Problems and The Promise," a surprising number of people seem to have no problem sharing the contents of their wills. "Just over 60%," the study found "say they either have discussed or will discuss their estate decisions with family members.'' The motivation to get everything out in the open, the researchers noted, is the hope of avoiding conflict and controversy later. The percentage among people who have written a will was even higher—94 percent. Only 6 percent of the people studied felt that a will is an intensely private matter that they would not discuss with others; however, the few who felt that way held that conviction intensely.

In our experience, some clients prefer not to talk about their estate plans. They may hope to avoid a possibly unpleasant confrontation. In other cases, they have left letters explaining to their heirs why they have made certain decisions. It's not a terrible idea to prepare such a document. However, you should do so with your attorney's assistance. You want the letter to be clear and not in conflict with anything in your will or other estate documents.

Of course, our hope is that you will be very candid with your loved ones. Just as important, we hope you will be concerned about what you have and how you'd like it to be distributed when you are gone. We began this book by talking about the legacy you would leave. Our purpose in writing the book was to give you a plain English guide that you could really use, not a tome to gather dust on the coffee table. If anything, this is a report from the front lines, written by a couple of guys who have spent years helping real people work these issues through.

We didn't assume that you'd become an expert on estate planning by reading the book. Rather, we wanted to inspire you to action. If you've gotten this far, there's only one course of action left. You are now armed with enough information to get started on a planning process that could have an impact on your family for generations. The ball is in your court. It's time to get moving.

Appendix A

Intestate Succession and Wills: Examples of State Laws

ARIZONA

Ariz. Rev. Stat. Ann. §§14–2102 through 14–2104, and
14–2106 (West 1975 & Supp. 1990), as amended
through Laws 1982, ch. 66

*Surviving Spouse and Child or Children**

If all children are issue of the surviving spouse also, surviving spouse gets all of decedent's separate property and all of decedent's share of community property. If any child is not issue of the surviving spouse, surviving spouse gets ½ of decedent's intestate separate property and none of decedent's share of community property; balance goes to issue of decedent equally if they are of the same degree of kinship to the intestate, but if they are of unequal degree the more remote take by representation.

*Surviving Spouse, But No Children**

Everything to surviving spouse.

*No Surviving Spouse, But Child or Children**

Everything to child or children equally if they are of the same degree of kinship to the intestate, but if they are of unequal degree the more remote take by representation.

---

*For purposes of intestate succession, any person who fails to survive the decedent by 120 hours is generally deemed to have predeceased the decedent and the decedent's heirs are determined accordingly.

Reprinted from *Advanced Sales Reference Service* with permission of the publisher, copyright 1991, The National Underwriter Company.

No Surviving Spouse, No Children*

Everything to parent or parents equally; if no parent or parents, everything to issue of parents or of either of them equally if they are of the
same degree of kinship to the intestate, but if they are of unequal degree
the more remote take by representation; if no issue of a parent, ½ to the
paternal grandparents equally or to the survivor of them or if none to
their issue equally if they are of the same degree of kinship to the intestate,
but if they are of unequal degree the more remote take by representation,
and ½ to the maternal relatives in the same manner; if no grandparent
and no issue of grandparent on one side, all to the other side in the same
manner as the ½.

ARKANSAS

Ark. Stat. Ann. §§28–9–204, 28–9–205, and 28–9–214
(1987), as enacted by Acts 1969, No. 303.

Surviving Spouse and Child or Children

All to children equally if they are related in equal degree to the intestate;
if they are related in unequal degrees, those in the nearest degree take
per capita and those more remote take per stirpes.†

Surviving Spouse, But No Children

Generally, all to surviving spouse. However, if married to deceased less
than 3 years, ½ to surviving spouse and ½ to parent or parents equally;
if no parents, parents' share to brothers and sisters and the descendants
of deceased brothers and sisters equally if they are related in equal degree
to the intestate but if they are related in unequal degree those in the
nearest degree take per capita and those more remote take per stirpest;
if no siblings and no descendants of deceased siblings, parents' share to
each surviving grandparent, uncle, and aunt equally, the share of any
deceased uncle or aunt goes to his or her descendants equally if they are

---

†The property passing is divided into as many shares as there are 1) surviving heirs
in the nearest generation (with living members, probably) and 2) deceased members of
that generation who left descendants surviving the intestate; each heir in the nearest
generation taking per capita takes one share, and the share of any deceased member of
that nearest generation who left descendants surviving the intestate passes to and is divided among those descendants in the same fashion.

related in equal degree to the intestate but if they are related in unequal degrees, those in the nearest degree take per capita and those more remote take per stirpes.†

No Surviving Spouse, But Child or Children

Everything to child or children equally if they are related in equal degree to the intestate; if they are related in unequal degrees, those in the nearest degree take per capita and those more remote take per stirpes.†

No Surviving Spouse, No Children

Everything to parent or parents equally; if no parent, to brothers and sisters and the descendants of deceased brothers or sisters equally if they are related in equal degree to the intestate, but if they are related in unequal degrees, those in the nearest degree take per capita and those more remote take per stirpes†; otherwise to each surviving grandparent, uncle, and aunt equally, the share of any deceased uncle or aunt goes to his or her descendants equally if they are related in equal degree to the intestate but if they are related in unequal degree those in the nearest degree take per capita and those more remote take per stirpes.†

CALIFORNIA

Cal. Prob. Code §§240, and 6401 through 6403 (West Special Pamphlet 1991), as amended through Stats. 1990, c. 79.

Community Property and "Quasi-Community Property"*[1]

The surviving spouse takes the deceased spouse's ½ interest in community and quasi-community property.

---

*A person who fails to survive the intestate by 120 hours is generally deemed to have predeceased the intestate for purposes of intestate succession.

1. "Quasi-community property" is, generally, 1) personal property wherever situated and California real property acquired by decedent while residing outside of California that would have been community property had decedent been a resident of California at the time of acquiring the property, and 2) the personal property wherever situated and California real property acquired in exchange for property that would have been community property if the decedent had been a resident of California at the time the exchanged property was acquired. Cal. Prob. Code §66 (West Special Pamphlet 1991).

Separate Property:
Surviving Spouse and One Child*

$1/2$ to surviving spouse; $1/2$ to child or his issue equally if they are of the same degree or kinship to the intestate, but if they are of unequal degree of kinship to the intestate the more remote take by representation.†

Surviving Spouse and More Than One Child*

$1/3$ to surviving spouse; $2/3$ to children equally if they are of the same degree of kinship to the intestate, but if they are of unequal degree of kinship to the intestate the more remote take by representation.†

Surviving Spouse, But No Children

$1/2$ to surviving spouse; $1/2$ to parent or parents equally; if no parent, to the issue of parents or of either of them equally if they are of the same degree of kinship to the intestate, but if they are of unequal degree of kinship to the intestate the more remote take by representation†; if no issue of a parent, to the grandparent or grandparents equally, or if there is no surviving grandparent to the issue of grandparents equally if they are of the same degree of kinship to the intestate, but if they are of unequal degree of kinship to the intestate the more remote take by representation.†

No Surviving Spouse, but Child or Children

Everything to child or children equally if they are of the same degree of kinship to the intestate, but if they are of unequal degree of kinship to the intestate the more remote take by representation.†

No Surviving Spouse, No Children

Generally the scheme is: everything to parent or parents equally; if no parent, to issue of parents or of either of them equally if they are of the

---

†When representation is called for, the property passing is divided into as many equal shares as there are 1) living members of the nearest generation of issue (with living members) and 2) deceased members of that generation who left descendants surviving the intestate; each living member of the nearest generation of descendants (with living members) receives one share, and the share of each deceased member of that generation who left descendants surviving the intestate is divided in the same way among that deceased member's descendants.

same degree of kinship to the intestate, but if they are of unequal degree of kinship to the intestate the more remote take by representation†; if no issue of a parent, to grandparent or grandparents equally. However, for the purposes of distributing real property, if decedent had a predeceased spouse who died not more than 15 years before decedent, and for the purposes of distributing personal property worth at least $10,000 in the aggregate and for which there is a written record of title or ownership, if the decedent had a predeceased spouse who died not more than 5 years before decedent, the portion of estate attributable to decedent's predeceased spouse[2] passes as follows: to the surviving issue of the predeceased spouse equally if they are of the same degree of kinship to the intestate, but if they are of unequal degree of kinship to the intestate the more remote take by representation†; if none, to the predeceased spouse's parent or parents equally; if none, to the issue of the predeceased spouse's parents or either of them equally if they are of the same degree of kinship to the intestate, but if they are of unequal degree of kinship to the intestate the more remote take by representation†; if none to the next of kin of the intestate in equal degree, but where there are two or more collateral kindred in equal degree claiming through different ancestors those claiming through the nearest ancestor are favored; if none, to the next of kin of predeceased spouse in like manner.

CONNECTICUT

Conn. Gen. Stat. Ann. §§45a–437, 45a–438, and 45a–439
(West Supp. 1991 & 1991 Conn. Legis. Serv. 131 and
186), as amended through 1991, P.A. 91–109.

---

2. "Portion of estate attributable to decedent's predeceased spouse" means:

(1) (One-half of the community property in existence at the time of the death of the predeceased spouse.

(2) One-half of any community property in existence at the time of death of the predeceased spouse, which was given to the decedent by the predeceased spouse by way of gift, descent, or devise.

(3) That portion of any community property in which the predeceased spouse had any incident of ownership and which vested in the decedent upon the death of the predeceased spouse by right of survivorship.

(4) Any separate property of the predeceased spouse which came to the decedent by gift, descent, or devise of the predeceased spouse or which vested in the decedent upon the death of the predeceased spouse by right of survivorship. Cal. Prob. Code §6402.5 (West Special Pamphlet 1991).

Note that for purposes of the "portion of the estate attributable to decedent's predeceased spouse," "community property" includes "quasi-community property." Cal. Prob. Code §6402.5 (West Special Pamphlet 1991).

Surviving Spouse and Child or Children

First $100,000 and ½ of excess to surviving spouse so long as all children of deceased are also issue of surviving spouse; balance in equal proportions to child or children and the legal representatives of any deceased children. Where one or more children of deceased is not issue of the surviving spouse, then ½ to surviving spouse; balance in equal proportions to child or children and the legal representatives of any deceased child or children.

Surviving Spouse, But No Children

First $100,000 and ¾ of excess to surviving spouse; ¼ of excess over $100,000 to parent or parents equally. While it is not clear, it seems that if there is no parent the surviving spouse takes the entire intestate estate.

No Surviving Spouse, But Child or Children

Everything in equal proportions to child or children and the legal representatives of any deceased children.

No Surviving Spouse, No Children

Everything to parent or parents equally; if no parents, equally to brothers and sisters and their legal representatives; if none, equally to the next of kin in equal degree.

FLORIDA

Fla. Stat. Ann. §§732.102 through 732.104 (West 1976 &
Supp. 1991), as amended through
Laws 1977, ch. 77–174.

Surviving Spouse and Child or Children

Real and personal property; surviving spouse takes $20,000 plus ½ of the balance if the child or children are the lineal descendants of the surviving spouse; remainder to child or children per stirpes.† Where one or more

---

†Florida adopts the strict understanding of the per stirpes system. See *In Re Davol's Estate*, 100 S.2d 188 (Fla. App. 1958). For an explanation of the strict understanding of the per stirpes system, see the second note following the digest of Delaware's statute. . . .

of the children are not lineal descendants of the surviving spouse, $^{1}/_{2}$ to surviving spouse; remainder to child or children per stirpes.†

Surviving Spouse, But No Children

Everything to Surviving spouse.

No Surviving Spouse, But Child or Children

Everything to child or children.

No Surviving Spouse, No Children

Everything to parents equally or to the surviving parent; if none, to brothers and sisters and the issue of deceased brothers and sisters per stirpes†; if none, half to paternal grandparents equally or to the survivor of them and half to the maternal grandparents equally or to the survivor of them.

GEORGIA

Ga. Code Ann. §53–4–2 (Supp. 1989), as amended
through Ga. L. 1985, p. 1257.

Surviving Spouse and Child or Children

Real and personal property: Surviving spouse shares equally with child or children; but surviving spouse entitled to at least $^{1}/_{4}$. Spouse and children take per capita; descendants of deceased children take per stirpes.†

Surviving Spouse, But No Children

Everything to surviving spouse.

---

†Georgia appears to apply the per stirpes system in its strict fashion, with the exception of per capita distribution when nieces and nephews are the sole heirs. For an explanation of the strict understanding of the per stirpes system, see the second note following the digest of Delaware's intestate succession statute. . . .

No Surviving Spouse, But Child or Children

Everything to child or children equally, the share of any predeceased child with surviving descendants passes to his descendants per stirpes.†

No Surviving Spouse, No Children

Everything to parents, brothers and sisters equally and issue of deceased brothers and sisters (but only as far as their children and grandchildren) per stirpes†; but if all brothers and sisters are dead, nephews and nieces inherit per capita. If there are no parents, siblings, nieces, nephews, and no children of nieces and nephews, then equally to paternal and maternal grandparents.

MONTANA

Mont. Code Ann. §§72-2-202 through 72-2-205 (1989), as amended through L. 1989, Ch. 582.

Surviving Spouse and Child or Children*

Real and personal property: If all surviving issue are also issue of the surviving spouse, entire estate to spouse. If one or more of the surviving issue are not issue of the surviving spouse, then: ½ to the spouse if there is only one child or the issue of one child, and the balance to the child or to the deceased child's issue equally if they are of the same degree of kinship, but if they are of unequal degrees then the more remote take by representation†; ⅓ to the spouse if there are at least two children, the issue of at least two deceased children, or at least one child and the issue of at least one deceased child, with the balance going to the children and/ or the descendants of deceased children equally if they are of the same

---

*Any person who fails to survive the decedent by 120 hours is generally deemed to have predeceased the decedent.

†When representation is called for, the property passing is divided into as many shares as there are 1) surviving heirs in the nearest generation (with living members) to the intestate, and 2) deceased members of that generation who left descendants surviving the intestate; one share goes to each living heir in the nearest generation, and the share of each deceased member of the generation who left issue surviving the intestate is divided among the deceased member's descendants in the same manner.

degree of kinship, but if they are of unequal degrees then the more remote take by representation.†

Surviving Spouse, But No Children*

Entire estate to surviving spouse.

No Surviving Spouse, But Child or Children*

Entire estate to child or children equally if they are of the same degree of kinship, but if they are of unequal degrees then the more remote take by representation.†

No Surviving Spouse, No Children*

Entire estate to parent or parents of the decedent, equally; if none, to brothers and sisters and children and grandchildren of deceased brother or sister by representation†; if none, to the next of kin in equal degree, one claiming through nearer ancestors preferred.

NEW YORK

N.Y. Est. Powers & Trusts Law §§4–1.1, and 1–2.14 (McKinney 1981), as amended through L. 1978, c. 423.

Surviving Spouse and One Child

Real and personal property: $4,000 out of money or personality plus ½ of the residue to the surviving spouse; rest to child or to his issue per stirpes.†

Surviving Spouse and More Than One Child

Real and personal property: $4,000 out of money or personalty plus ⅓ of the residue to surviving spouse; rest to child or children and to the issue of deceased child or children per stirpes.†

---

†The issue take, in equal portions, the share their deceased ancestor would have taken if living. However, if the issue are all in the same generation, they take equal shares.

Surviving Spouse, But No Children

Real and personal property: First $25,000 and 1/2 of the residue to surviving spouse; rest to parents equally or to the surviving parent. If no parent, entire intestate estate to the surviving spouse.

No Surviving Spouse, But Child or Children

Everything to child or children and the issue of deceased child or children per stirpes.†

No Surviving Spouse, No Children

Everything to parents equally or to the surviving parent; if none, to brothers and sisters and the issue of deceased brothers and sisters per stirpes†; if none, to grandparents equally or to the surviving grandparent.

PENNSYLVANIA

20 Pa. Cons. Stat. Ann. §§2102 through 2104 (Purdon Supp. 1991), as amended through 1980 P.L. 565, No. 118.

Surviving Spouse and Child or Children*

Real and personal property: If all children are also children of surviving spouse, first $30,000 plus 1/2 of balance to spouse, rest to children†; if any child is not also child of surviving spouse, 1/2 to spouse, 1/2 to children.†

---

*Any person who fails to survive the decedent by five days is deemed to have predeceased the decedent.

†If the heirs (other than the surviving spouse, if one) are in the same generation, they take equal shares. If the heirs (other than the surviving spouse, if one) are in different generations, the property passing is divided into as many equal shares as there are 1) surviving heirs (other than the surviving spouse, if one) in the nearest generation with living members, probably) and 2) deceased members of that generation who left descendants surviving the intestate; one share goes to each surviving heir (other than the surviving spouse, if one) in the nearest generation, and the share of each deceased member of that generation who left issue surviving the intestate goes to that member's issue per stirpes. While it is not clear, it seems that the "per stirpes" distribution scheme is a strict one that requires the counting of predeceased generations.)

*Surviving Spouse, But No Children**

Real and personal property: First $30,000 and ½ of excess to surviving spouse, rest to parents or parent; if none, everything to spouse.

*No Surviving Spouse, But Child or Children**

Everything to child or children.†

*No Surviving Spouse, No Children**

Everything to parents or parent; if none, to issue of each of the parents†; if none, but at least one grandparent survives, then ½ to the paternal grandparents or the survivor of them or if both are dead to their issue† (but only as far as their grandchildren), and the other ½ goes to the maternal side in the same manner; if there are no grandparents on one side, and no children or grandchildren of them, the whole to the other side in the same manner as the half.

TEXAS

Tex. Prob. Code Ann. §§38, 43, 45, and 47 (Vernon 1980), as amended through Acts 1979, ch. 713.

Community Property

Upon death of either husband or wife, ½ belongs to survivor* and ½ is subject to testamentary disposition. If deceased dies intestate, latter half goes to children equally, the descendants of any deceased child take the share of their deceased parent; if none, all to the surviving* spouse.

*Separate Property: Surviving Spouse and Child or Children**

Real property: Life estate in ⅓ to surviving spouse; remainder to child or children equally if they are in the same generation, but if they are in different generations the more remote take per stirpes.†

---

*Any person who fails to survive the decedent by 120 hours is generally deemed to have predeceased the decedent.

†That is, the descendants of the deceased "heirs" take the share their deceased parent would have taken if that parent had survived.

Personal property: $1/3$ to surviving spouse; $2/3$ to child or children equally if they are in the same generation, but if they are in different generations the more remote take per stirpes.†

Surviving Spouse, But No Children*

Real property: $1/2$ to surviving spouse; $1/2$ to parents equally; if only one parent, $1/4$ to parent, $1/4$ to brothers and sisters and the descendants of predeceased brothers and sisters equally if they are in the same generation, but if they are in different generations the more remote take per stirpes†; if no brothers and sisters and no descendants thereof, the whole $1/2$ to surviving parent; if no parent, the whole $1/2$ to brothers and sisters and the descendants of predeceased brothers and sisters equally if they are in the same generation, but if they are in different generations the more remote take per stirpes†; if none, all real property to the surviving spouse.

Personal property: All to surviving spouse.

No Surviving Spouse, but Child or Children*

Everything to child or children equally if they are in the same generation, but if they are in different generations the more remote take per stirpes.†

No Surviving Spouse, No Children*

Everything to parents equally; if only one parent, $1/2$ to parent and $1/2$ to brothers and sisters and the descendants of predeceased brothers and sisters equally if they are in the same generation, but if they are in different generations the more remote take per stirpes†; if no brothers and sisters and no descendants thereof, all to surviving parent; if no parent, all to brothers and sisters and the descendants of predeceased brothers and sisters equally if they are in the same generation, but if they are in different generations the more remote take per stirpes†; if none, $1/2$ to the paternal grandparents equally or if only one survives then $1/4$ to that survivor and $1/4$ to the descendants of the deceased grandparent (usually if they are in the same generation, but if they are in different generations the more remote take per stirpes†) or if there are no descendants of paternal grandparent the whole $1/2$ to the surviving paternal grandparent, the other $1/2$ goes to the maternal side in similar fashion.

WEST VIRGINIA

W. Va. Code §§42-1-1, 42-1-3, and 42-2-1 (1982),
as amended through 1957, C.53.

Surviving Spouse and Child or Children

Real property: All to children.†
Personal property: ⅓ to surviving spouse; ⅔ to children.†

Surviving Spouse, But No Children

Everything to surviving spouse.

No Surviving Spouse, But Child or Children

Everything to child or children.†

No Surviving Spouse, No Children

Everything to parents equally or to surviving parent; if no parent, to brothers and sisters and to the descendants of brothers and sisters†; if none, ½ to the paternal grandparents equally and ½ to the maternal grandparents equally; if only one grandparent on either side, ¼ to that grandparent and ¼ to the uncles and aunts on that side and their descendants, but if no uncles, aunts, and descendants the whole ½ to the surviving grandparent on that side; if no grandparent on one side, the ½ to that side's uncles and aunts and their descendants†, or if none to other kin

---

†West Virginia's distribution system is not entirely clear. The relevant statute provides:

Whenever the children of the intestate, or the brothers and sisters of the intestate, or the uncles and aunts of the intestate, or the brothers and sisters of the intestate's lineal ancestors of the same degree come into partition, they shall take per capita, or by persons; and where, a part of them being dead and a part living, the descendants of those dead have right to partition, such descendants shall take per stirpes, or by stocks, that is to say, the shares of their deceased ancestors; but whenever the persons entitled to partition, other than those whose shares are definitely fixed by the statute of descents, are all in the same degree of kindred to the intestate, they shall take per capita or by persons.

on that side†; if no grandparents and no other kin on one side, then the whole to the other side in the same manner as the ½.

WISCONSIN

Wis. Stat. Ann. §§852.01, and 852.03(1) (West 1991), as amended through
1987, Act 393.

Surviving Spouse and Child or Children*

If decedent leaves descendants all of whom are descendants of the surviving spouse, everything to surviving spouse. If decedent leaves descendants, one or more of whom are not issue of the surviving spouse, surviving spouse gets one-half of net intestate estate consisting of decedent's property other than marital property and "deferred marital property" (i.e., property acquired during marriage and before the determination date[1] that would have been marital property had it been acquired after the determination date); descendants get the remainder of the estate equally if they are in the same generation, if they are in different generations the more remote take by representation.†

Surviving Spouse, But No Children*

Everything to surviving spouse.

No Surviving Spouse, But Child or Children*

Everything to child or children equally if they are in the same generation, if they are in different generations the more remote take by representation.†

---

*Any person otherwise an heir who fails to survive the decedent by 72 hours is considered to have predeceased the decedent.

1. "Determination date" is the last to occur of following: (a) marriage, (b) the date of establishment of a marital domicile in Wisconsin, (c) January 1, 1986.

2. When representation is called for, the property passing is divided into as many shares as there are 1) surviving heirs in the nearest generation with living members and 2) deceased members of that generation who left issue surviving the intestate; one share goes to each surviving heir in the nearest generation, and the share of each deceased member of that generation who left issue surviving the intestate is divided among the deceased member's issue in the same manner.

No Surviving Spouse, No Children*

Everything to parents or parent; if no parent, to brothers and sisters and the issue of deceased brothers and sisters by representation† (but if there are no brothers and no sisters, the issue take equally if they are in the same generation, if they are in different generations the more remote take by representation†); if none, to the grandparents.

United States Estate (and Generation-Skipping Transfer) Tax Return

Form **706** (Rev. October 1991) Department of the Treasury Internal Revenue Service	**United States Estate (and Generation-Skipping Transfer) Tax Return** Estate of a citizen or resident of the United States (see separate instructions). To be filed for decedents dying after October 8, 1990, and before January 1, 1993. For Paperwork Reduction Act Notice, see page 1 of the instructions.	OMB No. 1545-0015 Expires 6-30-93

Part 1.—Decedent and Executor

1a Decedent's first name and middle initial (and maiden name, if any)	1b Decedent's last name	2 Decedent's social security no.
3a Domicile at time of death (county and state, or foreign country)	3b Year domicile established	4 Date of birth	5 Date of death
6a Name of executor (see instructions)	6b Executor's address (number and street including apartment or suite no. or rural route; city, town, or post office; state; and ZIP code)
6c Executor's social security number (see instructions)	
7a Name and location of court where will was probated or estate administered	7b Case number

8 If decedent died testate, check here ▶ ☐ and attach a certified copy of the will.   9 If Form 4768 is attached, check here ▶ ☐

10 If Schedule R-1 is attached, check here ▶ ☐

Part 2.—Tax Computation

1	Total gross estate (from Part 5, Recapitulation, page 3, item 10)	1
2	Total allowable deductions (from Part 5, Recapitulation, page 3, item 20)	2
3	Taxable estate (subtract line 2 from line 1)	3
4	Adjusted taxable gifts (total taxable gifts (within the meaning of section 2503) made by the decedent after December 31, 1976, other than gifts that are includible in decedent's gross estate (section 2001(b))	4
5	Add lines 3 and 4	5
6	Tentative tax on the amount on line 5 from Table A in the instructions	6
7a	If line 5 exceeds $10,000,000, enter the lesser of line 5 or $21,040,000. If line 5 is $10,000,000 or less, skip lines 7a and 7b and enter -0- on line 7c. 7a	
b	Subtract $10,000,000 from line 7a 7b	
c	Enter 5% (.05) of line 7b	7c
8	Total tentative tax (add lines 6 and 7c)	8
9	Total gift tax payable with respect to gifts made by the decedent after December 31, 1976. Include gift taxes by the decedent's spouse for such spouse's share of split gifts (section 2513) only if the decedent was the donor of these gifts and they are includible in the decedent's gross estate (see instructions)	9
10	Gross estate tax (subtract line 9 from line 8)	10
11	Maximum unified credit against estate tax 11 192,800 00	
12	Adjustment to unified credit. (This adjustment may not exceed $6,000. See instructions.) 12	
13	Allowable unified credit (subtract line 12 from line 11)	13
14	Subtract line 13 from line 10 (but do not enter less than zero)	14
15	Credit for state death taxes. Do not enter more than line 14. Compute the credit by using the amount on line 3 less $60,000. See Table B in the instructions and **attach credit evidence** (see instructions)	15
16	Subtract line 15 from line 14	16
17	Credit for Federal gift taxes on pre-1977 gifts (section 2012) (attach computation) 17	
18	Credit for foreign death taxes (from Schedule(s) P). (Attach Form(s) 706CE) 18	
19	Credit for tax on prior transfers (from Schedule Q) 19	
20	Total (add lines 17, 18, and 19)	20
21	Net estate tax (subtract line 20 from line 16)	21
22	Generation-skipping transfer taxes (from Schedule R, Part 2, line 10)	22
23	Section 4980A increased estate tax (from Schedule S, Part I, line 17) (see instructions)	23
24	Total transfer taxes (add lines 21, 22, and 23)	24
25	Prior payments. Explain in an attached statement 25	
26	United States Treasury bonds redeemed in payment of estate tax 26	
27	Total (add lines 25 and 26)	27
28	Balance due (or overpayment (subtract line 27 from line 24)	28

Under penalties of perjury, I declare that I have examined this return, including accompanying schedules and statements, and to the best of my knowledge and belief, it is true, correct, and complete. Declaration of preparer other than the executor is based on all information of which preparer has any knowledge.

Signature(s) of executor(s)   Date

Signature of preparer other than executor   Address (and ZIP code)   Date

Cat. No. 20548R

Form 706 (Rev. 10-91)

Estate of:

Part 3.—Elections by the Executor

Please check the "Yes" or "No" box for each question.	Yes	No
1 Do you elect alternate valuation?		
2 Do you elect special use valuation? . . . . If "Yes," you must complete and attach Schedule A-1		
3 Do you elect to pay the taxes in installments as described in section 6166? . . . . If "Yes," you must attach the additional information described in the instructions.		
4 Do you elect to postpone the part of the taxes attributable to a reversionary or remainder interest as described in section 6163?		

Part 4.—General Information (Note: *Please attach the necessary supplemental documents.* **You must attach the death certificate.**)

Authorization to receive confidential tax information under Regulations section 601.502(c)(3)(ii), to act as the estate's representative before the Internal Revenue Service, and to make written or oral presentations on behalf of the estate if return prepared by an attorney, accountant, or enrolled agent for the executor:

Name of representative (print or type)	State	Address (number, street, and room or suite no., city, state, and ZIP code)

I declare that I am the ☐ attorney/ ☐ accountant/ ☐ enrolled agent (you must check the applicable box) for the executor and prepared this return for the executor. I am not under suspension or disbarment from practice before the Internal Revenue Service and am qualified to practice in the state shown above.

Signature	CAF number	Date	Telephone number

1 Death certificate number and issuing authority (attach a copy of the death certificate to this return).

2 Decedent's business or occupation. If retired, check here ► ☐ and state decedent's former business or occupation.

3 Marital status of the decedent at time of death:
☐ Married
☐ Widow or widower—Name, SSN, and date of death of deceased spouse ► ....
....
☐ Single
☐ Legally separated
☐ Divorced—Date divorce decree became final ►

4a Surviving spouse's name	**4b** Social security number	**4c** Amount received (see instructions)

5 Individuals (other than the surviving spouse), trusts, or other estates who receive benefits from the estate (do not include charitable beneficiaries shown in Schedule O) (see instructions). For Privacy Act Notice (applicable to individual beneficiaries only), see the Instructions for Form 1040.

Name of individual, trust, or estate receiving $5,000 or more	Identifying number	Relationship to decedent	Amount (see instructions)
All unascertainable beneficiaries and those who receive less than $5,000 . . . . ►			
Total			

(Continued on next page)   **Page 2**

Federal Estate Tax Rates

If the amount with respect to which the
tentative tax to be computed is: The tentative tax is:

Not over $10,000 ....18 percent of such amount.

Over $10,000 but not over $20,000 ....$1,800, plus 20 percent of the excess of such amount over $10,000.

Over $20,000 but not over $40,000 ....$3,800, plus 22 percent of the excess of such amount over $20,000.

Over $40,000 but not over $60,000 ....$8,200, plus 24 percent of the excess of such amount over $40,000.

Over $60,000 but not over $80,000 ....$13,000, plus 26 percent of the excess of such amount over $60,000.

Over $80,000 but not over $100,000 ....$18,200, plus 28 percent of the excess of such amount over $80,000.

Over $100,000 but not over $150,000 ....$23,800, plus 30 percent of the excess of such amount over $100,000.

Over $150,000 but not over $250,000 ....$38,800, plus 32 percent of the excess of such amount over $150,000.

Over $250,000 but not over $500,000 ....$70,800, plus 34 percent of the excess of such amount over $250,000.

Over $500,000 but not over $750,000 ....$155,800, plus 37 percent of the excess of such amount over $500,000.

Over $750,000 but not over $1,000,000 ....$248,300, plus 39 percent of the excess of such amount over $750,000.

Over $1,000,000 but not over $1,250,000 ....$345,800, plus 41 percent of the excess of such amount over $1,000,000.

Over $1,250,000 but not over $1,500,000 ....$448,300, plus 43 percent of the
excess of such amount over
$1,250,000.

Over $1,500,000 but not over $2,000,000 ....$555,800, plus 45 percent of the
excess of such amount over
$1,500,000.

Over $2,000,000 but not over $2,500,000 ....$780,800, plus 49 percent of the
excess of such amount over
$2,000,000.

Over $2,500,000 ....$1,025,800, plus 50% of the excess over $2,500,000.

(2) Phase-in of 50 percent maximum rate.—
(A) In general.—In the case of decedents dying, and gifts made, before 1993,
there shall be substituted for the last item in the schedule contained in paragraph (1) the items determined under this paragraph.
(B) For 1982.—In the case of decedents dying, and gifts made, in 1982, the
substitution under this paragraph shall be as follows:

Over $2,500,000 but not over $3,000,000 ....$1,025,800, plus 53% of the ex-
cess over $2,500,000.

Over $3,000,000 but not over $3,500,000 ....$1,290,800, plus 57% of the ex-
cess over $3,000,000.

Over $3,500,000 but not over $4,000,000 ....$1,575,800, plus 61% of the ex-
cess over $3,500,000.

Over $4,000,000 ....$1,880,800, plus 65% of the excess over $4,000,000.

(C) For 1983.—In the case of decedents dying, and gifts made, in 1983, the
substitution under this paragraph shall be as follows:

Over $2,500,000 but not over $3,000,000 ....$1,025,800, plus 53% of the ex-
cess over $2,500,000.

Over $3,000,000 but not over $3,500,000 ....$1,290,800, plus 57% of the ex-
cess over $3,000,000.

Over $3,500,000 ....$1,575,800, plus 60% of the excess over $3,500,000.

(D) After 1983 and before 1993—In the case of decedents dying, and gifts
made, after 1983 and before 1993, the substitution under this paragraph shall
be as follows:

Over $2,500,000 but not over $3,000,000 ....$1,025,800, plus 53% of the ex-
cess over $2,500,000.

Over $3,000,000 ....$1,290,800, plus 55% of the excess over $3,000,000.

(3) Phaseout of Graduated Rates and Unified Credit.—The tentative tax determined under paragraph (1) shall be increased by an amount equal to 5 percent of so much of the amount (with respect to which the tentative tax is to be computed) as exceeds $10,000,000 but does not exceed $21,040,000 ($18,340,000 in the case of decedents dying, and gifts made, after 1992).

(d) Adjustment for Gift Tax Paid by Spouse.—For purposes of subsection (b)(2), if—

(1) the decedent was the donor of any gift one-half of which was considered under section 2513 as made by the decedent's spouse, and

(2) the amount of such gift is includible in the gross estate of the decedent, any tax payable by the spouse under chapter 12 on such gift (as determined under section 2012(d)) shall be treated as a tax payable with respect to a gift made by the decedent.

(e) Coordination of Sections 2513 and 2035.—If—

(1) the decedent's spouse was the donor of any gift one-half of which was considered under section 2513 as made by the decedent, and

(2) the amount of such gift is includible in the gross estate of the decedent's spouse by reason of section 2035, such gift shall not be included in the adjusted taxable gifts of the decedent for purposes of subsection (b)(1)(B), and the aggregate amount determined under subsection (b)(2) shall be reduced by the amount (if any) determined under subsection (d) which was treated as a tax payable by the decedent's spouse with respect to such gift.

Credit for State Death Taxes

(b) AMOUNT OF CREDIT.—The credit allowed by this section shall not exceed the appropriate amount stated in the following table:

If the adjusted taxable estate is:	The maximum tax credit shall be:
Not over $90,000	8/10ths of 1% of the amount by which the adjusted taxable estate exceeds $40,000.
Over $90,000 but not over $140,000	$400 plus 1.6% of the excess over $90,000.
Over $140,000 but not over $240,000	$1,200 plus 2.4% of the excess over $140,000.
Over $240,000 but not over $440,000	$3,600 plus 3.2% of the excess over $240,000.
Over $440,000 but not over $640,000	$10,000 plus 4% of the excess over $440,000.
Over $640,000 but not over $840,000	$18,000 plus 4.8% of the excess over $640,000.
Over $840,000 but not over $1,040,000	$27,600 plus 5.6% of the excess over $840,000.
Over $1,040,000 but not over $1,540,000	$38,800 plus 6.4% of the excess over $1,040,000.
Over $1,540,000 but not over $2,040,000	$70,800 plus 7.2% of the excess over $1,540,000.
Over $2,040,000 but not over $2,540,000	$106,800 plus 8% of the excess over $2,040,000.
Over $2,540,000 but not over $3,040,000	$146,800 plus 8.8% of the excess over $2,540,000.
Over $3,040,000 but not over $3,540,000	$190,800 plus 9.6% of the excess over $3,040,000.
Over $3,540,000 but not over $4,040,000	$238,800 plus 10.4% of the excess over $3,540,000.
Over $4,040,000 but not over $5,040,000	$290,800 plus 11.2% of the excess over $4,040,000.
Over $5,040,000 but not over $6,040,000	$402,800 plus 12% of the excess over $5,040,000.

Over $6,040,000 but not over $7,040,000 ....$522,800 plus 12.8% of the ex-
cess over $6,040,000.
Over $7,040,000 but not over $8,040,000 ....$650,800 plus 13.6% of the ex-
cess over $7,040,000.
Over $8,040,000 but not over $9,040,000 ....$786,800 plus 14.4% of the ex-
cess over $8,040,000.
Over $9,040,000 but not over $10,040,000 ....$930,800 plus 15.2% of the ex-
cess over $9,040,000.
Over $10,040,000 ....$1,082,800 plus 16% of the excess over $10,040,000.

For purposes of this section, the term "adjusted taxable estate" means the taxable
estate reduced by $60,000.

Appendix E

Examples of State Death Taxes

Generally speaking, these are three types of state death taxes:

1. An estate tax, assessed against the nature of the taxable estate similar to the federal estate tax

2. An inheritance tax, levied against the share passing to each beneficiary of the estate. There are different tax rates for various classes of beneficiaries.

3. A "sponge tax," which simply soaks up the maximum state death tax credit allowed against the federal estate tax

Examples of each type of tax follow.

EXAMPLE 1: ESTATE TAX

New York

> Tax Law, §§951–998, as amended through
> LL. 1982, Chs. 916, 917, eff. 12-19-82.

Estate Tax

New York does not have an inheritance tax. The New York estate tax is assessed against the entire estate, and not against the share passing to each beneficiary. New York has with modifications adopted the federal rules for determining the gross estate and allowable deductions.

Rates

Tentative Tax Base				
From *Col. 1*	*To* *Col. 2*	*Tax on* *Col. 1*	*Plus*	*Of Excess* *Over*
$ 0	$ 50,000	$ 0	2%	$ 0
50,000	150,000	1,000	3%	50,000
150,000	300,000	4,000	4%	150,000
300,000	500,000	10,000	5%	300,000
500,000	700,000	20,000	6%	500,000
700,000	900,000	32,000	7%	700,000
900,000	1,100,000	46,000	8%	900,000
1,100,000	1,600,000	62,000	9%	1,100,000
1,600,000	2,100,000	107,000	10%	1,600,000
2,100,000	2,600,000	157,000	11%	2,100,000
2,600,000	3,100,000	212,000	12%	2,600,000
3,100,000	3,600,000	272,000	13%	3,100,000
3,600,000	4,100,000	337,000	14%	3,600,000
4,100,000	5,100,000	407,000	15%	4,100,000
5,100,000	6,100,000	557,000	16%	5,100,000
6,100,000	7,100,000	717,000	17%	6,100,000
7,100,000	8,100,000	887,000	18%	7,100,000
8,100,000	9,100,000	1,067,000	19%	8,100,000
9,100,000	10,100,000	1,257,000	20%	9,100,000
10,100,000	....	1,457,000	21%	10,100,000

Computation. A tentative tax is computed using rates shown in the table on the sum of the "New York taxable estate" and the amount of "adjusted taxable gifts." The New York taxable estate is the New York gross estate less allowable deductions. The New York gross estate of a deceased resident means his federal gross estate[1] (see Sec. 54, ¶44.3) reduced by the value of real and tangible personal property outside New York state and increased by the value of certain limited powers of appointment created prior to September 1, 1930 and exercised by the decedent as described in §957 of the N.Y. Tax Law. "Adjusted taxable gifts" means the total amount of New York taxable gifts (see summary of New York gift tax law, below) made by the decedent after 1982 other than New York taxable gifts includable in the decedent's gross estate. From the tentative tax is

---

1. Where, however, it is provided in federal law that the three-year bringback rule of IRC Sec. 2035 does not generally apply to estates of decedents who die after 1981, the New York law provides that the three-year bringback rule does not generally apply to transfers made after 1982 by decedents who died after 1982.

deducted the aggregate amount of gift tax payable on post-1982 gifts after subtracting the gift tax credit. (Split gifts (see Sec. 55, ¶57.8) are handled for purposes of the New York estate tax the way they are handled for purposes of the federal estate tax (see section 54, ¶44.2).) The result is the estate tax before credits.

Deductions. Deductions from the gross estate of a resident decedent are those allowed for purposes of the federal estate tax (see Sec. 54, ¶44.5) but with appropriate reductions attributable to the transfers relating to real and tangible personal property outside New York. The election of the marital deduction for qualified terminable interest property must be made on the estate tax return as required by §955(c) of the New York Tax Law.

Unified Credit

If the tentative tax is	the unified credit is
$ 0 to $2,750	Full amount of tax
2,750 to 5,000	$5,500 less amount of tax
5,000 or more	$500

Credit to be determined before application of credits for exemptions, tax on prior transfers and gift tax.

Credit for exemption for special use of qualifying property. New York has adopted with modifications, the provisions of IRC §2032A. A credit is available against the estate tax on the exempted value of qualifying property. The credit is 2% of the first $50,000 in value; 3% on the next $100,000; 4% on the next $150,000; and 5% on the next $100,000. The exemption for qualifying property plus one-half of the value of qualifying property in excess of $400,000.

Credit for gift tax paid. A credit is allowed for the amount of gift tax paid with respect to property which is included in the decedent's New York gross estate. The credit is determined in generally the same manner as the federal credit for gift taxes under IRC §2012 (see section 54, ¶44.6(c)), except that the credit cannot be taken with respect to gifts made after 1982, rather than after 1976.

Credit for tax on prior transfers. A credit is allowed for any New York estate tax paid with respect to property passing to the decedent within 10 years before, or two years after, the decedent's death. The credit is determined in the same manner as the federal credit for previously taxed property.

Property subject to tax (residents). Real property tax and tangible personal property in New York and intangible personal property wherever located. The gross estate includes taxes paid on transfers within three years of death.

Special use valuation. The provisions of Internal Revenue Code §2032A (relating to the special use valuation of certain farming or closely-held business property) are adopted with modifications. Where qualified property passes to a qualified heir, a special exemption and tax credit is also available (see above). (See, also, ASRS Sec. 54, ¶44.4(a) for the federal rules.)

Nonresidents. Real property and intangible personal property in New York is subject to tax. Intangibles of nonresidents are not taxed. The tax on nonresident estates is computed in the following manner: Ascertain what the tax would have been if the decedent had been a resident except that the value of any intangible personal property otherwise includable in the deceased's New York gross estate is excluded for purposes of computing the tentative tax and the tax on prior transfers. (A special provision applies to works of art belonging to nonresidents but on loan for exhibition in New York.)

Taxable transfers. Same as federal law, except for exercise of a limited power of appointment as described in §957 of the N.Y. Tax Law.

Life estates and annuities. Valued according to federal rules.

Life insurance and annuities. Same as federal law.

Employee benefit plans. Same as federal law except that no deduction is allowed for the federal estate tax on excess accumulations.

Additional estate tax. An additional tax is levied, if necessary, to absorb the maximum credit allowable under the federal estate tax law. (See introduction.)

Payment. If the tax is not paid within 6 months from the date of death but is paid within 9 months from date of death, interest is charged on the unpaid tax at the rate of 1/2% if paid in the 7th month, 1% if paid in the 8th month. 1-1/2% if paid in the 9th month. However, no such interest charge is made if 80% of the tax as finally determined is paid within 6 months from date of death. If the tax is not paid within 9 months from date of death, interest compounded daily is charged from date of death at a rate 2% higher than the federal short term interest rate applicable for the quarter in which payment is delinquent. If failure to pay tax is due to willful neglect, a penalty of 1/2% of the tax is added if failure is for one month, plus 1/2% for each additional month of failure, but not exceeding 25% in the aggregate.

Extension for payment. New York has adopted Internal Revenue Code §6166 with modifications. These provisions permit an extension of up to 15 years for payment of taxes where the estate consists largely of an interest in a closely-held business. (See, also, ASRS Sec. 54, §44.7(c) for the federal rules.)

Generation-Skipping Transfer Tax

Tax Law, §§1020 to 1025, as added by L. 1990,
Ch. 190, eff. 5-25-90.

A generation-skipping transfer tax is imposed on every generation-skipping transfer (as defined for federal tax purposes, see section 56 of this service, at ¶100) which includes New York property. The amount of the tax is the maximum credit for state generation-skipping transfer taxes allowed by IRC Sec. 2604 multiplied by a fraction representing the portion of the generation-skipping transfer which is New York property. "New York property" includes (1) real and tangible personal property in New York, (2) intangible personal property in New York used in carrying on a trade, business, or occupation in New York, and (3) intangible personal property where the original transferor was a resident of New York at the time of the original transfer.

EXAMPLE 2: INHERITANCE TAX

Connecticut

C.G.S.A. §§12-340 to 12-392, as amended through
L. 1990, Act 148, eff. 7-1-90

Inheritance Tax

Rates

Value of Property Passing to Class		Class A	
From (1)	To (2)	Tax on Col. 1	Rate on Excess
$ 0	$ 50,000	$ 0	0
50,000	150,000	0	3%
150,000	250,000	3,000	4%
250,000	300,000	7,000	5%
300,000	400,000	9,500	5%
400,000	600,000	14,500	6%
600,000	1,000,000	26,500	7%
1,000,000	....	54,500	8%

Value of Property Passing to Class		Class B		Class C	
From (1)	To (2)	Tax on Col. 1	Rate on Excess	Tax on Col. 1	Rate on Excess
$ 1,000	$ 6,000	$ 0	0	$ 0	8%
6,000	25,000	0	4%	400	8%
25,000	150,000	760	5%	1,920	9%
150,000	250,000	7,010	6%	13,170	10%
250,000	400,000	13,010	7%	23,170	11%
400,000	600,000	23,510	8%	39,670	12%
600,000	1,000,000	39,510	9%	63,670	13%
1,000,000	....	75,510	10%	115,670	14%

Additional Inheritance Tax. An additional inheritance tax is imposed equal to 30% of the basic inheritance tax. With respect to the estate of any person dying after July 1, 1983, an additional 10% tax is imposed. The 10% tax does not apply to certain farm land in the estate passing to a descendant.

Relationship Exemptions
(See *Computation*, below.)

Class AA: Husband or wife.

For deaths occurring on or after July 1, 1988, amounts passing to the surviving spouse are exempt from inheritance tax.

Class A: Parents, grandparents, lineal descendant, adopted child, adoptive parent and lineal descendant of any adopted child.

Exemption: $50,000 for the class.

Class B: Husband or wife or unremarried widow or widower of natural or adopted child stepchild, brother or sister of full or half-blood; adopted brother or sister or any descendent of such brother or sister.

Exemption: $6,000 for the class.

Class C: All others.

Exemption: $1,000 for the class.

Computation. The tax is on the entire share going to each class, and not upon the share of each beneficiary. Each beneficiary of the same class pays the same proportion of the tax payable by his class as the property passing to him bears to the property passing to the entire class. Applicable exemptions are allowed for in the rate table.

Exempted property. Joint checking or savings accounts in banks, savings banks, savings and loan associations or credit unions, or United States war or savings bonds are exempt if in the aggregate they do not exceed $5,000. A fractional share of any excess over $5,000 is subject to tax.

Employee plans. Value of survivor benefit payable to named beneficiary under a qualified trust, plan or annuity (see section 59) is excluded from gross estate to extent attributable to employer contributions; and, provided at time of decedent's separation from service or earlier termination of plan, "payments to or in respect of such trust, plan or annuity were exempt from federal income taxation. . . ." CGSA § 12–349(b). Value of survivor benefit payable to named beneficiary under a self-employed qualified plan (see section 60) is excluded from gross estate "with respect to which payments to the credit of such plan were exempt from federal income tax." CGSA § 12–349(c). Annuity payments receivable by an eligible survivor, upon the death of a retired serviceman, under the Retired Serviceman's Family Protection Plan or the Survivor Benefit Plan are exempt irrespective of whether the payments are attributable to contributions made by the decedent.

Charitable exemptions. Transfers to the United States, any state or territory, or any political subdivision thereof, including the District of Columbia, any corporation or institution, society, association or trust, incorporated or organized in Connecticut or in any other state that provides similar exemptions to Connecticut organizations, formed for charitable, educational, literary, scientific, historical or religious purposes, or any association or corporation, in trust, for care of cemetery lots, are entirely exempt from tax.

Property subject to tax. Residents: real property and tangible personal property in Connecticut, and intangible property wherever located.

Special farm valuation. Farm land may be valued according to provisions similar to the federal statute (see section 54,¶44.4(a)).

Nonresidents: Tax imposed on real property and tangible personal property in Connecticut. No tax on intangibles of nonresidents. Special deductions for nonresidents. Exemptions are same as for residents. Nonresidents are not subject to the additional estate tax.

Taxable transfers. The tax is imposed on transfers when made: (a) by will or intestate law; (b) in contemplation of death (gift is presumed to have been made in contemplation of death if made within 3 years of death), or to take effect in possession or enjoyment at or after death (including revocable trusts); (c) by vesting of decedent's fractional interest in jointly held property (except joint checking or savings accounts or U.S. savings bonds up to $5,000); (d) by vesting of statutory substitute for dower or curtesy; (e) as transfers in lieu of executor's commission as to excess over reasonable allowance. Transfers of property in trust with powers reserved to revoke, alter or amend in favor of settlor are taxable, but "property" does not include proceeds of life or health insurance payable to named beneficiary or to insured's estate. Transfer of property subject to a power of appointment are taxable on approximately the same basis as such transfers are taxable under the federal estate tax (see sec. 54, ¶44.3(i)).

Life estates and annuities. Value based on American Men's Ultimate Table of Mortality with interest at 4%.

Life insurance. Proceeds of life or accident insurance payable to a named beneficiary, or to a trustee under an inter vivos or testamentary trust, or to the insured's estate, are exempt. Proceeds of government insurance are exempt regardless of beneficiary designation. Proceeds of policy assigned as collateral security not taxable even though a portion is used to satisfy the debt. *Connelly v. Wells*, 115 A.2d 444.

Deductions. Debts; property taxes that were a lien at date of death; income taxes accrued before death; funeral expenses; executor's and administrator's commissions; attorney's fees; administration expenses; unpaid mortgages; family allowance for one year. Federal estate taxes and death taxes to other states are not deductible.

Additional estate tax. An additional estate tax is imposed on resident estates to absorb the maximum credit for state death taxes allowable under the federal estate tax law. The amount of the tax equals the excess, if any, of the maximum federal credit over all death taxes paid to Connecticut and other states. C.G.S.A. §§12-391 to 12-399. (See introduction.)

Payment. Inheritance tax due at date of taxable transfer and payable within 6 months after death—15% interest charged thereafter. The additional 30% inheritance tax is payable at the same time as the basic inheritance tax. No discount allowed for early payment. Additional estate tax is payable 6 months after death—15% interest charged thereafter.

EXAMPLE 3: SPONGE TAX

Florida

Estate Tax

F.S.A. §§198.01-198.44, as amended through L. 1989, Ch. 89-356.

Florida has no inheritance tax. An estate tax is levied to absorb the maximum credit allowed for state death taxes under the federal estate tax law.

The provisions of the federal estate tax law are adopted for state estate tax purposes.

If the decedent's adjusted taxable estate (taxable estate less $60,000) does not exceed $40,000, the federal credit for state death taxes is zero. Consequently, the Florida estate tax is generally not applicable to gross estates of $100,000 or less.

Rates. See maximum federal credit table in introduction.

Residents. Tax is amount by which the credit allowed for all state death taxes exceeds all state death taxes actually paid to states other than Florida. In general, a person will be considered a Florida resident if he was in Florida during the greater part of any 12 consecutive months in the 24 months preceding death.

Nonresidents. Tax is upon the transfer of Florida real estate, tangible property with an actual situs in Florida and intangible personal property with a business situs in Florida, including securities of corporations organized under the laws of Florida (but not bank deposits or insurance proceeds). The tax is imposed on the proportionate share of the estate which the Florida property bears to the entire estate.

Death benefits payable to trustee. Death benefits of any kind, including but not limited to, life and health insurance and annuity proceeds and proceeds from pension, profit sharing or stock bonus plans, payable to the trustee of an intervivos or testamentary trust, are not subject to estate tax to any greater extent than if payable directly to the trust beneficiaries.

Computation. Computation is based upon decedent's federal estate tax return, a copy of which must be filed with the Commissioner of Revenue for the state of Florida.

Payment. Tax is due and payable on the last day prescribed for payment of any federal estate tax due; interest at 1% per month (on an extension of time) is charged thereafter. Interest at 5% per month is charged on delinquent taxes, together with a penalty. No discount for early payment. If federal estate tax is subsequently increased, causing increase in Florida tax, 1% interest per month is charged on the increase from the due date of the tax.

Generation-Skipping Transfer Tax

Florida enacted, through L. 1980, Ch. 80–153, amended through L. 1989, Ch. 89–356, a generation skipping transfer tax which is patterned after the federal tax.

Residents. Where the original transferor is a resident of Florida at the date of the original transfer, the tax is equal to the amount allowable as a credit for state legacy taxes under IRC Sec. 2604, to the extent that such credit exceeds the aggregate amount of all taxes on the same transfer actually paid to other states.

Nonresidents. Where the original transferor is not a resident of Florida, but the transfer includes real or personal property having a tax situs in that state, the tax is equal to the amount allowable as a credit for state legacy taxes under IRC Sec. 2604, reduced by an amount which bears the same ratio to the total state inheritance tax credit allowable for federal generation skipping transfer tax purposes as the value of the transferred property taxable by all other states bears to the value of the gross generation-skipping transfer for federal generation-skipping transfer tax purposes.

Payment. The person liable for payment of the federal generation-skipping transfer tax is liable for the Florida tax. The tax is due upon a taxable distribution or taxable termination as determined under the federal tax. If any portion of the tax becomes delinquent, that portion will bear interest at the rate of 1% per month for each month (or fraction thereof) that it remains delinquent.

Appendix F

United States Gift (and Generation-Skipping Transfer) Tax Return

Form **709**	**United States Gift (and Generation-Skipping Transfer) Tax Return**	
(Rev. November 1991)	(Section 6019 of the Internal Revenue Code) (For gifts made after October 8, 1990, and before January 1, 1993)	OMB No. 1545-0020 Expires 8-31-93
Department of the Treasury, Internal Revenue Service	Calendar year 19 .... ► See separate instructions. For Privacy Act Notice, see the Instructions for Form 1040.	

Part 1.—General Information

1 Donor's first name and middle initial	2 Donor's last name	3 Social security number
4 Address (number, street, and apartment number)		5 Legal residence (Domicile)
6 City, state, and ZIP code		7 Citizenship

		Yes	No
8	If the donor died during the year, check here ► ☐ and enter date of death......................., 19		
9	If you received an extension of time to file this Form 709, check here ► ☐ and attach the Form 4868, 2688, 2350, or extension letter		
10	Enter the total number of separate donees listed on Schedule A—count each person only once .... ☐		
11a	Have you (the donor) previously filed a Form 709 (or 709-A) for any other year? If the answer is "No," do not complete line 11b.		
11b	If the answer to line 11a is "Yes," has your address changed since you last filed Form 709 (or 709-A)?		
12	Gifts by husband or wife to third parties.—Do you consent to have the gifts (including generation-skipping transfers) made by you and by your spouse to third parties during the calendar year considered as made one-half by each of you? (See instructions.) (If the answer is "Yes," the following information must be furnished and your spouse must sign the consent shown below. If the answer is "No," skip lines 13–18 and go to Schedule A.)		

13	Name of consenting spouse	**14** SSN	
15	Were you married to one another during the entire calendar year? (See instructions.)		
16	If the answer to 15 is "No," check whether ☐ married ☐ divorced or ☐ widowed, and give date (see instructions) ►		
17	Will a gift tax return for this calendar year be filed by your spouse?		
18	**Consent of Spouse**—I consent to have the gifts (and generation-skipping transfers) made by me and by my spouse to third parties during the calendar year considered as made one-half by each of us. We are both aware of the joint and several liability for tax created by the execution of this consent.		

Consenting spouse's signature ►   Date ►

Part 2.—Tax Computation

1	Enter the amount from Schedule A, Part 3, line 15	1	
2	Enter the amount from Schedule B, line 3	2	
3	Total taxable gifts (add lines 1 and 2)	3	
4	Tax computed on amount on line 3 (see Table for Computing Tax in separate instructions) . .	4	
5	Tax computed on amount on line 2 (see Table for Computing Tax in separate instructions) . .	5	
6	Balance (subtract line 5 from line 4)	6	
7	Maximum unified credit (nonresident aliens, see instructions)	7	192,800 00
8	Enter the unified credit against tax allowable for all prior periods (from Sch. B, line 1, col. C) . .	8	
9	Balance (subtract line 8 from line 7)	9	
10	Enter 20% (.20) of the amount allowed as a specific exemption for gifts made after September 8, 1976, and before January 1, 1977 (see instructions)	10	
11	Balance (subtract line 10 from line 9)	11	
12	Unified credit (enter the smaller of line 6 or line 11)	12	
13	Credit for foreign gift taxes (see instructions)	13	
14	Total credits (add lines 12 and 13)	14	
15	Balance (subtract line 14 from line 6) (do not enter less than zero)	15	
16	Generation-skipping transfer taxes (from Schedule C, Part 3, col. H, total)	16	
17	Total tax (add lines 15 and 16)	17	
18	Gift and generation-skipping transfer taxes prepaid with extension of time to file	18	
19	If line 18 is less than line 17, enter BALANCE DUE (see instructions)	19	
20	If line 18 is greater than line 17, enter AMOUNT TO BE REFUNDED	20	

Under penalties of perjury, I declare that I have examined this return, including any accompanying schedules and statements, and to the best of my knowledge and belief it is true, correct, and complete. Declaration of preparer (other than donor) is based on all information of which preparer has any knowledge.

Donor's signature ►   Date ►

Preparer's signature (other than donor) ►   Date ►

Preparer's address (other than donor) ►

(left margin: Please attach check or money order here.)

For Paperwork Reduction Act Notice, see page 1 of the separate instructions for this form.   Cat. No. 16783M   Form **709** (Rev. 11-91)

Form 709 (Rev. 11-91)   Page **2**

SCHEDULE A — Computation of Taxable Gifts

Part 1.—Gifts Subject Only to Gift Tax. *Gifts less political organization, medical, and educational exclusions—see instructions*

A Item number	B Donee's name, relationship to donor (if any), and address and description of gift. If the gift was made by means of a trust, enter trust's identifying number below and attach a copy of the trust instrument. If the gift was securities, enter the CUSIP number(s), if available.	C Donor's adjusted basis of gift	D Date of gift	E Value at date of gift
1				

Part 2.—Gifts Which are Direct Skips and are Subject to Both Gift Tax and Generation-Skipping Transfer Tax. You must list the gifts in chronological order. *Gifts less political organization, medical, and educational exclusions—see instructions. (Also list here direct skips that are subject only to the GST tax at this time as the result of the termination of an "estate tax inclusion period." See instructions.)*

A Item number	B Donee's name, relationship to donor (if any), and address and description of gift. If the gift was made by means of a trust, enter trust's identifying number below and attach a copy of the trust instrument. If the gift was securities, enter the CUSIP number(s), if available.	C Donor's adjusted basis of gift	D Date of gift	E Value at date of gift
1				

Part 3.—Gift Tax Reconciliation

1	Total value of gifts of donor (add column E of Parts 1 and 2)	1	
2	One-half of items . . . . attributable to spouse (see instructions)	2	
3	Balance (subtract line 2 from line 1)	3	
4	Gifts of spouse to be included (from Schedule A, Part 3, line 2 of spouse's return—see instructions) .	4	
	If any of the gifts included on this line are also subject to the generation-skipping transfer tax, check here ▶ ☐ and enter those gifts also on Schedule C, Part 1.		
5	Total gifts (add lines 3 and 4)	5	
6	Total annual exclusions for gifts listed on Schedule A (including line 4, above) (see instructions) . . .	6	
7	Total included amount of gifts (subtract line 6 from line 5)	7	

Deductions (see instructions)

8	Gifts of interests to spouse for which a marital deduction will be claimed, based on items . . . . of Schedule A	8		
9	Exclusions attributable to gifts on line 8	9		
10	Marital deduction—subtract line 9 from line 8	10		
11	Charitable deduction, based on items . . . . to . . . . less exclusions .	11		
12	Total deductions—add lines 10 and 11		12	
13	Subtract line 12 from line 7		13	
14	Generation-skipping transfer taxes payable with this Form 709 (from Schedule C, Part 3, col. H, Total)		14	
15	Taxable gifts (add lines 13 and 14). Enter here and on line 1 of the Tax Computation on page 1 . . .		15	

(If more space is needed, attach additional sheets of same size.)

Appendix G

Examples of State Gift Taxes

DELAWARE

Gift Tax

D.C. Title 30 §§1401–1406, as amended through L. 1982, Ch. 296, eff. 6–29–82.

Description of the tax. Beginning with the calendar year of 1971, a tax imposed on the transfer of property by gift by any individual resident of Delaware. A taxable gift for Delaware gift tax purposes is defined the same as a gift for federal gift tax purposes. The tax is an aggregate tax computed in the same manner as the federal gift tax.

Rates: Tax rates are as follows:

Amount of gift		Rate of Tax
From	*To*	
$ 0	25,000	1%
25,001	50,000	2%
50,001	75,000	3%
75,001	100,000	4%
100,001	200,000	5%
200,001	....	6%

Payment. Tax must be paid by donor by 15th day of April following close of calendar year in which gifts were made. Interest at the rate of 1% per month is charged if tax is not paid when due.

LOUISIANA

Gift Tax

L.S.A.-R.S. 47:1201–1212,
as amended through L. 1989, Act 3, First Extra. Session.

Annual exclusion. $10,000 may be excluded annually in computing the amount of gifts made to any single donee during any one calendar year. Gifts made by a married person to a third party may be considered to be joint gifts if both spouses indicate on their gift tax return their consent to make all such gifts joint gifts for that year.

Specific exemption. In addition to the annual exclusion, above, a lifetime exemption of $30,000 is allowed to each donor in computing the amount of gifts subject to tax.

Rates. The tax is computed by applying the following rates to the aggregate sum of the gift made by a given donor in excess of the applicable annual exclusion and in excess of any portion of lifetime exemption claimed and allowed: The rate on the cumulative excess as determined below (see *Computation*), up to $15,000 is 2%, and on the cumulative excess above $15,000 is 3%.

Computation. For each calendar year the tax is computed as follows: (1) A tax is computed (see *Rates*, above) on the aggregate total of (a) all taxable gifts made in the current calendar year and (b) all taxable gifts made in prior years after allowing the annual exclusion and any amount of lifetime exemption applicable. (2) A tax is computed on the aggregate total of all taxable gifts made in the preceding calendar year after allowing for the annual exclusion and applicable lifetime exemption. (3) The amount of tax due in the current calendar year is the amount by which the tax computed in (1) above exceeds the amount of tax computed in (2) above.

Charitable exemption. Gifts to religious, charitable and educational institutions within the state and to the United States, the state of Louisiana, or any of its political subdivisions, and civic organizations are exempt from gift tax. Transfers to nonresident charitable, religious or educational institutions are exempt if such state grants reciprocal exemptions.

If the aggregate net gifts for any calendar year exceed the maximum single exemptions, the gift tax is applicable only to the extent that the gifts (other than gifts of a future interest) to each donee exceed $3,000. However, the total exemption allowed shall not be less than the maximum single exemption for each class.

RATES

Value of Gift to Class		Class A		Class B	
From (Col. 1)	To (Col. 2)	Tax on Col. 1	Rate on Excess	Tax on Col. 1	Rate on Excess
$ 0	$ 40,000	$ 0	5.5%	$ 0	5.5%
40,000	200,000	2,200	6.5%	2,200	7.5%
200,000	240,000	12,600	6.5%	14,200	9.0%
240,000	300,000	15,200	7.5%	17,800	9.0%
300,000	440,000	19,700	7.5%	23,200	11.0%
440,000	....	30,200	9.5%	38,600	13.0%

Charitable exemption. Same as under inheritance tax law.

Marital deduction. Where the donee is the donor's spouse, a marital deduction is available (as determined under IRC §2523).

Joint gifts. A gift-splitting provision, similar to that under IRC §2514(c), is available. Gifts will be treated as being made one-half by the donor and one-half by the donor's spouse.

Computation. The tax is computed on net gifts made to each class during the calendar year. The tax is not cumulative, so prior years need not be taken into account. Creation of a tenancy by the entirety is not a taxable transfer unless there is an unmistakable intention to make a gift and a return is filed.

Payment. Return must be filed and tax paid on or before April 15 following the year in which the gift was made.

WISCONSIN

Gift Tax

WS §§72.75–72.87, as amended through L. 1987, Act 27.

RATES[1]

Note: The gift tax is repealed as to gifts made on or after January 1, 1992. In the meantime, the gift tax is being phased out. These rates are reduced by 20% for gifts made in 1988, by 40% for gifts made in 1989, by 60% for gifts made in 1990, by 80% for gifts made in 1991, and by 100% for gifts made in 1992 and thereafter. L. 1987, Act 27, §§1541m,3203(47)(zf).

Value of gift Before Exemption[2]		Surviving Spouse		Class A[3]		Class B	
From (Col. 1)	To (Col. 2)	Tax on Col. 1	Rate on Excess	Tax on Col. 1	Rate on Excess	Tax on Col. 1	Rate on Excess
$ 0	25,000	$ 0	1.25%	$ 0	2.5%	$ 0	5.0%
25,000	50,000	313	2.5%	625	5.0%	1,875	10.0%
50,000	100,000	938	3.75%	1,875	7.5%	4,375	15.0%
100,000	500,000	2,813	5.0%	5,625	10.0%	11,875	20.0%
500,000	....	22,813	6.25%	45,625	12.5%	91,875	25.0%

Value of Gift Before Exemption[2]		Class C		Class D	
From (Col. 1)	To (Col. 2)	Tax on Col. 1	Rate on Excess	Tax on Col. 1	Rate on Excess
$ 0	$ 25,000	$ 0	7.5%	$ 0	10.0%
25,000	50,000	1,875	15.0%	2,500	20.0%
50,000	100,000	5,625	22.5%	7,500	30.0%
100,000	....	16,875	30.0%	22,500	30.0%

[1]Subject to a statutory limitation that the tax shall not exceed 20% of the clear market value of property transferred to any donee in a single calendar year.
[2]The total of all transfers to one donee by one donor within the same calendar year is considered a single transfer for the purpose of gift taxation.
[3]Does not include surviving spouse.

Classification of Donees   Donees are classified as shown below, according to their relationship to the donor. For purposes of the gift tax, the relationship of an adopted person to a donor is treated the same as the relationship to the donor of a naturally born person of the same degree of kinship.

Class A: Spouse, lineal issue, lineal ancestor, mutually acknowledged parent, wife or widow of a son or husband or widower of a daughter. For the purpose of this classification, a mutually acknowledged child, his spouse and issue, are treated the same as a natural child, its spouse and issue.

Class B: Brother, sister, or a descendant of the brother or sister.

Class C: Brother or sister of the father or mother, or a descendant of the brother or sister.

Class D: All others.

Appendix H
Estate Settlement Costs Worksheet

Gross Estate		$
less:	Administrative and legal fees	
	Last illness expenses	
	Burial expenses	_____
	Adjusted gross estate	$
less:	Marital deduction	_____
	Net taxable estate	$
less:	Tentative federal estate tax	
	Federal estate tax credit	_____
	Net federal tax	
less	Credit for state death tax	_____
	Net federal tax	

Cost Summary		
	Administrative, final expenses	$
	Federal estate tax	
	Florida estate tax	_____
Total expenses		$

Estate		
less:		
	Total expenses	$
	Net to heirs	$

Shrinkage

Ages of Majority

State	Age
Alabama	19
Alaska	18
Arizona	18
Arkansas	18
California	18
Colorado	18
Connecticut	18
Delaware	18
District of Columbia	18
Florida	18
Georgia	18
Hawaii	18
Idaho	18
Illinois	18
Indiana	18
Iowa	18
Kansas	18
Kentucky	18
Louisiana	18
Maine	18
Maryland	18
Massachusetts	18
Michigan	18
Minnesota	18
Mississippi	21
Missouri	18
Montana	18
Nebraska	19
Nevada	18
New Hampshire	18

New Jersey	18
New Mexico	18
New York	18
North Carolina	18
North Dakota	18
Ohio	18
Oklahoma	18
Oregon	18
Pennsylvania*	21
Rhode Island	18
South Carolina	18
South Dakota	18
Tennessee	18
Texas	18
Utah	18
Vermont	18
Virginia	18
Washington	18
West Virginia	18
Wisconsin	18
Wyoming	19

*Pennsylvania provides a special age at which minors may enter into a contract, may sue, and may be sued: 18.

Note: In some states, marriage may accelerate the age of majority.

Index

Other books of interest to you from Business One Irwin . . .

SOONER THAN YOU THINK
MAPPING A COURSE FOR A COMFORTABLE RETIREMENT
Gordon K. Williamson

If you are over 35, it's time to start thinking about your retirement goals! Packed with useful charts, checklists, warnings, pro and con lists, fill-in timelines, information sources, and a unique tickler system that alerts readers when an important decision needs to be made, this lively book removes the mystique of retirement planning. (275 pages)
1-55623-541-0

ASSET ALLOCATION
BALANCING FINANCIAL RISK
Roger C. Gibson

Earn long-term income for your clients and satisfied, profitable customers for yourself! Gibson gives you step-by-step guidelines for designing and implementing portfolio allocation strategies that make tough decisions easy. (220 pages)
1-55623-164-4

THE BUSINESS ONE IRWIN GUIDE TO USING
THE WALL STREET JOURNAL
FOURTH EDITION
Michael B. Lehmann

More than 200,000 copies sold in previous editions! Discover how to use the comprehensive information in the *Journal* to make more informed business and investment decisions. Includes an expanded investment section and highlighted tips to steer you to the best opportunities in the 90s. (450 pages)
1-55623-700-6

THE HANDBOOK FOR NO-LOAD FUND INVESTORS
12TH EDITION
Edited by Sheldon Jacobs

The complete books on mutual fund investing to help you make the most profitable decisions! A comprehensive directory that includes advice on choosing the right fund for your situation, performance data, and more. (530 pages)
1-55623-772-3